"*G.O.A.T. Wisdom* may be the most practical, most commonsense business book you'll ever read. You'll be both entertained and enlightened, picking up strategies that fueled Beekman 1802's success and learning how to avoid the mistakes its two founders made along the way. Highly recommended!"

—**PAMELA N. DANZIGER**, founder, Unity Marketing; author, *Meet the Henrys: The Millennials That Matter Most for Luxury Brands*; and coauthor, *The Corporateneur Plan*

"Written with a deeply authentic voice and powerful personal narratives, *G.O.A.T. Wisdom* is a practical guide for navigating the complexities of building a brand for the long term. A must-read for every aspiring entrepreneur."

—**NINI ZHANG**, Managing Director, Investment Banking, Bank of America

"Both fascinating and immediately useful, *G.O.A.T. Wisdom* offers insight after insight for smart people seeking not just to grow a successful business but to stay true to their values in the process."

—**MICHAEL NORTON**, Harold M. Brierley Professor of Business Administration, Harvard Business School; author, *The Ritual Effect*

"I began my career—with no formal business education—behind a department store makeup counter and rose to become president of Kiehl's. I grew that company from one store to a global powerhouse. The best, strongest businesses are grown the old-fashioned way. *G.O.A.T. Wisdom* shows you how this is done, and I use these lessons now as the founder of my own company."

—**CHRIS SALGARDO**, founder, ATWATER; author, *MANMADE*

"I met Brent Ridge and Josh Kilmer-Purcell in 2018. At that time I had been working for ten years on acquisitions at L'Oréal, so I have seen a lot of brands and met a lot of founders. I have always tried to judge a brand's DNA by understanding its soul, its layers of meaning, and its founders' personal resilience. The success of Beekman 1802 exemplifies the best of these qualities."

—**CAROL HAMILTON**, Group President, Acquisitions, L'Oréal

"Brent and Josh were at the forefront of the "makers" movement. They took something as simple as artisanal soap and turned it into something sexy and desirable. Beekman 1802 was not just a collection of products but a lifestyle. In *G.O.A.T. Wisdom* you see an entrepreneurial journey fueled by transparency and innovation, both personal and professional."

—**WENDY WURTZBURGER**, former Global Copresident, Chief Merchandising and Design Officer, Anthropologie

"TikTok became a global leader by harnessing the power of personal authenticity to build community, one connection at a time. This is exactly how Ridge and Kilmer-Purcell built Beekman 1802, neighbor by neighbor. It's the future of how big businesses will be built, because it's exactly how great businesses have always been built. That's the message in *G.O.A.T. Wisdom*."

—**CHRISTINA TRAN**, Head of Cosmetics, TikTok Shop US

G.O.A.T. WISDOM

G.O.A.T. WISDOM

HOW TO BUILD A
TRULY GREAT BUSINESS–

FROM THE FOUNDERS OF
BEEKMAN 1802

DR. BRENT RIDGE AND
JOSH KILMER-PURCELL

HARVARD BUSINESS REVIEW PRESS
BOSTON, MASSACHUSETTS

Library of Congress Cataloging-in-Publication Data

Names: Ridge, Brent, author. | Kilmer-Purcell, Josh, 1969- author.
Title: G.O.A.T. wisdom : how to build a truly great business—from the
   founders of Beekman 1802 / Dr. Brent Ridge and Josh Kilmer-Purcell.
Other titles: Greatest of all time wisdom
Description: Boston, Massachusetts : Harvard Business Review Press, [2025] |
   Includes index. |
Identifiers: LCCN 2024056714 (print) | LCCN 2024056715 (ebook) |
   ISBN 9781647829773 (hardcover) | ISBN 9781647829780 (epub)
Subjects: LCSH: Dermatologic agents industry—New York (State) |
   Cosmetics—New York (State) | Goat milk industry—New York (State) |
   Beekman 1802 Farm (N.Y.)
Classification: LCC HD9675.D474 B66 2025 (print) | LCC HD9675.D474
   (ebook) | DDC 338.7/6685509747—dc23/eng/20250217
LC record available at https://lccn.loc.gov/2024056714
LC ebook record available at https://lccn.loc.gov/2024056715

ISBN: 978-1-64782-977-3
eISBN: 978-1-64782-978-0

The paper used in this publication meets the requirements of the American National Standard for Permanence of Paper for Publications and Documents in Libraries and Archives Z39.48-1992.

To all the Neighbors who grew this

CONTENTS

PREFACE

We launched Beekman 1802 in one of New York State's poorest counties with no funding—during a punishing recession. As our story illustrates, it doesn't matter where you live, how you identify, or how many resources you have at your disposal. If you dedicate yourself to following tried-and-true wisdom, you can do it too.

Our adventure started in 2008, at the beginning of the devastating global financial crisis. Both of us lost our glamorous New York City jobs within the space of a month—Brent was a physician and the senior vice president of health and wellness for Martha Stewart Living Omnimedia. Josh was an executive creative director at a top advertising agency. Suddenly unable to pay the mortgage on our historic farm in Sharon Springs, New York, which we'd bought as a weekend getaway only one year earlier, we made a major decision. Rather than declaring bankruptcy and walking away from our debt as so many other homeowners were doing, we decided that we would try to find a way to run our farm as a profitable business.

At first, the odds seemed stacked against us. The Great Recession was raging, and we lacked capital, having sunk our life savings into buying the farm. We'd never earned our living as entrepreneurs before, and knew little about farming. For the first two months after making our decision, we hunkered down on our property, depressed and wondering what to do. We had long been on a track toward conventional material success, and now that we had abandoned it—or it had abandoned us—the challenges before us seemed insurmountable.

Our salvation came from a herd of eighty-five beautiful goats and a community of Kind, caring Neighbors.

Months earlier, while we were still employed, we'd helped a local farmer who was losing his farm, agreeing that he could move to a small caretaker's cottage on our property and keep his dairy goats on our land. In lieu of rent, he agreed to share some of his goat milk with us. Another Neighbor showed us how to craft soap with the milk, and we taught ourselves how to code an e-commerce site, take product photography, and process online payments.

Other local farmers and artisans were struggling financially and lacked media and marketing skills, so we began helping them market their products as well as our own on our website. At first, Beekman 1802, as we called our business, didn't generate much profit—it had been strictly a fun hobby we pursued during precious time off from our city jobs. But after losing our jobs, we realized we'd have to turn our hobby into a real business that would allow us to pay the mortgage and keep the farm.

To grow the business beyond simply e-commerce, Brent dropped by New York City department stores, showing them samples of our soap. Everyone turned him down except Henri Bendel, a luxury department store then located on Fifth Avenue. Bendel's allowed Brent to set up a small table during the holiday season with Beekman products. Each day for two months, Brent got up at 4 a.m., made the three-hour trip into the city, spent the entire day manning our display and interacting with shoppers, then returned to the farm late at night.

The work was exhausting, but it led to our company's first major order—52,000 bars of soap for the retail chain Anthropologie. We had no money to hire workers, but fortunately, our Neighbors helped us fulfill the order as a favor, coming to our farmhouse and wrapping bars of soap around the dining room table.

Over the next few years, we sold our handmade, locally sourced products via our website and a small storefront we opened in Sharon Springs. As we first envisioned it, Beekman 1802 was to be an umbrella lifestyle brand selling products in multiple consumer categories. But as the years went by, our science-backed goat milk personal-care products grew more and more popular, and we eventually pivoted to focus exclusively on the beauty category.

By 2020 we were one of the largest independent beauty companies in America, and after taking on additional investment in 2021, we've expanded globally.

From those early days when we celebrated our first "grand weekend" (over $1,000 in revenue at our Sharon Springs store) to today when our annual retail sales surpass the nine-figure mark, our day-to-day operations are still guided by the maxims you'll find in this book.

We are voracious readers of biographies, especially those of business leaders reflecting on their own journeys. It always strikes us that no matter the vertiginous heights of success or the specific industry, almost every single business icon will attribute their success to some basic principle. Warren Buffett (*The Lessons and Rules for Success*) said, "The price is what you pay, the value is what you get." Mark Cuban (*How to Win at the Sport of Business*) referenced, "The best way to predict the future is to invent it." "Simplicity is the ultimate sophistication," is attributed to Steve Jobs in *Think Differently*. Howard Schultz, the founder of Starbucks, who changed how many of us start our day, wrote in his book *From the Ground Up* that "how you spend your money shows your values." Sir Richard Branson (*The Virgin Way*) has a few gems: "Say less, contribute more"; "Zig when everyone else is zagging"; "Hire your weaknesses"; and "Fortune favors the bold."

Virtually every business book ever written and every commencement speech ever given has encouraged readers and listeners to "follow your passion" if you want to find success. Doesn't this all sound familiar? They are all variations of things you've heard before. We fully anticipate that absolutely nothing that you read in the next hundred or so pages will be new to you. But what we hope *will* be new is how we teach you to listen and actually incorporate this advice into your own life and business.

. . .

While this is a business book, it's also a book about love. Passion. Diligence. Dedication. And most of all, Kindness. A book built on forty years of hard work, big successes, and shattering failures. A book that's a lot like life.

When we first launched, we didn't know the specifics of our eventual business model. But we did know one thing: we wanted to build a good company, not merely a successful one. We wanted to sell high-quality products that would enrich our customers' lives and create a strong, diverse, caring community. We wanted to make the world a better place by spreading Kindness and Neighborliness. And we wanted to build a business that would last.

We were determined that our personal and corporate mission of spreading Kindness would be real, not an empty marketing slogan. (Please note that we always capitalize "Kindness" to illustrate and constantly remind ourselves just how important it is.) We wanted to build our business the right way, and that meant treating buyers of our products not as generic customers but as Neighbors—members of a community who deserved care, respect, and recognition. In fact, we actually don't use the word "customer" or "consumer" when referring to our own. As you'll see throughout this book, we, and our entire company, call our customers "Neighbors."

While other startups took investor money, sought explosive but unprofitable growth, and aimed for a quick, lucrative exit, we focused on winning over one new Neighbor at a time—both online and in person. Rather than mobilizing expensive advertising to attract throngs of new customers, we eschewed investor money and relied primarily on generating positive PR around our personal stories and business values. It was a less glamorous but far more satisfying way to build a business, and it enabled our brand to create a community of highly enthusiastic Neighbors and grow it organically and in an enduring fashion.

Marrying the traditional sensibility we encountered in our little town with our big-city media savvy, we parlayed our experiences as gentlemen farmers into a book deal and a reality TV show, *The Fabulous Beekman Boys*, aired on Planet Green and the Cooking Channel, both of which gained significant exposure for Beekman 1802.

In 2012, thanks to help from one of the show's fans, we were invited to appear on the twenty-first season of *The Amazing Race*. Although we were clearly underdogs, we wound up winning the competition, again bringing awareness of Beekman 1802 to an audience of millions.

Seventeen years later, Beekman 1802 is one of America's most admired companies, and we've built it around simple, old-fashioned human values. Millions of Beekman Neighbors turn to our all-natural, ethically sourced soaps, skin-care products, and other offerings to help them stay healthy and look their best. While trendier competitors have come and gone, Beekman 1802 has grown into a thriving community devoted to the ideal of Kindness.

To succeed with Beekman 1802, we had to figure out our own formula. The strategies and tactics that worked best for us embodied timeless proverbs that our parents and grandparents had taught us—the greatest-of-all-time principles for good living that also can be applied to any business. We chose to turn our backs on the trendy management advice of the day, and we took principled actions instead. We soon realized that this insight amounted to a fresh playbook that anyone can use to build a Kinder and more profitable business in the twenty-first century.

They say in business that "timing is everything"—you'll read how we certainly learned that the hard way—and it seems that people are hungry for this type of advice now more than ever. A 2024 national Job Satisfaction Survey revealed that workers are unhappier with almost every aspect of their current job, and multiple studies have shown that younger generations are much more inclined toward entrepreneurship as a way to right the course of their own lives.[1] In fact, 54 percent of Gen Zers ages twelve to twenty-seven want to become entrepreneurs.[2]

G.O.A.T. Wisdom shares our business playbook for the first time, helping a wide audience of entrepreneurs, owners, managers, and leaders tune out the hype and build real and enduring businesses of their own. With business more competitive and volatile than ever, taking an elevated approach to business often can seem different, even impossible. The profusion of both disruptions and facile management fads can leave leaders shaking their heads, unsure of how to proceed. Offering a wealth of tactics and exercises, we'll show you how classic proverbs such as "Love Thy Neighbor," "Make Hay While the Sun Shines" and "A Bad Workman Blames His Tools" can help business owners and entrepreneurs navigate today's fast-paced marketplace and build truly good businesses.

These are not outdated, old-fashioned clichés. They're deeply nuanced and oftentimes not fully understood actionable insights and guideposts. Isn't it interesting that most of these well-worn bits of advice have some sort of agrarian origin? That might be because farmers have the longest history of entrepreneurship—going all the way back to when the first hunters and gatherers started to cultivate their first crops. We've had many thousands of years to confirm their veracity. These homespun maxims aren't only useful as general life lessons but rather comprise a powerful and accessible approach for building and sustaining any modern business.

We *truly* fully believe that there is wisdom in these time-tested sayings. They're time-tested for a reason. In fact, they're so popular that every culture has its own version of them. Unfortunately, these maxims have also become so ingrained in our collective vocabulary that most people don't reflect on what the words really mean. (Admit it: Do you fully understand what "You can lead a horse to water, but you can't make him drink" *really* means? Hint: It's not an ad for Coca-Cola!)

If you dream of starting, owning, or growing a multimillion-dollar business but feel stuck or believe that you don't have what it takes, *G.O.A.T. Wisdom* will give you the conceptual foundation you need to tune out the chatter, return to what's real, and make consistently wise business decisions. This book will also inspire you to take a deeper look at your own heritage and traditions, reconnecting with the kernels of wisdom and the gut feelings you already have but might not be applying in your business practices. And it will provide you with a strong dose of motivation to get started or redouble your efforts to start your own business or to utilize an entrepreneurial mindset in the company in which you already work (we call this intrapreneurship!).

Throughout this book you'll find exercises to help you become a G.O.A.T. The first one starts right now. On this page, on your phone, or on anything else you have handy, write down the best piece of advice that you've ever been given. You don't have to look at it again, just remember where it is, because you'll need it again in a few hundred pages.

As we frequently say, "All Beekman 1802 products have two key ingredients: Goat Milk and Kindness." We're glad to welcome you as a new Beekman Neighbor, and hope that wherever you find yourself on your own business or career path, you find some bit of Kindness in this book that furthers you toward you own goals and your success, however you define it for yourself.

G.O.A.T. WISDOM

Chop Your Own Wood and It Will Warm You Twice

How to Delegate

It was midnight in January 2010, and we'd just finished wrapping our thirty-thousandth bar of goat milk soap. We were exhausted. Cranky. Tissue paper and string were coming out of our ears. A few weeks earlier, we'd gotten a huge order from Anthropologie, the stylish clothing, home decor, accessories, and beauty retailer, for 52,000 bars of soap. At this point, we were only selling online, not in any physical stores. We just wanted to make a profit. Anthropologie is one of the largest specialty retailers in the United States, so being in its stores would put our products in front of affluent customers and also provide us with cash to fund further product development. We were thrilled.

Our celebration didn't last long. Because once the elation subsided, the harsh reality set in: *now we had to execute it*. Make the soap, cure it, wrap it, and shepherd all 52,000 bars out the door. And *that* was going to be a problem.

We'd been in the soap-making business for just over a year and had been contracting out production to a Neighbor, Deb McGillycuddy. (Seriously, that's her last name.) Deb had been making soap for her own business for decades, so it seemed like a natural fit for her to use goat milk from our farm to create bars for Beekman 1802.

Initially, Deb delivered the finished bars to us wrapped in craft tissue paper, tied with a bow, and ready for us to sell. It was a magnificent package, but due to her labor costs, it ran us an extra $1.50 for her to deliver a wrapped bar versus a naked one. (Plus, sometimes the people she hired to wrap the bars didn't share our sense of perfectionism.) This extra cost cut deeply into our profits, and we very much wanted (and needed) to make a good profit.

We had always set out to be a business that would be profitable because we refused to take loans or investments. Not only would we be warmed by the extra $1.50 on our bottom line, we'd also be more comfortable knowing that we were more in control of delivering the kind of consumer experience we'd hoped to deliver.

Now, if we had to do it all over again, we would have set a specific margin goal. If you have a margin you're trying to hit, that will inform all the decisions you're trying to make, like what ingredients you use, the kind of paper you use to wrap the item, and so forth. You're more conscientious about everything that goes into the product. We weren't good at this. We erred more on the side of "Let's just make this product!" That did slow down our growth.

Still, we had managed pretty well until this first massive order came in. It had been placed around Christmas 2009 and had to be delivered within months. Missing the deadline would cost us nearly $10,000 in charge-back fees for the product arriving late to the company's warehouse, which we obviously couldn't afford. Deb and her team cost us money. But *we* worked for free.

On that winter's night in 2010, a phrase popped into Brent's head: "Chop Your Own Wood and It Will Warm You Twice." It was something we'd both heard growing up in rural America, Brent in Randleman, North Carolina, and Josh in Oconomowoc, Wisconsin. And it was the sort of thing that we'd both kept in our heads over the years.

The phrase is often attributed to Henry Ford, of automobile fame, who had it carved into a plaque above the mantelpiece in his

Dearborn, Michigan, home.[1] But it actually predates him by (at least) a hundred years: Henry David Thoreau, who was concerned with all things arboreal, used a version of the maxim in *Walden*, which came out in 1854: "Every man looks at his woodpile with a kind of affection. I love to have mine before my window, and the more chips the better to remind me of my pleasing work. I had an old axe which nobody claimed, with which by spells in winter days, on the sunny side of the house, I played about the stumps which I had got out of my bean-field. As my driver prophesied when I was plowing, *they warmed me twice—once while I was splitting them, and again when they were on the fire*, so that no fuel could give out more heat [italics added]."[2]

Whatever its true origin, the moral is pretty straightforward: the process, the *journey,* is as rewarding as the end result. And if you learn how to do something, you can enjoy its benefits later. Looking at our own profit margins, which were razor-thin, we decided that it was more prudent to bring our soap wrapping in-house. (Quite literally—to our dining room table.)

At first, we decided to continue doing it all ourselves—just faster. It would be a ridiculous, humongous undertaking, but we were game. We stacked all the bars of soap in our doorway and set up a fulfillment center at our dining room table. As a teenager, Brent had worked at McDonald's, where efficiency is critical. He knew we had to figure out ways to make the process more efficient. We realized that if we precut the wrapping paper and the string, we could be quicker. So we did.

Josh also timed Brent as Brent wrapped each one. Forty-five seconds! Thirty-two seconds! Twenty-five seconds! It sounds anal, we know. But it was a matter of survival. Time was, quite literally, money.

Brent eventually got it down to twelve seconds per bar, but that still wasn't fast enough. Plus, we had other orders coming in from other customers, whom we always refer to as: "Neighbors." (The idea is that we're all one big community. We care about them the same way we care about the people who live in the house next door. And we mean it.)

We were overwhelmed.

We faced a dilemma. Continue to chop our own wood and risk missing the deadline? Or farm it out again and chip away at our profits? As entrepreneurs, we've faced this question hundreds of times as we grew, and we've realized that the answer is more complicated— but also simpler—than it seems.

To Chop or Not to Chop?

Most entrepreneurs know they must "chop their own wood"—that is, do the operational grunt work, the menial tasks that are seemingly beneath them—when first starting a business. It's not like they're incapable of doing it, 82 percent of successful business owners admit they're qualified and experienced enough to do various tasks while running a company.[3] But many of them aren't excited about it.

They regard being a jack-of-all-trades as a necessary evil, something unglamorous and stressful that they must do when their budgets are small and the company's future is uncertain. As the business grows and stabilizes, most entrepreneurs are happy to abandon a do-it-themself attitude and delegate, bringing in employees and vendors to handle areas of the business they prefer not to do, or know little about, or don't want to learn about.

According to research from *Entrepreneur* magazine, a startup founder can spend as much as 40 percent of their working hours on things that don't generate income, like payroll, hiring, or HR.[4] That's a high percentage. But we believe it's worth it. Because, though it's wise to *eventually* delegate and outsource, especially as a company increases in size, washing your hands entirely of frontline work is a mistake.

As we've learned firsthand, every business owner must continue to stay in touch with diverse functional areas, chopping at least a small part of the wood themselves or directly overseeing others as they do it. For example, because we had spent so much time packing individual orders off our website, we knew how to optimize product design and packaging to fit into standard-size shipping boxes. We didn't waste money on oversized boxes, which can lead to increased shipping charges.

If you don't have some fundamental understanding of what your employees are doing, you won't be able to pick out the things they're doing wrong. Yes, you will get splinters. But that's part of the gig.

There are scientific reasons for this, most notably educational theorist David Kolb's 1984 experiential learning theory. Experiential learning is basically learning by doing; it comprises four elements: concrete experience (experiencing something firsthand); reflection on and observation of that experience (thinking about the experience); abstract conceptualism based on the reflection (learning from the experience and its meaning); and active experimentation (putting your learning into action).[5]

About three-quarters of organizations use experiential learning to train employees and develop leaders, according to the Association for Talent Development, an international group for organizational talent creators.[6]

It's also an effective way to build so-called "soft skills"—attributes that include teamwork, creativity, adaptability, problem-solving, and conflict management—in the office. Statistics show that companies whose employees learn experientially have a 90 percent retention rate.[7]

As Brent can attest, medical school is a terrific example of experiential learning. Med students go to school for years and years. But they don't get to become full-fledged doctors until they go through a one-year internship, a residency, and often a fellowship. Brent recalls the common mantra when he was in medical training at the University of North Carolina, Chapel Hill: "See one, do one, teach one." In other words, first you watch a procedure being done, then you do one yourself, then you teach another student to do one. By that point, you've mastered it.

Research has also found that leaders who learn experientially—
that is, by performing various business functions themselves—have
an opportunity not just to understand various skills but to think
through the business more deeply and identify themselves personally
with it.[8]

The reality TV show *Undercover Boss* illustrates this beautifully.
Undercover Boss started in 2010, about a year after we launched our
first product.[9] We watched it religiously.

Each episode featured a business executive who went incognito
as a low-level employee in their company. The executive used a fake
name and résumé and spent about a week working in various areas
of the company, meeting colleagues and eventually bonding with
them. Chaos ensues, along with a whole lot of humility. The boss invariably learns to appreciate his employees, promotes a few of them,
and becomes more accessible to everyone.

In one episode, Todd Ricketts, the co-owner of the Chicago Cubs,
cleans bathrooms, parks cars, operates the manual scoreboard, and
sells hot dogs at Wrigley Field.[10] Yankee Candle Company CEO Harlan Kent goes undercover at his company's retail stores and packaging
center.[11] Stacy Anderson, brand president of the workout franchise
Anytime Fitness, works as a gym manager in Lebanon, Indiana. She
later poses as a personal trainer somewhere else. The show ran for
eleven seasons and was nominated for two Emmys.[12] It's entertaining and fast-moving, a lot of fun. But what struck us most was how
out of touch so many bosses are with their own companies and the
people who work there. And that's precisely why the show resonated
with so many people (the US version was based on a British TV program): everyone has heard horror stories of executives who hole up
in their corner office and are oblivious to the daily grind.

These, of course, are stories of bosses who grew wildly out of touch
with the basics of what makes their businesses successful. Most entrepreneurs can only dream of being that out of touch because most
entrepreneurs have no money. According to Small Business Trends,
one in three business began with less than $5,000 dollars.[13]

We had a million-dollar mortgage on the farm and were trying to start a business with no savings. We had to chop our own wood, two, three, four times. In fact, we literally needed that firewood to keep us warm, since, to save money, we kept our house at a balmy forty-five degrees. (We would've kept it even lower, but we didn't want the pipes to freeze.) It was so cold that snow would blow in under the kitchen door and not melt.

We had little choice but to learn how to do everything needed to get our business off the ground ourselves. Google was our first, and most valuable, employee. We barraged it with queries: "How to register a dot-com?" "How to code a website?" "How to take good product photos?" "How to process credit card transactions?" Perhaps the most interesting thing we learned during this period was that most of the tasks that business owners think they need to throw money at can actually be done (or learned) for free.

With the popularity of shows like *Shark Tank*, or stories of tech companies that raise hundreds of millions of dollars before their first day of work, many people believe that the very first task of any new company is to raise money to pay woodchoppers. They chase venture capital, raise money from friends and family, and start hiring. But unless you have some proof of concept for your business idea, how do you even know how to best spend that money? This is where the benefits of chopping your own wood really start to become apparent.

The Perks of Sharpening the Axe

That's the first thing you learn when you chop your own wood. All those nitty-gritty tasks we learned how to do ourselves from Google? They began revealing efficiencies that saved us money and fueled more sales. We learned that taking product photos with specific dimensions and specs meant that they could be used across more platforms. We didn't have to take new photos for each use.

LEARN FROM A G.O.A.T.:

Martha Stewart

Martha Stewart earned G.O.A.T. status by starting her lifestyle company, Martha Stewart Living Omnimedia, at the age of fifty-six, and became the first self-made female billionaire when the company went public.

Please tell us your favorite saying or piece of homespun wisdom, the one that has meant the most to you personally or professionally.

"Learn something new every day." That's my favorite saying that I made up. That's it. Just learn something new every day. Because I'm a teacher, and if I don't learn something new every day, there's no way I can be a good teacher.

How did you first discover or learn of this maxim?

My parents had six kids, and they sort of let us do our own thing. But they encouraged us to learn. If we wanted to go to the library every day, we could go every day, as long as we did our chores. Chores came first, and then the rest of life came after the chores. I read every biography I could read. That was very important. I loved reading those books. I learned a lot about American history that way too.

We learned that choosing the right bookkeeping application could help us seamlessly connect our e-commerce transactions with our bank account and our tax program, rather than creating dozens of different spreadsheets and manually synchronizing them.

If we'd farmed these tasks out to separate freelancers or employees (which we couldn't afford, anyway), we never would have realized these efficiencies. Deep-diving into every aspect of any business or organization and breaking down every step of unfamiliar processes can yield exponential results.

An early great example for us was when we were forced to explore ways to bring down the cost of producing our soap so that we could

Why is this maxim so wise and valuable in business and beyond?

I often use the phrase, "Don't go down the same street twice." You're not going to be inspired going down the same road every single day. I make my drivers crazy because I don't allow them to go down the same street twice. They can't go down 23rd Street. They have to go down 22nd Street or 21st Street or 25th Street. If I go down 25th Street, I might find a store that sells different kinds of nuts and bolts. I find new things going down another street. Without curiosity, I just couldn't exist.

How has this maxim contributed to your own success? Any particular stories come to mind?

I'm always looking for a void in the world and trying to fill it. That's with a product or with an idea or with a book. When I wrote my first book, *Entertaining*, that filled a very big void. There was no book like that. There was no cookbook or inspirational book as well as a beautiful, beautifully photographed book that existed at that time.[14]

sell it on the wholesale market. Soap maker Deb was producing bars of soap for us for just over $4 a bar, which gave us a healthy enough margin to sell to Neighbors directly from our own website. But we needed to get that down closer to $3 to sell at wholesale. Rather than negotiating with Deb without any knowledge of her process, we decided to help her make soap for a day to see where any hidden costs might lie.

After a long day of mixing, heating, pouring, molding, and unmolding, we set the bars of soap on racks to cure. The three of us sat down to add up the price of ingredients, the theoretical labor costs of our time, equipment costs, and so on.

It was under $2. Even with a standard markup for Deb, it seemed like we could come to an agreement of $3 a bar.

But then Deb gave us the rest of the story.

> "After the soaps are done naturally curing," Deb told us, "a fine layer of ash forms on the bottom of the soap, and I have to pay someone to come in and meticulously shave it off before sending it to you. It's a massive time and labor suck."

Our wheels started spinning.

> "So this fine layer of ash forms because they cure naturally?" we asked.

> "Yep," she answered. "It's just aesthetic. It washes away on the first use."

> We knew we had our solution: we would simply leave that fine layer of ash on the bars. And from that day on for the next five years of our company, we included a small card with every bar of soap that read: "You know this is a naturally cured bar of soap because it has a fine layer of ash that washes away after the first use."[15]

The moral of the story? We turned a time- and money-saving efficiency into a marketing benefit, which we never would have realized had we not made a batch ourselves.

People Like to Buy Chopped Wood from Woodchoppers

You might be wondering how we got to Anthropologie in the first place. The answer? By making ourselves visible so a company like Anthropologie could find us.

When Beekman 1802 began, Brent would go to the city and show up unexpectedly at luxury department stores. This was no time to be shy, and he wasn't. He'd ask to speak to the beauty buyer, and once he got them, he'd show them our products.

The beauty buyer at the late Henri Bendel, the luxury Fifth Avenue boutique known for discovering new brands, was intrigued. She saw something real in us. She offered us a three-by-three table where we could set up shop for eight weeks during the holiday season. We would have to stand there all day and sell our products ourselves, but we jumped at the chance.

Every morning, Brent would load up the truck, drive three-and-a-half hours to the city, hawk our wares at that tiny table, and then turn around and drive three-and-a-half hours home. That's right—he drove more than *six hours* a day. But he had to. We sold out every day, so he had to go home to replenish the stock.

One afternoon, a woman came into Bendel's, wandered over to Brent's table, and started asking a lot of questions about the soap. Like, *a lot* of questions. Brent knew this wasn't a normal customer, so he probed back. Eventually she revealed herself to be a buyer for Anthropologie. They exchanged cards, and two weeks later we had our order for 52,000 bars of soap.

This never would have happened if we'd hired a freelance salesperson to monitor the table. The Anthropologie buyer liked the soap, but she liked our story even more. And she loved hearing the story directly from the horse's (or goat's) mouth.

So when we got our next big break, we decided to replicate Brent's little table at Bendel's, but this time in over 90 million homes across the country.

A buyer from a TV shopping channel called Evine had stumbled across our website and blog and contacted us about selling our soap on television. We knew nothing about television retail other than they were channels we scrolled by looking for our favorite shows. But, always seeking new sales opportunities, we said yes.

Everyone who goes on a shopping network must go through training. Whether you're Joan Rivers or Jamie Kern Lima (the billionaire founder of IT Cosmetics), you have to do the same training program. They tell you what to wear, what to say, and how to demonstrate the product in the best light. You memorize your product's three main attributes and benefits, and practice repeating them over and over and over. The goal, after all, is to sell, sell, sell, and the networks have years of experience in the best ways to close that deal with a viewer.

Many companies hire brand ambassadors to peddle their products on air. We could have brought in a professional salesperson, but that would've cost money, and we knew from experience that our Neighbors liked to hear directly from us. We also knew that by personally selling our products on live television, we would learn about our Neighbors and their preferences in real time . . . down to the second. We could learn what sold, what didn't sell, what price points connected with consumers, and what their trigger points were. We would then be able to use that intel when overseeing product design and making marketing decisions.

Being dumb outsiders and more than slightly rebellious, we decided not to follow the network's training to the letter. The way we saw it, we faced two main hurdles: to get people to stop changing the channel, and to make people who love shopping on TV love us.

Now, TV retail was operating much the same as it operated when it began more than thirty-five years earlier. But a lot changed during that time. Not only were there endless channels, the internet and mobile platforms competed for buyer's attention. We knew that if we wanted to reach Neighbors, we'd have to break the mold.

Instead of wearing tasteful, professional outfits as they suggested, we wore our farm plaid shirts and muck boots. We brought in real live baby goats who pranced, played, pooped, and peed on live television, making it almost impossible for any casual viewer to change the channel.

Since we knew the ins and outs of soap making, we were able to credibly talk about the details of the product on TV. But rather than only focusing on the three top attributes and benefits of the soap, we told stories about life on the farm. We were *authentically authentic*.

As you're probably aware, "authenticity" is a big buzzword right now. Celebrities and influencers start businesses just because they have an audience, not because they know anything about what they're actually selling. So, while they might be successful out of the gate, there's no great foundation. Consumers know this. The scent of fake seeps through the airwaves.

But we had firsthand knowledge! We knew exactly how the soap was made! We could wax poetic on *everything*.

We did everything we weren't supposed to do on TV. We bickered with each other, which reminded viewers that we were a real live couple, like them. We didn't wear any makeup, which proved that we truly stood behind our skin care products. Josh even took a bath, live on air, which showed that . . . well . . . we're still not sure what that accomplished. But viewers loved it.

In short, viewers knew that we were the real deal. We'd chopped our own wood. They could trust what we were telling them. This is what made us the number one beauty brand on the channel, and eventually across HSN and QVC, the video shopping giants with a combined reach of more than 100 million homes in the United States, and among the top five retailers in America.[16]

And guess what? Now when new on-air guests go in for TV shopping training, the channels show clips of *our* on-air presentations as examples and tell trainees to "just be themselves."

The Warms-You-Twice Part . . .

Most people are familiar with the adage "A jack-of-all-trades is a master of none." The implication is that if you spread yourself too thin, you won't accomplish anything of substance. So you have to home in on one thing and be really good at it. What people don't know is that there's more to the original quote: "A jack-of-all-trades is a master of none, *but oftentimes better than a master of one.*"

We subscribe to this theory 100 percent. In our opinion, every entrepreneur needs to be a generalist—that is, someone who's still in the field or once was. But also, a generalist who's not afraid to admit when they're lost.

Now that we're a large company, we may have team members who are far more advanced in their respective job responsibilities than we ever were, whether it's digital marketing, coding, or finance. But oftentimes when they have a problem, we're able to come up with a solution not because we know more than they do, but because we know a very little bit about what they do. Our knowledge in their field is so foundational and rudimentary. But because we built the company doing a little bit of their job way back when, we often come up with a very basic question that they don't think to ask themselves.

Because we're generalists and our company's history keepers, we know what works and what doesn't. When our creative team first started taking pictures for the website, they didn't have lather on the soap. If you're only used to taking straightforward product shots, you wouldn't know that lather is the big selling point of soap. You also wouldn't know that a picture of lemon-scented soap with a wedge of lemon sitting next to it sells better than one without the lemon for two reasons: people instinctively smell the lemon in their imagination, and that lemon wedge also gives them an idea of how giant the bar of soap next to it is. But if you've been there before, as we had, you'd get it.

The risk, of course, is that *because* you've been in the trenches, and *because* you know the company so well, you could end up looking over your employees' shoulders and micromanaging the bejesus out of them. Not only will this annoy your employees; it will also overwhelm you, the founder.

Ultimately, we view the founder/CEO as the translator between different silos. The founder doesn't micromanage but connects all the people doing specific tasks. The founder must delegate and monitor wisely. The way we see it, every CEO needs to learn how to chop their own wood. Because by the time you get to be the CEO of a company, working around many people, you'll be able to warm yourself the second time because you have that foundational knowledge. So, you'll be able to translate between the different silos.

The warmth comes not from just having people around you, but because each person is chopping their own wood. Not only can that chopping generate heat, but it can really grow a business.

Still Chopping after All These Years

Growing a business isn't a linear narrative for any employee. There's no beginning, middle, and end. The minute you start patting yourself on the back because you've hired the perfect team and everything is running smoothly, someone quits. Or a supply line breaks. Or a tax law changes. Or—and this is a stretch—there's a global pandemic.

Which is why, even if or when you're lucky enough to successfully delegate most of the roles in your organization, there will be moments when you should, or must, remember how to chop wood.

Thirteen years into our business, and despite being active delegators, we still handle certain core operational areas ourselves. To this day, Brent reads every single Neighbor (customer) service email that arrives at our company—a practice that allows him to spot problems early on and to help our teams avoid repeating previous mistakes. Josh still writes the copy for select marketing projects that he knows have the most potential based on what has worked with Neighbors in the past. And our historical generalists' knowledge has helped avert more than one disaster.

In 2018, we created a novelty line of chocolate confections called "Goat Poop" for the holiday season. Even though we're a beauty company, it was the kind of out-of-the-box, fun marketing idea that we'd become known for, and our customer base went wild for it. It sold out within a month. One of the most popular products in the line was a "chocolate Goat Poop bomb"—a hollow chocolate globe filled with marshmallows that you drop in a glass of hot milk. They melt and dissolve and voila! You get a rich, frothy glass of "Goat Poop" hot chocolate.

They sold like mad. People worshipped them! But there was one teensy little problem: they all broke in shipping. Every. Single. One. Neighbors opened their packages and just had smashed shards of chocolate with smushed marshmallows. It was, in fact, a chocolate *bomb*.

Not surprisingly, we got thousands of complaints. Brent read every single one. Of course, we refunded every single purchase and averted disaster . . . until the next holiday season.

Our inventory purchaser never saw any of the previous year's complaints. After all, she didn't work in the Neighbor service department. All she saw in 2019 was a spreadsheet that said that we completely sold out of the bombs in 2018. The only obvious action she should take was to order a ton more of them for the upcoming holiday season, right?

Luckily, we were able to catch the mistake in time and no order was placed. But it reinforced the importance of nurturing and maintaining communication between employees who hold institutional knowledge based on their years of chopping wood themselves.

We've been happy to discover that chopping our own wood warmed us twice by allowing us to be better managers. All of this allowed us to get more out of everyone—and generate more fire. We tend not to micromanage, but instead use our knowledge to ask better questions, pay heed to warning signs, and guide our colleagues in order to find new solutions. All of this, in turn, allowed us to get more out of everyone.

Chop Wood. But Know When to Let Others Help Carry It

Many entrepreneurs struggle with the idea that if they hire someone else, then they're going to be making less money or profit. But sometimes the smartest thing to do is to hire a person to make your time management more efficient and more productive. This will make you more money.

One of the most critical things an entrepreneur can know is when it's time to hire someone better than they are. Let's be real: there are going to be things you don't like to do or aren't in your wheelhouse. Consequently, you'll be spending a lot of time learning things you hate doing or doing things that you're not good at. You will be way more valuable to the company if you're spending your time doing things that you're actually good at.

But delegating is *good* for the bottom line. In 2014, Gallup studied 143 CEOs on the *Inc.* 500 list.[17] High delegators' three-year growth rate was (on average) 112 percentage points higher than CEOs who were less-adroit delegators. What's more, CEOs who delegated well generated 33 percent greater revenue in 2013 than those with low or limited levels of the talent. This allowed the better owners to create more jobs at a faster rate (twenty-one jobs in three years, compared with seventeen new jobs for the less awesome delegators).

This is something our friend Steven Satterfield learned quickly. Steve is the executive chef and owner of the famed Atlanta restaurant Miller Union, a cookbook author, and an old friend of ours.

Steven opened Miller Union in 2009, and it has since become an award-winning enterprise. He created it from nothing, and he had to find the balance between staying true to his original vision and his real need to give others some control.

"I had to learn delegating very quickly," he says. "It takes a village to manage a village. Because I care, I'm overseeing and making sure things are the way I want them to be. But I can't physically make it all, so you need a team. I try to download as much information about what I'm creating so they have the tools to recreate it. It's like air traffic control at that point."

About thirteen years ago, when he was forty-two, Steven was diagnosed with testicular cancer. He was out of work for almost six months dealing with surgery and chemo and wasn't able to do much else. When he returned to work, he realized he had to make some serious life changes.

"I wasn't paying attention to my health and was really focused on the business and restaurant and super worried about what people thought and if we would succeed," he admits. "Then I had to let that go. It allowed me to be myself more. I learned that you have to give yourself time to focus, to learn when to delegate, to take the time to teach people.

"I think delegation is a daily practice," he continues. "Sometimes you just want to get the job done and you know how to do it yourself, so it seems that if you can handle it, it would save everybody's time. But there are many occasions daily when it doesn't make sense for me to do it, but it needs to be done. So I say, 'Can we take care of this? If you have any questions I'm right here.'"

Fourteen years into his business, Steven still spends a good eight to ten hours at the restaurant almost every day. And while he'll always be tethered to it, "My leash gets longer every year," he says. "If I delegate enough, then I can do whatever I want. That's the goal. Sometimes it takes a little time to delegate and teach, but the freedom that it grants you is going to be exponential."[18]

Back to wrapping those 52,000 bars of soap. We'd precut the wrapping paper. We'd cut our wrapping time down to twelve seconds per bar. But still, Josh pulled out a calculator and did the math. Even if we both worked 18 hours a day wrapping soap, it would still take both of us 288 straight days to complete the order. Clearly, we needed help. But if we hired all the help we needed, we would lose money on every single bar that went out the door.

Luckily, we knew whom to ask.

Maria worked in our local post office, which, in our tiny town of only 547 people, was constantly on the verge of being closed due to lack of mail volume. A small town losing its post office is practically a death knell for the community. Shipping 52,000 bars of soap to Anthropologie's warehouse from our little post office would surely get some US Postal Service higher-up to notice and keep our branch open.

Maria and our whole community had a stake in getting this order out. Which is why we weren't surprised when nearly a dozen local Neighbors showed up to sit around our dining room table and help us wrap soap. We got the order out. Sure, we didn't chop all of the wood by ourselves, but our community warmed us with their generosity.

And besides . . . remember the poster boy for self-reliance who came up with this maxim, Henry David Thoreau? Here's a little-known fact: while most everyone believes that he was chopping wood all by himself near his isolated Walden Pond cabin, his sisters occasionally brought lunch out to him. And every Sunday, he went to his mother's home for a chicken dinner. Clearly, he understood that he could accomplish more on a full stomach, especially if he wasn't doing all the cooking himself.

 CHEW ON THIS

- Lean into a do-it-yourself attitude as you grow, while also taking care not to micromanage.

- Delegate, but always stay in touch with what's going on in the company.

- In areas where you delegate the most, hire people who can explain the nuances to you in plain English so that you can continue to learn about them. Ideally, you should make that part of the interview process before you even hire them.

- Use your generalist's knowledge of the business to solve or prevent problems by purposefully forging connections between silos.

BECOME A G.O.A.T.:
Are You Chopping Enough Wood, or Too Much?

Consider the key functional areas of your business: marketing, sales, operations, and creative.

For each one, assess how much knowledge you possess in that area, evaluating it on a scale of one to ten.

Now calculate the average of your rankings. If you average between four and six overall, congratulations! You're a master delegator, sharing the wealth equally while maintaining a meaningful degree of contact across and throughout your business.

If your average is a seven or higher, you're probably micromanaging, so try to step back a bit more. Your people will appreciate it, and so will you.

If it's a three or lower, you're excessively distanced. Take steps to familiarize yourself with operational details, starting with those areas in which you ranked lowest.

When the Well Is Dry, We Know the Worth of Water

How to Budget, Allocate, and Be Scrappy

Many people don't like to step outside their comfort zone when it comes to asking for assistance or favors. They worry about being a nuisance or a pest, or appearing too opportunistic. Luckily, neither one of us has that worry gene. We're both exceptionally skilled at seeing an opportunity, going after it, and grabbing it.

This trait came in handy in 2014, a few years after we built and launched our flagship Beekman 1802 Kindness Shop in our hometown of Sharon Springs, New York. Our online business had been growing quite steadily, but we were having difficulty luring traffic to our brick-and-mortar store, which was over an hour from the nearest major population center.

This challenge became particularly acute during the holiday season. Consumers have always wanted their seasonal shopping to come with a side of glitz and glamour, and so most go to the nearest malls and large box stores to shop among their ornate Christmas decorations. We wanted to compete, but we had no budget to decorate the store, let alone the entire village. Sharon Springs wasn't exactly a hot destination. What to do?

As it happens, we had partnered with the Lenox Hotel in Boston, which stocked our products. One day we were chatting with a worker there who told us that her husband ran a company that decorates commercial buildings and offices for Christmas. Giant wreathes. Municipal-grade seasonal installations. Holiday lighting displays. Our eyes shone as bright as Rudolph's nose.

"What do they do with the decorations after they've been used?" we asked.

"Usually they're stored in a warehouse and reused the next season, but eventually no one wants them anymore and they're just tossed out," she said. "In fact, they're cleaning out one of the warehouses right now."

We had a proposition: What if instead of throwing them out, we paid for a truck to deliver all their obsolete decorations from the warehouse to Sharon Springs? He said sure.

So we rented the largest box truck we could afford and loaded it full of commercial-grade decorations: wooden soldiers, trees, candy canes, wreathes, giant ornaments, and lights. We invited all the small businesses in our town to help unload and take whatever they wanted for their stores. That year, our whole village was lit up like, well, a village lit up for Christmas. It was magical. Sharon Springs looked like the perfect country village from a classic holiday movie. Word got around, and people drove from all over the region to see and shop in the Beekman 1802 store. We even fielded a query from Hallmark about filming one of its Yuletide movies there. Talk about a Christmas miracle.

Now, many years later, we're still as frugal and scrappy. One of our habits that probably doesn't endear us to our employees is how we respond when one of them tells us, "We don't have enough in the budget to do [fill in the blank]!" Instead of asking them how much more they need, we say, "Well, what could you do instead if you had *no* budget?" Having built our company's sales into the high eight figures before taking on any outside investment, we accomplished a heck of a lot when all of our budgets equaled a big, fat whopping zero.

At most companies, including ours in recent years, budgeting creates a perverse incentive to spend excessively. It makes sense: team members are given a certain budget, and they feel compelled to spend all of it even if they don't need to. They know that if they achieve their goals yet have money left over at the end of the fiscal year, they'll get a smaller budget the following year—a de facto punishment for operating efficiently. We feel it's far better to instill a mindset where people assume they have zero budget and then try to engineer creative experiments that add value, receiving more money the following year when those experiments bear fruit. We call it the "dumpster-diving approach" to business.

Until we took on our first investors—in November 2022—we never really had a budget. Our philosophy was always, "Don't spend a dollar until you've made two."

The idea behind our approach is that any time the company needs something, the first response shouldn't be, "How much does this cost?" but "How can I do this for less than it costs?" Our starting point in any endeavor is: we need to accomplish X. But we have no money to spend. So how do we accomplish what we want to for as little as possible (ideally, nothing)?

As we've said before, we are both frugal. One might use the word "cheap," but there's a difference. Cheap has a negative connotation, a stinginess, whereas frugal has intelligence behind it. Frugal is strategic: a penny saved, a penny earned, and all that jazz. In business, a penny saved goes straight to the margin. It's worth noting that our friend Abby worked at McDonald's as a teenager. She was forbidden from ever letting a customer pay less than the full amount—not even one red cent less—because all those pennies accrued and would negatively impact the bottom line. There is a reason why gas stations and delis have a little tray with a sign attached that says, "If you have a penny, leave a penny. If you need a penny, take a penny." Because every penny literally counts.

The Beekman 1802 way of thinking about money is very deliberate and best illustrated by the edict, "When the Well Is Dry, We

Know the Worth of Water." The phrase was uttered by none other than founding father and famous kite-and-key guy Benjamin Franklin in the 1746 edition of *Poor Richard's Almanack*, a yearly digest he wrote under the pseudonym "Poor Richard."[1]

The adage resonated with us literally and metaphorically, and still does. It's so obvious, yet so many businesses don't follow the philosophy. On a literal level, of course, we all need water to survive. That's a no-brainer. Metaphorically, the implication is that we can't understand the true value of resources, or even opportunities, until we no longer have access to them. The maxim encourages us to recognize and cherish what we have while we still have it, rather than realizing its value once it's gone or depleted.

To channel Joni Mitchell: "Don't it always seem to go that you don't know what you've got till it's gone."

We have firsthand experience gauging the value of water, which has also led to our own variation: "Scrappiness pays." For years, we both led somewhat high-flying lives, until we were laid off and the rug was unceremoniously yanked from under us. Not only did we have no water, we were *parched*. Remember: we had a $1 million mortgage, homeless goats, and a homeless farmer to feed.

After losing it all, we learned how to be highly resourceful. We had no option. Nothing makes a stomach rumble more than incredible thirst and nothing to quench it.

Water, Water Nowhere

Most entrepreneurs find that they have few resources on which to draw when launching their businesses—the well is bone dry. To survive, they learn to improvise and make do.

You can realize important benefits when you cultivate frugality, even after your business has grown and the financial pressure has dwindled. Just because you have resources at your disposal doesn't mean you have to *use* them.

One of the greatest benefits of maintaining a frugal mindset is continued creativity and adaptability. In our case, that mindset has not only allowed for greater efficiency but also opened up entirely new revenue opportunities.

This brings us to the notion of *frugal innovation*, also known as "frugal engineering" or "*jugaad* innovation." (*Jugaad* is a South Asian word loosely translating to "make do and mend.")[2]

Frugal innovation is a concept within engineering that focuses on creating simple, affordable, and practical solutions to complicated problems, especially in low-income areas or settings with limited resources. It involves developing innovative products, services, or systems that are cost-effective, efficient, and accessible to a wide range of people. (It doesn't only apply to engineering. It can also apply to health care, energy, banking, technology, agriculture, and yes, beauty, along with any other business.)

Frugal innovation aims to maximize value while minimizing costs and making solutions affordable and applicable in diverse contexts. This approach doesn't prioritize high-end technology or expensive infrastructure, but instead leverages creativity, resourcefulness, and simplicity to address the inevitable challenges.

We are big proponents of frugal innovation, especially since it allows companies to operate more sustainably.

It also helps people live more sustainably. A 2014 meta-analysis in the *Journal of Personality and Social Psychology* found a connection between materialism and poor health.[3] The researchers also found that those who lived more frugally had better physical and mental health.

Not eating junk food, for example, saves money while helping people stay healthy. Another study found that saving money might increase consumers' likelihood of seeking preventative health treatment, which makes them live longer.[4]

Our thriftiness also contributed to our own emotional and physical well-being. About eight years into our business, we really wanted (and needed) to take a vacation. We were working a hundred hours a week and were physically and emotionally drained. We needed to regroup somewhere far away.

But there was one major hurdle: we had no money for a vacation. We weren't even paying ourselves a salary yet. But then we thought: What if we organized a trip for our Neighbors, partnering with a travel agency so that we could be chaperones of sorts? We would benefit, sure, but so would Neighbors who would enjoy a new way to connect with the Beekman brand.

Cuba had recently opened to US travelers, and we desperately wanted to go. Many other people also wanted to travel with a community of like-minded individuals. So we worked with an independent travel agent with experience in Cuba, crafted a Beekman 1802–style itinerary that would immerse us in local culture, posted information about the trip online, and crossed our fingers that enough Beekman Neighbors would put down a deposit on this "Beekman 1802 Trip of a Lifetime." On each excursion, in every location, we had different pillars of things we wanted to address: an agriculture day, an arts-oriented day, a food-focused day, and a give-back-to-the-community volunteer day in each location that we went to. It sold out within days.

That was the first of our Beekman 1802 Trips of a Lifetime, which continued for the next five years. We accompanied groups of Beekman Neighbors to Peru, India, Germany, Czechoslovakia, England, Kenya, Tanzania, and Iceland.

So, with a budget of zero, we'd been able to turn our desperation for a vacation into a brand-building, loyalty-deepening, educational, and charitable adventure for Beekman 1802's best customers.

How Much Is Water Worth?

When we first started as a direct-to-consumer (DTC) company, we couldn't even afford packing materials. We saved every bit of packing material to come our way (thank you, Amazon)—crinkle, peanuts, bubbles, foam—and asked our friends to do the same. Back then, Beekman Neighbors would never know what would surround their packages when they arrived. Sometimes it was newspaper. Sometimes it was Bubble Wrap, sometimes it was straw, and once even the Styrofoam beads from the inside of an unused bean bag chair. We actually hit the gold mine when one of our employees found a resource at the local hospital that had trash bags full of shredded paper, medical records, and financial statements. It was a pillar of scrappiness.

This is an example of a circular economy business model.[5] These models aim to minimize waste, maximize resource efficiency, and create sustainable practices by keeping materials and products in use for as long as possible. They prioritize reuse, recycling, and regeneration. Some common circular economy business models include offering products as services, like fashion company Rent the Runway, online auctions like eBay or Facebook Marketplace, Airbnb, and Uber, and even the old-fashioned yard sale (a staple of the entrepreneurial economy). Instead of owning a product, customers pay for the use or access to it, or they buy someone's castoffs.

When it works, it works beautifully. But it doesn't always work.

Consider the case of Interface, an Atlanta-based commercial flooring company. In the 1990s, its founder and CEO, Ray Anderson, wanted to turn his firm into, in his words, "the first sustainable corporation in the world."[6] So he decided to shift Interface's business model from leasing floors to selling, and launched something called the Evergreen Services Agreement (ESA) program.[7] The ESA included installing, maintaining, and removing flooring bundled under one monthly fee. This allowed the company to keep used flooring materials out of landfills and recycle the valuable raw materials in them.

Interface tried really hard, even going so far as to develop a network of carpet distributors across the United States. But after seven years of strenuously trying to sell the idea, it had only landed a smattering of lessees. Most customers, it turned out, wanted to purchase their carpets instead of leasing them. Interface was unable to grow the ESA program.

By 2000, Interface began producing modular carpet tiles using recyclable nylon fibers and vinyl backings. Manufacturing the new carpet tiles emitted 75 percent less carbon than the industry average, and after the company began using renewable energy on production sites, Interface's total carbon footprint was lowered by 69 percent, the company reported.[8] Unlike leasing, the focus on recycling leveraged Interface's strength: manufacturing and selling rugs. And now, when you walk into any office environment and see those alternating square patterns of carpet—that's this idea incarnate.

The point is that creating a sustainable circular business model depends on many factors, but it's critical that it aligns with a company's capabilities and resources—and addresses the constraints on its operations. It also takes into consideration what the customer wants.

Because we work with a few different companies—Ulta Beauty, Amazon, QVC—it gets expensive to keep creating new visuals and images. Each organization has its own standards and little peccadillos: one wants you to use models, one wants close-ups, one wants a different color background, and so on. So, when we're planning our content photo shoots, we have to think about how we can reuse the same image or video so we're laying out money for shooting only once.

We can even apply this tactic to how we gather and use marketing insights from our consumers. The development process for a new product from conception to formulation to marketing takes us about eighteen months. All along in this process, we are thinking about what are the compelling aspects of the product that are going to entice the consumer. Is it a never-before-used ingredient? A powerful clinical trial result? A strong before-and-after image? Creative and unique packaging? Any one of these could be the thing that makes the product leap off the shelf, and as much time as we spend thinking about these things, it often comes down to the very last minute—the minute we launch the product on TV. When we launch a new product on TV, we get real-time feedback on what is resonating with buyers. Did the orders go up when we talked about the new ingredient?

Did the calls come in when we showed a certain photo? By the time we are finished with the sell (usually around ten minutes for a new product), we know exactly what messaging will work when we are talking to the customer in our store, at Ulta, and even on our own website. That information becomes its own sort of circular economy. But you don't need to be on TV to do this. You can get similar results by building your own online community and then posting or livestreaming your various marketing messages and seeing which one generates the most excitement.

Just how powerful and powerfully efficient is the circular economy? The most discussed new technology in the last couple of years—generative AI, a type of artificial intelligence technology that creates text, images, audio, and synthetic data—is the ultimate example of the circular economy, recycling content that has been online for a completely new use. That's why there have been whole books written about how generative AI is going to change nearly every industry. Will it put writers, photographers, musicians, and other content producers out of work? Some, naturally. But it will also free up many of them from spending their energy rehashing well-worn concepts, and instead reward them for creating new and never-before-seen types of work.

Putting on Your Own Life Jacket

At any point in a company's life, operating frugally and maintaining a scarcity mindset can allow the business to swing above its weight class, fueling growth. Knowing the worth of water does this in part by pushing leaders to seek out new partners and build strong, mutually beneficial relationships rather than trying to solve problems by simply throwing more resources at it.

One of the most triumphant examples of cross-category success is the partnership between Barnes & Noble and Starbucks. When brick-and-mortar bookstores across the country were being put out of business by the emerging Amazon juggernaut in the early 2000s, Barnes & Noble realized that its one competitive advantage was having a place to sit and read or meet a friend. This "third space" concept (a place to gather that isn't home or work) was first coined by Ray Oldenburg in his book *The Great Good Place*. Barnes & Noble realized that having a place to grab a coffee or quick snack would help strengthen its competitive third-place advantage, but it lacked the resources and business expertise to open food service capabilities in all of its many stores. Starbucks was also trying to expand rapidly at the time, and what better way than to sign leases inside hundreds of retail locations in one fell swoop? To this day, analysts credit this partnership with the survival of Barnes & Noble when almost all of its competition has long since been felled by Amazon.

When we look to partner up for the sake of expanding our reach and marketing muscle, the question is always: What people or businesses can we link up with who will benefit enough from their association with us that they're going to want to give us something for free? (Or for very, very cheap?) How can we find someone who stands to benefit from the buzz around a collaborative idea that they could never do on their own?

This approach harkens all the way back to the early aughts, when Brent was practicing medicine at Mount Sinai Hospital in New York. The Department of Geriatrics wanted to create a new center for the study of aging and care for aging patients. But it was chronically underfunded. Part of his responsibility was to figure out how to build this center. While New York City is filled with lots of people with pockets so deep they could literally fill a well, Brent knew he could only approach them with an amazing proposition and design. He made a list of all the star architects in the city. At the top of the list was I. M. Pei, who had designed, among other things, the Rock and Roll Hall of Fame and the renovation of the Louvre. Brent wrote him a letter explaining what he was doing and how he wanted to show the world that just because you're older, it doesn't mean you can't come up with great ideas and *age better*. I. M. Pei was about eighty at the time, and the concept fed directly into what he was dealing with in his own life. He and his son came up with a beautiful design for the space.

But then Brent realized that wasn't enough. He needed a household name, someone who could give massive exposure to the place. Someone like . . . Martha Stewart. At the time, Martha was in prison for insider trading, presumably with lots of time on her hands. Brent didn't know her at all, but he wrote her a letter, cold. He told her how impressed he was with her, noting that she had built her company when the baby boomers really cared about creating the perfect home. And he explained that by helping to build this new academic center, she could help shepherd boomers into their next phase of life. And also, not coincidentally, a large charitable donation could help burnish her own brand with the very demographic her business depended upon. He sent the letter to Alderson Federal Prison Camp, Attn: Martha Stewart, in a gigantic envelope normally used for housing x-rays. He figured that the envelope's medical connotation and sheer size might help it stand out from all the other fan mail she was likely getting.

Two weeks later, he got a response from her daughter, Alexis, saying Martha had read the letter and wanted to speak with him. When Martha returned home five months later, Brent went to visit her at her farmhouse in Bedford, New York. She happily wrote a check to fund the new center in honor of her mother, who was in her nineties at the time. Ultimately, Martha made healthy living a vertical in her company and hired Brent to become its head. To this day, the Martha Stewart Center for Living at Mount Sinai stands as one of the preeminent facilities of its kind in the world.

If you can figure out how someone else can benefit from what you want from them, it will always be a win-win. But beware: money isn't everyone's primary need. They often need something else. Like value. Or association. If you can figure out what they need and give it to them some way in this project, you'll get what you need back.

LEARN FROM A G.O.A.T.:

Bethenny Frankel

Bethenny Frankel became a G.O.A.T. by realizing that her small role on a reality show, The Real Housewives of New York, *was just a stepping stone. She's built a $100 million business (SkinnyGirl), become a significant philanthropist, and continues to find opportunities everywhere.*

Please tell us your favorite saying or piece of homespun wisdom, the one that has meant the most to you personally or professionally.

"Don't buy into all the love or all the hate."

How did you first discover or learn of this maxim?

Because we believe our own BS and it gets us into trouble. No one is too big for the game. I've known it my whole life.

Why is this maxim so wise and valuable in business and beyond?

Everything can be taken away in an instant. The wolves are always at the end of the bed.

Does this maxim have any special relevance given what's currently going on in the world?

Not particularly, but social media is a land of love and hate, and in many cases, it's parasocial and also not unconditional. We have to know any media is like the ocean. It's beautiful but you can't always trust it.

How has this maxim contributed to your own success? Any particular stories come to mind?

I never forget where I came from. I know exactly why I'm here and I never overplay my hand.[9]

Marketing offers huge opportunities to save money by forging unconventional relationships. As with many other situations, we found creative ways to build relationships.

Such was the case between Beekman 1802 and Nestlé Toll House. Josh had an old connection there from his days in advertising, who invited him and Brent to speak on creative marketing at the annual Nestlé national sales conference. While mingling with the Nestlé Toll House Team after the speech, both sides realized how several of their business needs aligned. Much of Toll House's annual revenue depended on sales during the holiday baking frenzy over the fourth quarter. Likewise, nearly 50 percent of Beekman 1802's revenue came from gifting purchases made during the same time frame. Getting free press during this period would greatly supplement the marketing budgets for both companies, and we knew the press liked nothing more than a fun collaboration between two beloved brands.

So we suggested that our marketing team create lip balm, body cream, and soap that smelled like milk and cookies, specifically Toll House cookies.

The Beekman team was skeptical. "How much money does Toll House want to license its brand for use on our products?" they wondered. Most licensing deals cost the licensee a percentage of the revenue generated from items sold using the brand.

"Nothing," we replied. While the arrangement was unusual, both sides recognized the equal value to be gained from the free press. And besides, we were removing all of Nestlé's risk by taking on all of the inventory production costs and being responsible for the sale of all of it.

When thought of this way, it seemed more than fair that there would be no licensing fee. In fact, maybe Nestlé should owe us something for all of the free fourth-quarter exposure.

(Just kidding. The best way to ruin any win-win is to try to turn it into a solo victory.)

Selling Ice Cubes to Penguins

We are always looking for ways to squeeze out unforeseen value and to maximize our "scraptitude."

Most companies waste a lot of money on ineffective marketing. They try to be prudent, but it's difficult. You can spend a lot of money for awareness, but if you're not making an emotional connection with your customer, there will be no conversion. And if there is no conversion, there can be no loyalty. And if there's no loyalty, there's no lifetime value. It's the emotional connection with the consumer, not the rational one, that's so critical to long-term brand growth.

Our first priority in marketing is to connect emotionally with our customers (well, we like to connect emotionally with everyone). That's one of the reasons we like to think of them as "Neighbors." Our first cookbook, aptly titled *The Beekman 1802 Heirloom Cookbook*, came out in 2011. Why would we publish a cookbook? Well, we'd been growing our own food, whipping up our own recipes, and then posting them to our website as search engine optimization (SEO) content to draw eyeballs to our DTC business. One day it occurred to us that if we put all of our recipes in a book and someone actually published it, we could use it as a marketing tool. We didn't get a huge advance for it, but it didn't matter. Our goal wasn't to get rich by writing a cookbook. It was to save money by getting a publishing house to use its PR department on its dime to promote the Beekman 1802 brand.

That was the same idea behind our reality TV show, *The Fabulous Beekman Boys*. No company of our small size has the funds to pay for TV ads, so we brainstormed other ways to get ourselves and our young company on TV. At the time, reality television was just beginning to boom, and we knew that if we had our own show, it could in effect be one giant TV ad. Now while it might seem as if getting one's own TV show is just plain dumb luck, remember that to pitch a reality TV show, you need to have a compelling concept that includes high stakes, drama, and the risk of potential scandal. It also includes giving up control of how you and your company are portrayed. It was a bit hard for us to let go, but ultimately, we knew it would be a way to turn zero marketing dollars into millions worth of exposure. We took the risk, managed it as best we could, and we still have many customers who say they first discovered us from that "silly little show" that ran for two years from 2010 to 2011.

Our 2013 wedding is another example. We would have been fine with just a small party with our family at our house, but we knew that a lot of our growing community of Beekman Neighbors would love the chance to be part of our special day and visit the farm. So we put two hundred free tickets on our website and on social media and posted: "OK, if you want to join in the celebration, go here and reserve your spot." Two hundred people—friends, neighbors, and Neighbors—did so.

Knowing that we could never afford the type of modern-day fairy-tale wedding reception that fills the pages of bridal magazines, we did what the original Beekman family would have done on our farm back in 1802. We supplied the grilled meats and asked everyone else to bring a side dish that was always included in their own most important family celebrations. We also asked them to bring along the recipe. A photographer friend took portraits of them with their special dish and the handwritten recipe. We then posted them on our website. It was a wonderful souvenir of the day for everyone who attended, and also a great way for those who didn't get tickets to take part in it as well. (And no one went home from our wedding hungry.) That way people who didn't make it to the wedding could at least sample the food.

Our frugality continues even now that we're more financially stable and have actual, competitively sized marketing budgets. During the fourth quarter of 2022, a new media company invited us to do a one-hour live-stream event in South Street Seaport in New York City. If you're not familiar with the Seaport, it's a busy, touristy area in downtown Manhattan where people come to wander, eat, and shop. Lots and lots of shopping.

There were some costs associated with the event, and all of our budget had already been spent for the entire year. But it was an excellent opportunity. The foot traffic at the Seaport alone was worth having any sort of presence there just for brand awareness. Our wheels began spinning. How to conquer this mountain?

We asked the director of the media company if anything else was happening in its studio space for the rest of the year. The studio was at street level and had huge windows. Passersby could see production in action, which made us think. *Plate glass windows + Street level = Pop-up shop!*

So we wondered aloud if, in exchange for doing the live-streaming event, we could borrow the space—for free—for the rest of the season and do a holiday pop-up there?

He said sure, which was good news all around. Free rent for a month, and free branding in a happening location! All seemed great, until the estimates came back for the window displays we needed for the pop-up: $15,000. But we only had about $5,000 in our budget.

Churn, churn, churn.

Then we remembered that one of our staff members used to have a sign company, so she knew how to print and install vinyl. We got the budget for printing the vinyl to $3,000, and then our team members went down and installed the signs. We knew we could recoup the cost in sales during the pop-up. What originally would have seemed impossible for a company our size—a retail location during the holiday season in one of the busiest foot-traffic areas of New York City—became a reality based on a little creative thinking and extra manual labor.

"But why limit frugality to marketing?" we wondered. "Why not expand to other areas?" And that is how we managed to snag state-of-the-art office space in a city near our home upstate.

For the first ten years of Beekman 1802, our offices were located in our farmhouse and, later, on the second story of our store in Sharon Springs. It was a nice commute from our farm to Main Street four miles down the road. But as we grew, our staff was crammed into one room. It had become increasingly difficult to convince the caliber of talent we needed to relocate from New York or LA to a small village in upstate New York, where the hottest new restaurant was also the gas station.

We scoured the nearest startup hubs: New York, Boston, Philadelphia. And of course, we couldn't afford any of them. So we began looking closer to home. The closest big city is Schenectady, about forty minutes from the farm. The town had once been a booming metropolis; General Electric was its major employer. But GE dwindled over time, and the city's fortunes had been sinking steadily since.

To revitalize itself, Schenectady began offering incentives for businesses to open up shop there. We were probably one of the most visible companies in our area. And we were looking to hire not just minimum wage labor, but the kind of professional talent that the region was losing every passing day. It had space and no jobs. And we had jobs and no space. The possibilities were too good for either of us to pass up.

And that's how we got free office space in Schenectady. We will repeat that: *we got free office space.* And the kicker? The space we took over was a brand-new, gleaming, class A office that had been built out by a startup tech company that took on too much investment too quickly and overspent itself into bankruptcy. Not only didn't it know the price of water, it didn't even know the true cost of its own offices (free).

Drowning in Freeness

But free isn't always free. We've learned to look for any hidden costs the hard way. In late 2014, we were offered the chance to sell a line of farm-to-table branded food at Target grocery stores. It was to be called Beekman Farm Pantry, and it encompassed everything from pasta sauce to salad dressings. We would be given a four-foot endcap—that's nearly twenty feet of shelf space—in nearly two thousand Target stores. We would need to develop about thirty different food SKUs. That's a lot of product on a lot of shelves. It's the kind of opportunity that giant consumer packaged goods companies like Unilever or Kraft would sell their employees' firstborn children for. And probably *their* firstborn too.

It was a fabulous opportunity, but was it too big for a company of our size? (At that time, we only had five employees with about $5 million in revenue.) Despite our hesitations, we fell back on what we usually did when something was offered to us for free . . . we said yes.

It nearly swamped us, but in less than a year's time, we found producers for all thirty different products. We designed the packaging, manufactured the products, and delivered them to Target distribution centers and onto shelves all on time. It was an amazing accomplishment by any measure.

When we finally stopped to exhale, we looked deep in our well. It was as dry as Georgia asphalt in July. We had no money left to market everything we'd just launched.

We'd been concentrating on getting the products on the shelf, and we naively assumed that they would either sell themselves or that Target would help us market and move product somehow. What we didn't know about wholesale grocery retail was that there are millions of dollars of extra costs even after products hit the shelves. Brands have to pay the retailer a certain amount to market the item. There are extra fees to get in the retailer's flyers, for signage, for sampling. We were expected to shoulder the costs of coupons and discounting. Nationwide third-party contractors needed to be hired to restock shelves. We even had to pay for the shipping on items returned to us if they didn't sell. We had no idea of the amount of investment it would take to make our line successful, and worse yet, we'd never even asked Target how it worked. It assumed we knew. We didn't know what we didn't know. We were in way over our heads.

In the end, we did everything we could with what little money we had. We asked our army of Neighbors to stop by their local Target and help straighten and restock shelves. We redirected any cash flow from other sales channels into supporting the Target line. And yes, we even handed out samples of food ourselves in stores around the country. But in the end, we couldn't make it work. The line tanked.

Did we feel bad? Of course. But something good came from it: we learned a lesson. An expensive and humiliating one, but a lesson nonetheless. After that experience, we implemented a rule to make sure that all partners know exactly what each side expects the other to bring to the table. We had learned the worth of water, but now we'd learned that even free water is sometimes too expensive.

In 2020, when we got our second big chance with a brick-and-mortar retail partner, Ulta Beauty, we knew exactly what to ask for. How much shelf space we could comfortably handle. How much we'd be able to contribute to promotions. How many freelance sales associates we could put into stores on high-traffic days. We knew what was nonnegotiable for our success, what was nonnegotiable for their success, and what we could both compromise on.

There have been plenty of other mistakes over the years too. For example, our Facebook marketing was wildly successful at the time when Instagram initially launched in October 2010. We'd picked up a quarter million followers in our first year alone. But because our marketing dollars were working so well on Facebook, we decided that we didn't really need to embrace an unproven new platform like Instagram. We didn't even create an Insta account until about two years after it came out. And even then, we didn't embrace it the way much of our competition had.

Bad, bad, bad move. Many of these early Insta adopter beauty brands like Glossier, Drunk Elephant, and Tula had taken on a lot of investment dollars. When Instagram had a massive rise in popularity and importance for the beauty industry, these companies had deep wells in which they could find cash to spend on social media advertising. They were able to gamble on new platforms. They were able to embrace the new phenomena of "influencing." Some were signing contracts with over a thousand individual social media influencers. None of this was free, as our Facebook following was. It was very expensive.

But sometimes, just as there are no free lunches, there's no free water either, no matter how creative and scrappy we could be. We lost out on that early Instagram wave in a big way.

That turned out to be one of our biggest failures, and it was partly because we had always been so hesitant to take on investment dollars. Because we didn't have the extra funds as our startup competitors did, we weren't able to jump on this huge new opportunity.

But we console ourselves by remembering: companies that are acquired by private equity firms are ten times as likely to go bankrupt as those that don't sell.[10] And now many of those companies that put all of their eggs in the Instagram basket (pardon the mixed maxims) are suffering now that the cost of working with mega-influencers has skyrocketed. We missed out, but it may have saved us in the long run. (We did hop on TikTok immediately, though.)

So many companies never learned the value of water during the last decade or so of "free" investment dollars: WeWork. Theranos. Quibi. Fisker. Peloton. The mattress company Casper. Each brand was touted as the "next big thing," guaranteed to revolutionize the employment, healthcare, exercise, entertainment, auto, sleep industries. They raised a ton of money and bought a lot of water. But guess what? The next big thing is rarely that. It's statistically proven. A good idea does not necessarily a good business make. (More on that in chapter 5.) Sometimes you get to the bottom of your well and you still need a life jacket.

 ## CHEW ON THIS

- Just because you have resources as you grow doesn't mean you should use them. Cultivate a mindset of frugality and set a personal example for others to follow as well.

- Reverse the conventional logic of budgeting. Have people assume that they have a small or nonexistent budget and that they must work with that. Reward them when they show an ability to do more with less.

- Constantly scan the horizon, seeking out ways to build innovative partnerships that allow you to do more with less and that benefit others as well.

BECOME A G.O.A.T.:
The Zero-Budget Business

Think of your core business functions: marketing, operations, finance, human resources, and so on. For each function, assume you have only half of your current budget. What creative adjustments might you make to accomplish as much with that reduced budget as you currently do? What creative partnerships might you forge?

Now go further and assume that you have zero dollars—the well is entirely dry. Are there any potential ways that you might still get the job done? Think hard here, sticking with these thought experiments even if they initially seem impossible. Hopefully, you'll wind up with new solutions that you can use in your business at its current spending levels to operate more efficiently and improve performance.

A Bad Workman Blames His Tools

How to Learn and Grow

In 2020, we launched a new line of skin-care products that incorporated an ingredient derived from probiotics, which are living organisms that have a positive effect on gut health. At the time, "probiotics" was a buzzword more popular than Taylor Swift. Many companies in the beauty category began launching products with probiotic derivatives: lip glosses, moisturizers, mascaras, blush. We were eager to let the world know that we had this hot new ingredient in our line of skin care, so we used the descriptor "probiotic moisturizer" on the packaging. It launched. It did great. We got served with a class action lawsuit notice.

The Food and Drug Administration (FDA) had recently mandated that only food products containing live cultures could be labeled "probiotic." Keep in mind that these regulations were only for the food category. While these regulations did not pertain to beauty products or any other category of goods, a class action law firm in the Midwest smelled potential. Surely, it posited, if the FDA regulation of probiotic labeling in foods meant that they had to include live cultures, the average consumer would assume that there were live cultures in similarly named beauty products. And if the consumer felt confused, then that amounted to fraud in the eyes of the law. And fraud results in class action lawsuits. Not just against us, but against several other beauty companies as well.

We were annoyed by the suit, and even more annoyed with our advisers. Why hadn't our lawyers, who were supposed to scour every new product claim with a fine-toothed comb, pointed out the risk? And what about the retailers? They certainly should have seen potential problems. Where were they?

We weren't sure what to do. We didn't know then that most, if not every, company will face a fairly regular flow of lawsuits once it reaches a big enough size. The vast majority of the suits are without merit or frivolous and are settled with nothing more than a stern letter from one's own counsel. But not all of them. And if just one lawsuit garners a little bit of judicial traction, it can literally bankrupt a smaller company.

Some of our competitors fought their probiotic lawsuits, incurring hefty legal fees. Some are still fighting them. Other companies settled. It took a few months of hand-wringing to figure out what to do with our own situation, and to acknowledge one very real truth: any potential customer confusion—even if it was just a handful of customers—*was* ultimately our responsibility. We had blamed everyone else for the legal challenge, but as the founders of the company, we needed to take ownership of the situation and rectify it. The buck stopped with us, as it does with every founder or CEO.

So we decided that it would be cheaper in the long run to simply eat the loss on producing new packaging without the word "probiotic" and promote our product's benefit to the skin microbiome instead. We were being probiotically proactive.

Yes, it cost us a bundle, but as a result of the shift in messaging, we ended up becoming one of the world's leading brands educating people about their skin's microbiome. By tackling our potentially multimillion-dollar headache and owning up to our inadvertent label confusion, we wound up in a better place than had we continued to blame others and defend ourselves.

Blaming your tools means you aren't learning from your mistakes. If you're constantly maligning others, then you're not stopping to analyze your own role in the mistake. And that's a problem.

Tilling the Land

Many times when a mistake happens, everything but the person who committed the error is held responsible. But part of the lesson is learning to blame yourself, or, in more compassionate language, learning to take responsibility for the error. Don't try to find the blame; try to find the *lesson* that can be learned from the problem. While a bad workman blames the tools, a good workman finds the right solution for a better outcome.

The idea of taking ownership of and learning from mistakes goes back to the seventeenth-century G.O.A.T. maxim, "A Bad Workman Blames His Tools."

Different cultures have their own version of the saying. A Polish speaker might recognize the phrase, "A bad dancer blames the hem of her skirt." Indonesians might say, "An ugly person blames the mirror." The idea is that dysfunction occurs when we don't take responsibility for our failings. If we want to achieve any level of competency at what we do, we must not only admit our mistakes but learn from them as well. If we try, we can usually find ways to turn mistakes to our advantage, beyond simply learning for the next time.

We're never afraid to ask a question. Our approach has always been that if *we* have a question, someone else probably has the same one. Nor are we afraid of looking stupid. Who cares if we look stupid? We've always tried to create a culture of questioning in our company.

"If you don't understand why someone's making a decision or call, whether it's product development, creative, financial, then *ask*," we tell our employees. "Because a lot of times people may be missing the forest for the trees."

Entrepreneurs and CEOs would do well to not merely identify and learn from mistakes, but to take a deeper kind of responsibility for their shortcomings. Because if you're in a leadership position and take the blame for a subordinate's mistake, you will have a longtime employee. It's not being charitable or gratuitously kind. At the end of the day, you *are* responsible. If a leader is the workman, their employees are their tools.

Back when Josh was an advertising executive, he discovered the power behind regularly taking the blame for other peoples' slipups. Almost every time there was an issue that prompted everyone else to start pointing fingers at each other, Josh would take the heat. Most times everyone was so grateful that someone stepped up to the plate. This made his team much more open and creative to solving issues, simply because they weren't perpetually worried about getting into trouble. (And let's face it: most mistakes are a collective responsibility.)

Recently, we decided to move all of our warehouses to a third-party logistics service (also known as 3PL), which businesses use to outsource their supply chain and logistics operations. Most big companies do this, but it's a huge transition—you're moving all your inventory. It took a little over a year; we had to hire an outside consultant to oversee the process. But the cost of the transition came up to half a million dollars more than we had budgeted for. It was a big, unexpected hit. We hadn't considered the labor cost of the time it took to unload the trucks and place the inventory on the shelves in the new 3PL. Everyone in our company had played some role in the step. We had no choice but to eat the cost. It didn't go down well.

The opposite of blaming your tools *after* mistakes occur is humbly acknowledging your own imperfections and lack of knowledge *before* mistakes occur. We've been so inspired by this G.O.A.T. proverb that we make acknowledging what we don't know, and asking supposedly "dumb" questions, a hallmark of our leadership. This behavior, in turn, has inspired others in our organization to do the same, giving rise to a powerful culture of learning.

That's because making a mistake can really capture people's attention—what's known as "intellectual humility."

Intellectual humility is, essentially, a willingness to be openly wrong. Whereas most businesspeople think they have to project a strong and confident image, intellectual humility is about expressing uncertainty and limitations.

Researchers at the University of Buffalo found that leaders are held in higher regard when they admit mistakes and a desire to learn.[1] A 2018 Ohio State University study noted that leader humility, which it characterizes as being open to admitting one's limitations and mistakes, spurred creative thinking throughout the organization.[2]

All brands want their product to be aspirational. But being infallible is not aspirational. To many people, in fact, being infallible is off-putting. People don't like perfection. It makes them uncomfortable, and they feel bad about themselves.

Many years ago, not long after we launched, we sent out an email to our entire Neighbor base with the wrong price listed for a new product launch. It was humiliating. As a small company trying to gain respect, you worry that any kind of mistake erodes your credibility. What to do? Pretend it never happened? Make a joke about it? Or own up to it and suffer the consequences?

We chose Door Number Three and sent out a second email with the subject heading of "Oops! We made a mistake!"

We braced ourselves for a massive drop-off in clients, but the opposite happened. The number of people who opened that email was about six times the average normal open rate; people were curious to see what mistake we had actually made. Mistakes can be beneficial.

Often, whenever we really want to get people's attention, we'll send out an email with the subject line: "WE GOOFED!" It works.

As Michael Houlihan and Bonnie Harvey, founders of the Barefoot Wine brand, note in their book *The Barefoot Spirit*, when you admit to mistakes in a positive way, you actually gain admiration and loyalty.

"You and your company are not judged by how well you do when you're good, but by how well you do when you're bad," they write. "The fact is, everyone—and every company—makes mistakes. Denying that they have happened usually exacerbates and magnifies an already awkward situation, because chances are, you aren't fooling anyone, and you appear insincere. In fact, in a very real way, trying to dodge responsibility can hurt your reputation more than simply owning up to the mistake in the first place."[3]

Founders are often portrayed as being big dreamers, winning against all odds, fighting the naysayers. This is negativity aversion, or magical thinking, which can cause as many issues as the opposite. Business culture tends to lionize and revere optimism in founders, but rarely the contrary. If this is your tendency, then you need to find your counterbalance. Just being a dreamer might help you see an opportunity first, but that won't necessarily make you successful.

Wharton professor and best-selling author Adam Grant, author of, among other books, *Originals: How Non-Conformists Change the World*, believes that the first mover—that is, the first to market—does not necessarily gain a competitive advantage just by being first.[4] In many cases, the first person to market can be too early.

"With most products and industries, the settlers enjoy more success than the pioneers because the pioneers have to fight an uphill battle to create the market, whereas the second or third movers have to make the product better," he said in an interview with TechCrunch.[5] The first-mover personality often lacks humility. By the time they learn from their mistakes, it's too late. The second mover has already seen their mistakes and subsequently built their company better.

"First movers, except in industries where there's a network effect or patents, have a disadvantage because you spend your time creating the market and getting people used to this idea and then someone else can swoop in and make it better," he added. "But you don't want to be the last mover because then it's too late."[6]

Most entrepreneurs are scared to lose customers. But admitting mistakes can actually help build loyalty.

We like to do special things for our loyal Neighbors every year. It's just something extra to make them know we see them, we recognize them, and we appreciate them.

Every holiday season we offer our best Neighbors an early chance to order our big, expensive, annual advent calendar. Because these are limited edition, sometimes they sell out immediately. But in 2022 we'd ordered a healthier amount than usual, and they didn't.

To move the final small amount of inventory, about three weeks later, our team ran a gift-with-purchase promotion: "Buy an advent calendar, get a free goat ornament!" About half a dozen people wrote in and effectively said, "Wait, you told me that because *I'm* your best customer, my gift was early access to purchase a calendar. And so I did. And now you're giving other people a free gift that I didn't get?!"

Six people may not seem like a lot. But if six people took time out of their lives to actually reach out and complain, that probably means that several hundred people felt similarly angry but just weren't motivated enough to email us. After all, it's the sort of thing that other companies do all the time.

Our team's first proposal to correct that mistake was to send an ornament to everybody who wrote in and complained. That would be the most cost-efficient way to make good on our mistake.

We said no. The smarter and more strategic thing to do would be to send it to *everyone* who bought the advent calendar right from the beginning. To admit we made a mistake and, in addition, to send them the free gift they lost out on, we would also send an extra discount as well, a discount that the second wave of purchasers didn't get. This way they would still feel like our most important Neighbors.

So that's what we did.

Ultimately, the loyal customers were so pleased that they took the coupon and returned to the website to buy additional gifts and *increased* their average holiday spending with us that year. This showed our employees that they can make a mistake and benefit from it. This philosophy makes work a lot less stressful, because if you're not spending every minute worrying about every little mistake you might make, you can focus on actually doing the work.

The real worry sets in if our employees *don't* learn from their mistakes. If you make the same mistake twice, then we get mad. But at first, if a mistake is made, we always say, "OK, well, what was the breakdown? What are we learning from it? What should I have learned from that? What process was out of place? What skill wasn't there?"

It's like doing a root cause analysis on every bad outcome, no matter how big or how small. Eventually, this will just become a habit.

In the immortal words of jazz musician Miles Davis, "If you're not making a mistake, it's a mistake."

Good Workman, Good Tools

The concept of learning from mistakes has grown in popularity over the years—at least in principle. In practice, not so much.

Businesspeople and thought leaders often talk about admitting to and learning from mistakes. Over the past decade or so, tech entrepreneurs have adopted the mantra "Fail fast and break things!" Only recently have they learned the limitations of that philosophy (over-hiring, running unprofitably, growing at all costs, and so on).

Harvard leadership professor Amy Edmondson has extolled the virtues of "learning organizations," where people feel safe to explore their failings and learn from them. And professor and bestselling author Brené Brown has been trying to get leaders to display their vulnerability, as this helps others admit and learn from their own failings as well.

But what businesspeople *say* and what they actually *do* are often pretty different things. The fact is that most individuals, teams, and organizations—even those in the tech world— still struggle to take responsibility for their shortfalls. We see it in the continued prevalence of pseudo apologies as well as in the failure of many companies to learn from their mistakes.

Consider the September 2016 flop of Samsung's Galaxy Note 7 phone. When batteries on thirty-five phones burst into flames, Samsung announced that it would stop producing the devices. Then it implemented an "exchange program" where users could trade in their defective phone for a new model. Except that not long after, consumers around the country reported that the replacement phones Samsung had distributed through other carriers were also combusting.

Industry observers blamed the failure on managers and employees to spot and correct mistakes, but that's not what actually happened. As an October 2016 *Fast Company* article noted, it was a failure in *leadership*.[7]

Until then, consumers had been feeling pretty loyal to Samsung. But after the second disaster, they began getting angry. Samsung had scurried to put a Band-Aid over the problem without fully researching, or admitting, that the rollout had been a disaster. Neil Cybart, the founder of the Apple tech analysis firm Above Avalon, blamed company leadership.

"Regardless of the root cause, the only way Samsung will be able to learn from this experience is to have strong leaders address shortcomings found within the company's culture and processes," he told *Fast Company*. Someone at the electronics company must have been listening. Samsung decided it had to figure out what had gone wrong. So it gathered upper-level executives for three months, with workdays sometimes lasting over twenty hours. "We basically lived in a war room, a conference room for those 120 days," Tim Baxter, Samsung's North America chief executive, told the *Washington Post*. Often, workdays would end at 4 a.m. or 5 a.m., he said, and sometimes pick back up at 6 a.m. "We learned more about working as a team in that time—almost operating as a start-up—than I'd ever experienced."[8]

After determining what had caused the problem, Samsung made sure it didn't happen again. So it set up new testing protocols and a "battery advisory group" with battery consultancy firms and intellectual heavyweights from Stanford, UCLA, and Cambridge University.

"In the end, they were painstakingly clear about the fact that this happened and it was their fault," said Ramon Llamas, a researcher at IDC, a provider of market intelligence and advisory services for the information technology, telecommunications, and consumer technology markets. The proof that this worked? In 2017, Samsung reported $50 billion in profit, according to the *Post* article. The reporter noted that Samsung's response to the crisis and position in the global smartphone market helped it avert disaster.[9]

Sometimes you have to take responsibility for things that *aren't* of your own doing. (Or at least take an amount that seems appropriate to your customers.) The hair-care brand Olaplex had been an industry darling since its launch in 2014. It held over one hundred patents for its shampoos, conditioners, and bond multipliers formulated especially for fragile and damaged hair. It revolutionized the industry. And it was rewarded when the company went public in 2021 and raised significantly more than estimated.

However, in 2023 it found itself the subject of a lawsuit claiming that the brand's products caused hair loss and damage. As we showed earlier, it's one of the worst positions a company can find itself in.

Olaplex immediately started fighting back. Forcefully. Its CEO personally posted a video on its social media denying that its products caused damage. That was followed by a full media campaign touting its previous safety testing, as well as results from independent labs that refuted the claimant's charges.

In fact, there has been no proof that the product caused hair loss or damage. And there were other issues plaguing the company at the time of the lawsuit as well. But was its swift and strongly defensive response effective? There was a viral backlash of consumer sentiment on social media that may have been impossible to quell by any response, and it quickly overtook any of the brand's efforts to regain stable footing.

Would more humility—even when it could be shown it had done nothing wrong—have helped? Or would a display of vulnerability have shifted consumer sentiment?

It's impossible to say now. Over the next year, the stock continued to drop precipitously. The same CEO who presided over the legendary IPO wound up stepping down only three years later, with the stock trading at less than 90 percent from its peak.

Perhaps the saddest part is that a judge eventually dismissed the claims entirely, and the original plaintiff dropped her suit a few weeks later.

Leaders of more traditional, small and midsize businesses might struggle to understand how a mantra like "think fast and break things" or talk of "vulnerability" really applies to them. But it does.

As total entrepreneurial novices, we knew we would make plenty of mistakes over the course of building Beekman 1802—and make no mistake, we were right about that. Fortunately, our G.O.A.T. practice of taking responsibility for errors—and even perceived errors—and learning from them helped our company to recover and grow regardless. As we discovered, you don't need to be a brainiac Harvard MBA to build a thriving business. And we can say that, because Brent has an MBA from a top ten business school, but his most valuable lessons have been learned from our entrepreneurial experiences, including being wise enough not to blame our tools when we've screwed up.

Remember the Beekman 1802 Target fiasco from the last chapter? When Target gave us the opportunity to sell a line of branded, shelf-stable food products in its stores? And remember how we hadn't budgeted any time or money for marketing the product to consumers in the store because we figured that Target would take care of that? And remember how it didn't? As newbies, we didn't understand how the retail business worked. Because of this error on our part, our food line at Target fizzled.

Now, ten years later, we're back in Target and Ulta Beauty. Luckily for us, management changed during that time, so we didn't have to announce to anyone that we had corrected our errors. All we had to do was make sure we did it correctly when given the second chance by hiring good people and budgeting properly for the marketing programs.

Ratcheting Up Responsibility

Beyond its clear business benefits, taking responsibility can benefit us personally, physically, and psychologically. Research links taking responsibility to individual happiness and well-being. That's because when we accept responsibility, we feel a sense of agency. That sense of control and power, in turn, helps us to feel more content.

You can also take deeper responsibility for your shortcomings by endeavoring not just to learn from mistakes but to move in the moment to turn them into opportunities.

Andy Stenzler is a serial entrepreneur who has founded or co-founded more than seven companies, including Kidville and the Rumble Boxing chain, which sold to Xponential Fitness for a cool $300 million.[10]

"I know the worth of having dry powder when things are tough," Andy, fifty-five, admits. "The most powerful thing for me was failure and mistakes. You can continue to make mistakes, and if they don't put the company out of business, then you become smarter and more powerful. The experience of navigating bumps—when to take money and at what valuation, when to sit on cash, that's a powerful lesson."

In 2005, Andy and his wife, Shari Misher Stenzler, founded Kidville, a play space for children. Three years later, the market crashed.

"You'd think the last thing people cut back on was classes or their kids [but they did], so we had to make sure we had enough capital," he says. "We had to be able to turn on and turn off variable expenses. Cut back on initiatives we wanted to do. Sometimes it involves cutting back on staff, which is never easy. You have to be as prudent and disciplined as possible."

To compensate, they ran fewer classes and cut back employee hours. It was painful, but Andy tried to be philosophical. "I always look at them as opportunities and challenges," he says. "A lot of entrepreneurs in today's world—their back is against the wall. Slow down your growth and make sure the conditions are right in the marketplace."

Andy did a similar pivot at Rumble, where he and his team noticed an issue with music. As at most gyms, music is hugely important to each class. And while the trainers were excellent, they weren't DJs. They were banging their heads against the wall trying to pick out the best music. This led to frustration for the trainers and, ultimately, a less optimal experience for the clients. People already find any excuse not to work out. They didn't need another.

This wasn't the kind of head-banging Andy had envisioned. So Rumble created a companywide playlist, with each song lasting three minutes (each round in boxing lasts three minutes, so it mimicked a real live match). There was something for everyone: classic, rock, pop, hip-hop. Trainers could pick from playlists, and the songs were mashed together with the right mix.

"It took a lot of stress off employees," he says. It also provided an extra branding opportunity because it was so Rumble-specific.[11] This is yet another form of taking ownership, seeing into the future and preventing mistakes from happening.

 CHEW ON THIS

- When you're with your teams, make a practice of asking lots of "dumb" questions and humbly emphasizing what you don't know.

- With every mistake that occurs, look for hidden ways to turn it into a meaningful opportunity.

- Consciously build imperfection into your brand identity, balancing humility and pride.

BECOME A G.O.A.T.:
Analyzing Our Errors

Think of the three biggest, most painful mistakes you've made in the course of running your business. Have you repeated that mistake? What has the mistake taught you? Was a process inside your organization flawed? Did you lack sufficient resources? Did you fail to communicate well? Finally, what would you do today to turn this mistake into a valuable opportunity?

Make Hay While the Sun Shines

How to Seize Opportunities

Date: December 24, 2013

Time: 12:01 a.m.

Place: The shipping room in the Beekman 1802 store in Sharon Springs, New York

It was a snowy evening in December, and our holiday orders were through the roof.

They were so big—more than two thousand packages had to go out—that we'd been frantically trying to assemble all of them so they could go out in time for the Christmas shipping deadline. We knew we were going to have to work throughout the night in shifts, with short napping and biological breaks. We were exhausted and unshaven, and possibly even unshowered. We were not happy about this—if nothing else, we Beekman Boys love our beauty sleep. But we had no choice. If we didn't do it, we'd have lots of unhappy Neighbors waking up on Christmas morning.

This was clearly a good problem to have. What entrepreneur wouldn't want an overabundance of customers clamoring for their products? It was a dream. But dreams sometimes cause problems. Answered prayers, and all that.

So, there we were on our assembly line—Josh slapping his 862nd label on our logoed box, Brent risking lingual paper cuts by licking yet another envelope—when a voice boomed from Beyond: "Make hay while the sun shines!"

Just like that. "Make hay while the sun shines!"

Now, you might be wondering why some otherworldly being would concern itself with the day-to-day intricacies of Beekman 1802. We wondered that, too. (We also wondered if we were experiencing auditory hallucinations. This is highly possible.) But we couldn't dwell on it because we had work to do. So, we focused on the message instead: "Make Hay While the Sun Shines."

This spoke to us, especially since, like many traditional sayings, it's rooted in agriculture. The phrase is credited to a German humanist named Sebastian Brandt, in his satirical book *Narrenschiff*, which came out in 1494. The book was later published in English in 1509 by Alexander Barclay. Its proper title back then was *Ship of Folys of the Worlde*, but it's also known as *Ship of Fools*.[1]

If you've ever lived or worked on a farm, you know that if there's rain in the forecast when you mow and bale your hay, you're asking for trouble. If your hay gets wet while drying on the field, the moisture will cause mold and bacteria to grow in the hay, creating heat and eventually flames. If you don't make hay while the sun shines, your barn just might burn down. This is not good for goats, or G.O.A.T.s.

In business terms, the proverb encourages people to take advantage of good fortune when it comes around, because you never know what kind of rainstorms are on the horizon.

In both business and life, it's important to grasp opportunities for gain promptly, and to then make the most of them. (*Carpe diem!*) Delaying or taking a more passive, lackluster approach might not cause a fatal conflagration, but it might well prevent you from reaping the kind of value you seek. Conversely, successes we notch increase the odds of even more success—if we're willing to lean into our successes. In business, we stand to gain if we can jump on these winning streaks when they appear and make the most of them.

Research has shown that winning streaks actually do happen. If you start sinking free throws in basketball, your chance of sinking even more of them increases, leading to what observers have called the "hot hand effect." Other people might call it "flow" or being "in the zone." Sometimes you just *kick ass*.

The idea is that a basketball player has a statistically better chance of scoring if they've been shooting that night with unusual accuracy, which Golden State Warrior point guard Stephen Curry did in 2022, when he made 105 consecutive three-pointers during a practice session.[2] A video of this went viral, which triggered conversation about whether there was any validity to the hot-hand theory or not.

In 1985, researchers published a paper in *Cognitive Psychology* in which they argued that the hot hand is nothing more than a coincidence, which they called the "hot hand fallacy."[3] Humans, they argue, simply want to make sense of random events in order to try and create some order in the universe. Nobel Prize–winning economist Daniel Kahneman, the author of *Thinking Fast and Slow*, put it this way: "The hot hand is a massive and widespread cognitive illusion."[4]

The legitimacy of hot-handedness became somewhat of a brouhaha in academic circles, and a July 2017 paper debunked the debunkers, arguing that three-point shooting was not a "widespread cognitive illusion" at all and actually regularly occurs.[5]

New Yorker editor David Remnick agreed. "What's clear is that when it comes to the life of the imagination, the hot hand is a matter of historical fact," he wrote in a 2015 article called "Bob Dylan and the 'Hot Hand.'" "Such golden periods, which usually take place just once, if at ever, in the life of an artist, are undeniable."[6]

He cited the Beatles, whose golden period lasted from 1965 to 1969; Dylan, whose "most intense period of wild inspiration and creativity ran from the beginning of 1965 to the summer of 1966"; and Stevie Wonder, whose creative heyday was from 1972 to 1976.

Whether you believe in the hot-hand theory or not (we do), the takeaway is the same: just like Ben Franklin, you must know when to hoist the key in the air. You have to know when the lightning is going to strike.

If you're winning, the only way to keep doing so is to keep playing. If you're losing, the only way to start winning is to keep playing. And when you're on a winning streak, the only 100 percent guarantee of breaking it is to kick back and coast. So in this instance, when we were swamped with holiday orders and at the point of exhaustion from fulfilling them, we doubled down.

To let Beekman Neighbors know that we were working hard to get their packages to them on time, we decided to turn on our laptop camera and livestream the last twenty-four hours of shipping on Facebook. As we worked to pack up the orders, we could see which Neighbors were leaving comments. We'd interact with them by text or even phone. When a box was ready to go out, we'd hold it up to the camera and let the recipient know that it was on its way. It made everybody feel good that their package was going out, while also connecting them to other Neighbors around the country.

Interestingly, our actual Sharon Springs Neighbors were also tuning in to the live feed. They saw how hard our team was working into the wee hours of the morning, and some decided to bring in homemade cookies for them. Our famously exuberant mayor, Doug Plummer, came by to sing Christmas carols with our team to keep their spirits high. And the local café brought in hot coffee and doughnuts when the sun came up.

All of this was captured on our camera and streamed live to thousands of Neighbors across the country. They loved watching our little community come together. It was about as pure an expression of the Christmas spirit as they'd ever seen, especially for a retailer.

They started sending messages of support. Many even put in second or third orders. Some even put in extra orders but kindly let us know that "it wasn't a rush . . . it could wait till after your team gets some sleep." As a result, our impromptu Beekman "Last Day of Shipping 24 Hour Live Marathon" became an annual tradition, and by far our busiest revenue driver of the entire holiday season, even besting Black Friday and Cyber Monday. By the fifth year, tens of thousands of people tuned in specifically to watch the ever-increasingly entertaining antics. The local high school band came to play outside the store. Farmer John brought in live goats. We had cooking and crafting demonstrations. Eventually the viewing audience grew so large that we started attracting celebrity call-ins from Beekman fans like Pioneer Woman Ree Drummond, actresses and singers like Vanessa Williams, Sharon Jones, Mindy Cohn, Tiffani Thiessen, and of course, Martha Stewart.

A side benefit of Beekman Neighbors watching the Beekman team working so hard to get their packages out was that if, for whatever reason, their holiday packages didn't reach them in time, well, they knew we tried our hardest. Our transparency helped avert many future irate Neighbor services calls.

That first livestream was just to let people know that we were working hard to get their packages to them on time. But if we hadn't noticed the level of engagement it generated, we wouldn't have invested to build upon it year after year. We made hay while the sun gleamed brightly on us. And then we spun that hay into gold.

Hay Fever

Most entrepreneurs naturally seek out opportunities where they can. But as we've learned, it pays to look far and wide to maximize opportunities, even going beyond the confines of your business itself. In business as in farming, the sun doesn't always shine. Quite often, it's raining or even downright stormy. It's best to squeeze every last bit of value out of opportunities when they arise, using all the creativity and ingenuity you can muster. And when the weather does turn bad, we can use that same creative spirit to make the best of it by finding still more opportunities to grasp.

The first time we faced this need was when we were doing *The Fabulous Beekman Boys* show, which aired on a small cable channel called Planet Green from June 2010 to May 2011. We got the show when Josh went on a freelance job interview at the network because we desperately needed some outside income to help pay the mortgage. When he realized mid-interview—with the network president, no less—that he wasn't a good fit for the job, he pivoted and turned the interview into a pitch for a reality TV show about two gay city slickers buying a farm in the middle of nowhere. She bit and ordered a pilot episode, which turned into two full seasons, a wedding special, and a holiday special.

Before the first season came out, Discovery, which owned Planet Green, sent us to various high-profile events in Manhattan, like the opening of a Broadway show or a hot new restaurant. The idea was that we would get photographed on the red carpets at said events, thus amplifying our visibility and drumming up some nice PR for the *Beekman Boys*. It was a brilliant strategy, but for one thing: nobody knew who we were. We would attend these events and there would be photographers there, but they were searching for Ryan Gosling or Keanu Reeves. They did not care a whit about the two randos before them. We understood; we were unknown entities. But we weren't going to let that get in the way of our future success.

So we asked ourselves: How can we stand out so these photographers will remember us the next time they see us? We decided we needed some sort of fashion trademark. The show was about two New York City professionals who were starting over on a farm in the country. So the next time we were sent out to a red carpet publicity event, we dressed in our finest business suits . . . and muck boots. It might not have been the most stylish look, but it was a look. The photographers who all shuttled between red carpet events started to remember us. Our pictures were snapped and resnapped and eventually landed in the pages of *People, Entertainment Weekly, Us Magazine*, and so on. In fact, our attire became such a statement that Swarovski crystallized a pair of muck boots for us, which we wore for *Vogue's* famous annual Fashion Night Out event. Ultimately, we signed on with the Original Muck Boot Company for a line of Beekman 1802 boots. Farmer bling!

Our entire short-lived reality show endeavor was a lesson in making hay while the sun shone. It wasn't just about taking advantage of the opportunity put before us (pivoting from a job interview for Josh) but capitalizing on it every step of the way. This will come as no surprise to anyone, but hundreds—if not thousands—of people appeared on some form of reality television in the early 2000s. Most of them were thrilled for their moment in the sun. The problem was that most of them just soaked it up. Very few worked to turn their moment in the sun into something sustainable.

Another time this maxim came into play was when we got the opportunity to do *The Amazing Race*, the Emmy award–winning reality series that has run on CBS for more than thirty-five seasons. (We were asked to audition because one of the network big-wigs turned out to be a fan of *The Fabulous Beekman Boys*. More sun. More hay. More sun . . . .)

The Amazing Race producers weren't planning on giving us or our company free advertising; promoting us wasn't their goal. But it was ours. Being on a national TV show with 11 million viewers was a spectacular opportunity to brand ourselves and our burgeoning business. Our initial goal was just to publicize the company and get as much exposure as possible. Winning never crossed our mind. For us, any Beekman 1802 awareness marketing was already prize enough.

We made up T-shirts with the words "Beekman Boys" emblazoned on the front in eighty-point font. When we introduced ourselves to people on the race, we didn't say, "Hi, we're Josh and Brent." We said, "We're the Beekman Boys!" We wanted to get the word "Beekman" on air as many times as possible. On one leg of the race, in Bangladesh, we had just completed the exhausting task of sorting and transporting huge loads of bamboo timber. (Long story. Watch the season.) As we were running toward the finish line in 102-degree heat, one of the last things we were thinking about was how to get free marketing for Beekman. But as you can probably tell, free marketing is never the very last thing we're thinking about.

As luck would have it, our sprint to the finish took place right when a nearby school was letting out for the day. About forty kids saw us running and began chasing behind us, hollering and laughing. We started shouting "Beekman Boys! Beekman Boys!" And all forty of those kids joined us in unison, running and shouting our name to the finish line. Not only was it incredibly motivating to have these fun kids excited and rooting us on when we were minutes away from passing out from exhaustion and heat, it was also another "Beekman" moment that was impossible for CBS to edit out. Win-win.

Each week, when a new episode aired, our website traffic and orders would see triple-digit increases. Over the course of the season, our sales grew over tenfold. When we eventually wound up winning the race—yeah, it was pretty amazing—our website traffic actually shut down not just our site, but nearly the whole platform we were hosted on. We may have been the first to break the internet. (Sorry, Kim Kardashian.)

We realize that some people might be thinking: "What a lucky break to be on TV while growing your small business." But remember, if Josh hadn't pivoted from a failing job interview to a winning show pitch, we would have been stuck waiting for the rain to stop to start making hay.

Before we continue, let us pause for a moment to explore the concept of opportunism. The word has a negative association, and we get it. An opportunist is typically thought to be someone who takes whatever they can, with few principles and little concern about anyone else. They don't care who suffers as long as they get ahead. Think Machiavelli, who advocated exploiting and manipulating others for his own benefit.

But being an opportunist doesn't have to be to the detriment of other people. For example, just because we promoted our business on *The Amazing Race*, that didn't stop any of the other contestants from doing the same thing. We're pretty sure it also didn't take away any of CBS's ad revenue. As far as we're concerned, recognizing and seizing an opportunity is smart business. The words we would use, in fact, are "savvy businessperson" or "entrepreneur."

The cold hard truth is that if you don't grab opportunities when they present themselves, you'll end up standing in the barn petting your goats while fire erupts around you. A little opportunism never hurt anyone. It's essential to getting ahead in life.

One of the ways we maximize every opportunity in our company is that we don't just do postmortems when something goes wrong like most companies do; we also debrief successes. Postmortems help avoid making the same mistakes twice. Post-success debriefs help us understand how something went right, so that we can replicate it.

When the pandemic erupted in 2020, we knew right away that Beekman 1802 was going to be inundated with orders. With handwashing now a national obsession, more people than ever would be looking for natural soap products like ours that were gentle on their skin.

Mindy Cohn is an original Beekman Neighbor, a regular customer who discovered us and became a good friend. Her name might sound familiar to some of you—she played Natalie on the TV show *The Facts of Life*, and she most recently appeared in the Apple TV hit show *Palm Royale*.

The three of us were having a chat, and she said: "If you're going to walk onto a stage of any sort, make sure it's memorable. Otherwise, it's a waste of your time."

So, Brent, who is a doctor, took the pandemic as a chance to educate Beekman fans on the proper handwashing technique he was taught in medical school. We filmed videos demonstrating the correct way to wash hands that people could share with their own social networks. We even helped develop an app that would send out reminders throughout the day to wash your hands. During the first scary weeks of lockdowns, Brent went live on our social media channels to answer Beekman Neighbors' medical questions and help them keep calm. In those early days of the pandemic, we even helped HSN and QVC edit together a public service announcement about proper handwashing.

LEARN FROM A G.O.A.T.:

Curtis Stone

Curtis Stone is a Los Angeles–based, Michelin-starred chef, restaurateur, author, and culinary entrepreneur.

Please tell us your favorite saying or piece of homespun wisdom, the one that has meant the most to you personally or professionally.

"You create your own luck in life. And the harder you work, the luckier you get."

How did you first discover or learn of this maxim?

I did an apprenticeship and worked for good people. I wasn't exceptional. I was like any other twenty-year-old kid wanting to be a good cook. Then, I moved to Europe, and everything changed. When I landed in London and began working for Marco Pierre White, another world opened to me. When you're in the company of someone as brilliant as Marco, and his equally impressive team, you quickly realize you have a whole lot to learn and need to keep your head down to keep up. After a period, I started believing in myself and realized that my focus on technique had gradually, day-by-day, resulted in improvement.

Why is this maxim so wise and valuable in business and beyond?

We have a limited capacity as human beings. All we can do is try our best and if that dedication doesn't cut it, we know we've done everything in our power.

Unlike many other companies, we didn't take advantage of soap shortages to raise our prices. Just because the sun is shining, it's not always necessarily a good time to make hay. Pandemics are temporary; consumer grudges last forever. In hindsight, the pandemic seemed like boom times for HSN and QVC—and for a soap company, for that matter. People were stuck at home with nothing to do but watch TV and worry about viruses.

Does this maxim have any special relevance given what's currently going on in the world?

We live in an uncertain time, especially in the restaurant business. Remaining creative and turning over every stone to look for opportunities is essential to my definition of success. During the pandemic, we had to change the way we cooked at the restaurants, there were massive pivots in the entire industry. We are fine-dining establishments, and we put down our tweezers and picked up our rolling pins. I remember the first chicken pot pie I made for delivery. It was such a trying time and the amplified gratification I got from making such a comforting and humble food was off the charts.

How has this maxim contributed to your own success? Any particular stories come to mind?

Diversification is critical in any business, and I've learned not to be solely reliant on the restaurants. While I love hospitality, when we were literally told during the pandemic, "You can't open for business," we didn't sit on our hands and hope that something changed. We got creative.[7]

But operationally, QVC and HSN depend on brand guests traveling to the studio with their hosts. With travel in complete lockdown, the model was broken. QVC and HSN tried selling with just the hosts alone, and then with brand guests phoning in, but none of it was working. An increased number of viewers and shoppers were tuning in, but they weren't buying.

Besides our regular sales on those channels falling due to our lack of personal appearances on air, we had another issue. Long before the pandemic broke out, we had been scheduled to be a "Today's Special Value" on QVC. That's its "big daily deal" that accounts for up to 80 percent of its revenue on the day. A TSV is a big deal for any brand. We had already purchased over $5 million in inventory for the day, which is entirely sold on consignment. Anything leftover at midnight we had to eat.

Our TSV date fell the second week of lockdown. We panicked. Actually, that's not the word for it. We aspirated. Like all companies our size, we finance our inventory with temporary loans. How were we going to move $5 million of inventory when we couldn't even be in the studio to sell it? And how pathetic would it be for a soap company to go bankrupt during a pandemic?

Rain clouds were forming over our hayfield. What to do?

We knew of a production company in Saratoga Springs that normally shot horse racing and other sports live events for network television. Of course, all of those had been canceled during Covid-19, so it was scrounging for work. Opportunity knocked.

We quickly hired it to build out a studio on the top floor of our store and contracted with it to find a way to broadcast us to QVC, which would rebroadcast over its airwaves. (This was before "Skyping" became the norm on all TV channels during the pandemic.) All of this cost us about $52,000. This was not cheap, but it was less expensive than losing $5 million and going bankrupt. We were the first TSV guests to appear "live" on air on QVC, and later again on HSN, and we sold all $5 million worth of product before the day was over.

Soon, every other brand followed suit. In fact, the sports production company we partnered with began contracting with many of QVC's other brands—including Martha Stewart—to set up studios in their locations, enabling it to keep all its staff working throughout the entire pandemic. It was a win-win-win for everyone, but most especially the customer, who had a way to get soap safely to their door without ever having to leave the house.

Bale, Don't Bail

One of our hay-making role models is thirty-six-year-old Australian entrepreneur Melanie Perkins.[8] In 2013, Perkins started Canva, a free online design platform, with the goal of making design easily accessible for everyone. Perkins was nineteen when she came up with the idea. In 2006, and she and her cofounder, Cliff Obrecht, were studying at university in Perth. To earn extra cash, they taught students how to use design programs like Microsoft and Adobe. But the programs were challenging, and Perkins decided there had to be a better way. So Obrecht created an online school-yearbook design business, Fusion Books, and launched a website for students to "collaborate and design their profile pages and articles." The pair then printed the yearbooks and delivered them to schools across Australia. The venture was so successful that Perkins started reaching out to investors. In 2010, she met venture capitalist and Silicon Valley entrepreneur Bill Tai, who introduced her to some folks in his network. He also invited her to Mai Tai, the exclusive gathering he held in Maui a few times a year for investors and kite-surfing fans.

Perkins did not know a kite from a surf (though she had been an ice skater since she was fourteen, so she understood discipline and training).[9] But she knew that it would serve her well to pick up a new skill that her new best friend loved. "Every time he [Tai] would say how was my business going, he'd also be like 'how's your kite surfing going?'" Perkins told CNBC. "I had not done it before—and, to be honest, it's not something that I would normally, naturally try," she said. "But yeah, I decided to give it a go because when you don't have any connections, you don't have any network; you just kind of have to wedge your foot in the door and wiggle it all the way through."

It paid off. By 2018, at the ripe old age of thirty, she had made it as one of tech's youngest female CEOs, and was featured on the *Forbes* billionaires list in 2023.

We are not advocating lying. No one wants to feel duped. But puffery is a real thing. Legally, puffery describes an exaggerated or vague statement about a product or service that's intended to encourage a potential buyer to buy it. Publicists know this. Donald Trump knows this. So do good businesses. Obviously, sometimes puffery can bite you in the back. To wit: Elizabeth Holmes, the Theranos founder, who fraudulently amped up her data, is now in jail for eleven years.

But Perkins didn't go Holmesian! She just never told Tai that she hadn't been a kite-surfing devotee before he came along. We're saying, capitalize on opportunities . . . or make hay while the sun shines. When a famous business media outlet once referred to us in a press release as "one of the fastest growing lifestyle brands in the country," we didn't let that fade away with yesterday's news. We had no idea what it had based its statement on, but we used that quote repeatedly in marketing and business materials for years to come. When the Universe sends you gifts to make hay with, bale as much as you can as long as you can.

 ## CHEW ON THIS

- When opportunities arise, think of ways to take it up a notch—and then another notch. Look for unusual actions you can take or partnerships you could forge to squeeze even more value. Think beyond your business, looking to your personal background or to those of your employees, customers, and other stakeholders.

- Create more future success by mobilizing your current success as a credential. Your performance might not allow you to claim that you're the number one lifestyle brand in the country, but can you claim that one of your products or services is number one or that you're number one in a certain region? The shrewder you are at building awareness of your present success, the greater the odds of bigger victories going forward. Everyone likes to associate with winners.

- Hold regular post-success meetings, not just the traditional postmortem meetings, to celebrate what went right so that you can replicate that and also to determine where you might have left opportunity on the table and build further to achieve your next success.

BECOME A G.O.A.T.:
Taking Opportunity Further

Make a list of the three biggest opportunities you've seized in the past. These could be commercial opportunities, such as the chance to increase sales or expand into a new market, but they could also be strategic (the chance to make an acquisition), organizational (the chance to hire new talent, make leadership changes, or improve internal processes), or financial (the chance to access new capital).

For each opportunity, think of two to three other steps you might have taken to squeeze out extra value. Now apply this same analysis to the opportunities that you find before you today.

An Empty Vessel Makes the Most Noise

How to Stay Focused

It was 2014, five years after we launched, and we were feeling pretty good about ourselves and the business we created. No, we weren't one of the *Fortune* 500, and no, we hadn't gone public. But that was never our goal. Our goal from day one was to build an enterprise that would last long after we were gone, while also doing some good in the world. Financially, we wanted to do well enough to pay our mortgage on the farm and enjoy a reasonably comfortable retirement. Our personal goal was around $5 million in liquid assets and no debt.

We realize that might seem like a lot to most people. And to most of the world, it is an awful lot. But if we were going to drop both of our lucrative careers to get Beekman 1802 off the ground, we needed a personal goal. However, we didn't need to aim for "F-U Money," which is what most entrepreneurial guides seem to promise. We didn't need a yacht, or private plane, or ritzy mansion in Gstaad. We just wanted enough so we didn't have to worry about not having any. It was a very realistic kind of goal—a lot more than many people have or achieve, but a lot less than a lot of other people think that they need.

We were on our way to achieving that goal and were feeling pleased with ourselves and convinced of our capabilities. We had a terrific product, and we truly believed that anyone who associated with us was also benefiting from our success. We weren't being snotty; we just knew the worth of our water. We'd been growing steadily, and every partner we'd worked with to date had made money with us. So, you can imagine our surprise when one of the country's leading beauty retailers refused to carry us in its stores.

"You're just not trendy enough," the buyer told us point blank.

Now, we both appreciate honesty, but this cut a bit close to the bone. This retailer perceived us as middle American, dare we say "boring" and unfashionable, instead of "urban" or "coastal," which is how it classified itself.

But we were also used to it. For years, the beauty industry had passed us over in favor of the latest celebrity skin-care collection and brands that spent millions on social media influencers. We were rarely mentioned in industry press, never invited to conferences, and other founders didn't reach out to network, even though we'd grown as big—and sometimes even bigger—than other hot beauty brands. Why were those companies getting all the attention from the industry, while we couldn't even get mentioned in holiday gift guides? What did they have that we lacked?

The questions gnawed at us, but the only answer we could come up with was that there was a lot of smoke and mirrors around these other brands. These companies—as the world would discover when many of them imploded a few years later—had nothing wafting beneath the surface.

It was frustrating and upsetting. But though the perceptions stung, we didn't let the naysayers get to us or derail us from our mission. Nor did we listen to other so-called experts in our industry who downplayed our early business model of not taking on excessive debt or outside investment to "grow at all costs" until we had several years of proof that our brand could survive and scale. We stuck with what we did well, striving to serve our Neighbors and live our core value of Kindness, while making enough money to support a slow but steady growth of our company. Maybe we were stubborn. Maybe— probably—we didn't know any better. Whatever the case, despite our own considerable failings and imperfections, we focused on building our core business, using what we now recognize were G.O.A.T. principles. And as we later learned, "boring" can be *good*. And, yes, slow and steady wins the race.

Broken Vessels

Over the last decade, unicorns have been hot. Everyone hunted for these privately held companies valued at a billion dollars or more, like Theranos, FTX, and WeWork. All of these companies once generated serious buzz and have buzzed themselves out of existence. These companies focused on acquiring new customers and the revenues that came with it, but they didn't build a strong, underlying brand promise to support that growth. There was no growth there.

Same with SPACs, or "special purpose acquisition companies," which were created for the purpose of acquiring or merging with an existing company. Around 2020, they were huge. Now, investors flee at the mere mention of them.

Many trendy companies flame out because they had no substance to start with. To belabor the metaphor, their phoenixes didn't rise from the ashes. We'd all do better to remember Plato's edict: that an "empty vessel makes the most noise." Rather than causing a ten-alarm fire, every business needs to focus on what's real, enduring, and unique about them. Yes, if an empty vessel is making a lot of noise, like many brands that rose during the dot-com, DTC, EV, and current AI booms, it gets a lot of attention. But it can be distracting. And when push comes to shove, it's still empty.

So many companies focus on simply making the initial sale, but they don't focus on the lifetime value of the customer. In other words, building loyalty is not high on their list. We don't just focus on the first sale, but also on the fifth. We focus on the journey between the customer and Beekman over the course of a year. If a customer comes through this point, where do they go next? If someone comes in through a bar of soap, what's their journey after? How can we give them content to get them further down the customer journey? We don't just think about the first transaction, but what is the journey going to be over the next twelve months. You want them to go deeper and deeper into the brand and not just one transaction.

Shakespeare referenced empty vessels in act 4, scene 4 of *Henry V*, in which he wrote: "Empty vessels make the loudest sound." (He credits Plato, whose full quote is: "An empty vessel makes the loudest sound, so they that have the least wit are the greatest babblers.")

We are happy to report that neither Shakespeare nor Plato were one-hit wonders. Neither are we. Over the years, we learned to trust our own inner voices, even when the business world was saying something much different.

How did we hone our coping skills and creativity? Interestingly, we both came to this without discussing it between ourselves. It's possible we both feel that way because we grew up in the 1970s, when it wasn't acceptable to be gay. Every day you were always trying to figure out how to pass as a straight person. That really honed our creative and strategic thinking skills, because every day was a strategy of "How am I going to make it through the day?" As a result, it honed our ability to suss out who we can trust and make decisions early on.

While we may have gotten a head start, that doesn't mean you can't think strategically every day and hone your own strategic thinking.

We knew that one day we'd get where we wanted to be, in the stores we wanted to be in, with investors we respected and whom we respected. We concentrated on building our company slowly, creating a "love brand" and filling our bucket to the top slowly and quietly. As a result, we were able to find the right retailers to carry our products and the right investors to inject capital into Beekman 1802.

The whole purpose of this book is to tell you, the reader, how to build a brand carefully, methodically, and yes—with love.

(Incidentally, if you're wondering about the physics of it all, an empty vessel makes a louder noise than a full one because the air molecules in an empty vessel have greater amplitude and hence greater intensity than liquid molecules in the filled vessel. We discovered this fun fact after spending endless afternoons filling countless numbers of five-gallon buckets to water the vegetable garden. While waiting for them to fill, we couldn't help pondering why the water makes the most noise when the bucket first starts to fill. Google explained it.[1])

Other leaders have stuck it out and stayed true to their vision even though their business didn't seem exciting by the standards of the day. Consider World of Wonder (WOW), a TV production company that started by promoting a drag competition long before mainstream culture paid attention. World of Wonder was cofounded in the 1980s as a record label and management company by Fenton Bailey and Randy Barbato, who met in NYU's graduate film program. They had been living deep in Manhattan's East Village in an apartment building laden with drag queens, part of a true underground counterculture. After producing some albums, they got into television production and documentaries. Around that same time, they met a drag queen named RuPaul, producing his album, *RuPaul Is Star Booty*, in 1986, and became his manager.[2]

Fenton, sixty-three, loves catch phrases. A favorite? "No is the beginning of yes." In fact, hanging on the wall of their conference room is a giant picture with the word "YES." "If you can needlepoint it on a pillow, it's got legs," he says, only half joking.

World of Wonder was the production company behind *The Fabulous Beekman Boys*. Fenton easily admits that his interest in our story when we were starting stemmed not so much from his love of goats, cheese, and soap (though he does love them), but because he wanted to transport two gay entrepreneurs into living rooms across the country. We were told that *The Fabulous Beekman Boys* was the first documentary series in history to focus on a gay married couple.

"TV has been this amazing way for us to change how the world sees us," he says. "It also lets people support gay men while not having to get a flag and march in a parade. It allows audiences to participate without feeling threatened or being confronted."

WOW's desire to showcase what he calls "Queer joy" informed every project it took on. That was its mantra, even if it wasn't stated aloud. Like us, it built the business without investors or big partners, who almost certainly wouldn't understand the pop culture potential of bringing the drag scene to the mainstream.

When RuPaul asked WOW to manage him—he had a song called "Supermodel (You Better Work)"—WOW jumped at the chance. But the company was met with rousing choruses of no from every record label except Tommy Boy Records.

WOW directed the video for "Supermodel," which was a "lean and mean" operation. Randy Barbato jokes about the "starving kitty syndrome."

"You'll do anything. You'll try anything." During the video shoot, WOW didn't even have a proper trailer where RuPaul could relax. It was more of a van, but they were elated that they actually had somewhere for him to go. They didn't have work permits from the city; they simply raced around the city shooting things. But they got it done.

Other record labels scoffed at RuPaul and WOW for taking a chance on him. But "Supermodel" was gigantic, hitting number two on the US dance charts. The video premiered on MTV in 1993. It hit an empty cultural void with a bang. It made a lot of noise, selling over 500,000 copies in 1993 and breaking into the Billboard top fifty in the United States, the UK, Canada, Australia, and the Netherlands. RuPaul was a cultural icon, especially in the LGBTQ+ community, but he didn't really hit the big time until 2009, when *RuPaul's Drag Race* launched on the gay-focused Logo network. In 2017 it became a breakout when it moved over to VH1, making it a mainstream hit. There have now been seventeen seasons, more than seventeen international versions with multiple spinoffs and thirty

Emmy awards. Six hundred and fifty queens have walked the runway over the course of almost 1,000 episodes.

So what does this all mean? You can make a big noise, but it still takes time to fill the bucket, and most importantly, *it doesn't mean it's going to stay full.* Even if you initially make a loud entrance, don't be fooled that it'll always be easy after that point. People think that if they have a big success in the beginning, afterward they can coast. But that's not how it always is. It could take years before you fill the bucket. (For more on that see Charles, RuPaul, above.)

Fenton credits WOW's success to its authenticity. "No TV show has ever been a hit because of research and development," he says. "The audience wants to be surprised. They want new things. They like to discover things. And they like things that are different. That's what makes a hit show."

"With the success of *Drag Race* we faced the challenge of how to keep the bucket full," Fenton says. "Investors didn't see us as a unicorn, they saw us as a one-trick pony, so we were on our own."

Using their own resources (and knowing how to stretch a dollar) he and Randy have built a drag race universe that—in addition to spin-offs like *Untucked, All Stars, Versus the World, Secret Celebrity, Queen of the Universe*, and *Slaycation*—also includes tours, a live show in Las Vegas (that has been running for 1,000 shows), and a line of ready-to-drink cocktails.

"And that's also how we came to launch our own streaming platform, WOW Presents Plus as a home for *Drag Race* and original content." In 2024, they launched almost 300 hours of new content and saw a forty percent growth in subscribers. "The popular wisdom is that streaming can only work if you are prepared to spend—and lose—billions," he says. "But since day one, WOW Presents Plus has been profitable and—again contrary to industry norms—has a 96% retention rate since its launch."

Fenton's entrepreneurial advice? "You just have to be you and have the courage of your convictions, and ignore the naysayers. There's really no alternative to being authentic." Fenton isn't using "authentic" as a sound bite. Nor does he mean saccharine or overly earnest. "Being you as in what brings you joy, what makes your eyes twinkle? At least if you just do you, you'll be reasonably happy. Or, at least, not potentially unhappy."[3]

How You Fill the Vessel Matters

When we were first starting on the farm and had to grow our own foods, we repeatedly had to fill our buckets to water the garden. We learned that if you fill the bucket incrementally—say, only halfway—you can get more water to its destination. But if you fill it to the tip-top, you'll end up spilling most of it along the way.

Research by New York University social psychologist Gabriele Oettingen has shown that balanced goal-setting leads to more progress overall, regardless of your ambitions.[4] In 2009, Oettingen did a peer review of a hundred research articles. She was fascinated by the "if you can dream it, you can accomplish it" mentality that's become so fashionable over the years. You can see it on wall plaques and posters in every possible language.

But she went against the grain of conventional wisdom. Instead of unfettered positivity, she subscribes to the idea of "mental contrasting." With mental contrasting, you visualize a desired future or outcome that contrasts with your current reality.[5] Rather than only focusing on the successful result, as positive psychology and Instagram would like you to do, Oettingen believes that only by managing your expectations can you avoid overcommitting or undercommitting to a goal that may be out of your grasp.

Here's an example from Nicole Celestine, a behavioral scientist and writer based in Perth, Western Australia:

> "A man wishes to buy a new Ferrari. Initially, the man may find himself captivated by images of himself driving along the coast with the roof down; he fantasizes about smiling to passersby, who are admiring his new vehicle. This posi-

tive imagined reality may motivate him to begin saving for the car, but when he realizes how much work is involved in saving for such a lavish purchase, he loses motivation and settles for a cheaper car.

An alternative scenario is that the man is considering saving for a Ferrari, but he dwells on the substantial amount of work and sacrifice that will be required to buy it: late nights at the office, disciplined budgeting, and so forth.

Consequently, these images of the reality involved in goal pursuit dampen his enthusiasm, and once again, he settles for a cheaper car."[6]

The idea is that you set smaller goals. Once you achieve them, you move on to the next goal. Oettingen adheres to the option that "the man could choose to balance fantasizing positively about owning a Ferrari while also contrasting these fantasies with negative aspects of his impending reality, such as the sacrifice involved in saving to make the purchase. The process of comparing and contrasting these positive and negative aspects of an impending future is what is known as mental contrasting. And the process of mental contrasting is valuable, as it triggers expectancies that can guide decisions about goal commitment and motivate sustained goal pursuit."

Remember: when we entered *The Amazing Race*, our initial goal was to only make it halfway. That was it. We didn't want to bite off more than we could chew (another G.O.A.T. chestnut). But once we accomplished that, we thought, "Well, maybe we can actually win this thing." And we did.

Our ultimate retirement goal was $5 million in the bank. But if we could save $1 million in retirement investments, then we decided that Josh could stop freelancing in New York City and move to the farm to work on Beekman 1802 full-time. We accomplished that within five years.

The thesis is that if you set your goal too high, you'll fail (and worse, think of yourself as a failure). That was another reason why only $5 million seemed like a viable option for our company. It was a little more

LEARN FROM A G.O.A.T.:
David Venable

David Venable is one of the G.O.A.T. Program Hosts on QVC, one of the world's leading retailers responsible for billions in sales per year. During his thirty-year career, David has been welcomed into the homes of millions of consumers and has helped thousands of entrepreneurs launch their products.

Please tell us your favorite saying or piece of homespun wisdom, the one that has meant the most to you personally or professionally.

"You gain strength, courage, and confidence by every experience in which you stop to look fear in the face. You must do the thing which you think you cannot do!" –Eleanor Roosevelt

How did you first discover or learn of this maxim?

I first read this online. I printed it and it hangs in my QVC dressing room. I read it every day!

than we would have saved if we stayed on our original career paths, but less than most entrepreneurs shoot for. It was Goldilocks. Just right.

Ryan Serhant is another seriously goal-oriented businessperson whom we met when he sold our Manhattan apartment before we moved to Sharon Springs full-time. Ryan started out as an actor before becoming a real estate mogul, CEO, and founder of Serhant, a mega brokerage comprising an in-house film studio, education arm, marketing division, and technology platform. He's also the author of *Sell It Like Serhant* and a star of Netflix's *Owning Manhattan* and Bravo's *Million Dollar Listing New York*—both, coincidentally, produced by World Of Wonder. He's also very good-looking, which can sometimes be a hindrance. People tend to underestimate an attractive vessel. That would be a big mistake in this case. Huge.

Ryan, forty, is incredibly focused, subscribing to the thousand-minute rule. "I've got 1,440 minutes in a day, just like everyone else," he says. This is how he moved from broke actor whose debit card was

Why is this maxim so wise and valuable in business and beyond?

It applies to all aspects of my work at QVC, from long shifts, to challenging product demonstrations, scheduling changes, and demanding on-camera presentations—this quote fuels me to always be at my best. I never let doubt or fear slow me down.

Does this maxim have any special relevance given what's currently going on in the world?

There are so many issues in the world that are tough right now—politics, the economy, and wars around the world. This quote reminds us to stand in our truth in all situations and never let nagging thoughts hold us back.

How has this maxim contributed to your own success? Any particular stories come to mind?

This quote has always pushed me to go beyond what I perceive as my limits. It encourages me to step outside my comfort zone and achieve all goals no matter how difficult they may seem.[7]

declined in a grocery store to power broker to some of the wealthiest clients in the world.

But rather than thinking about time as a unit of measurement, he thinks about it as money. He is the CEO of his own day. Once you eliminate sleeping, eating, and kissing your family, you've got about a thousand minutes left to be productive. "If you think about being the CEO of your own time, your day is a commodity and not just a Tuesday," he says. "If those minutes were actual money, you'd never get on TikTok or watch the *Housewives* because you wouldn't want to pay for it."

He takes a similar approach to goal-setting, structuring his year with macro and micro wins. In December—what he calls "the Sunday of the year"—he sits down with his president and CFO and together they hammer out their goals for the upcoming year. They set up repeatable, achievable goals. "I don't like sailing, but I do know that if you don't know where you're going to sail to, it's *Bad News Bears* for everyone on the boat. You don't do it with your own life."

In 2024, one of his goals was to say the words "No." "I'm so good at saying yes and I set myself up for failure," he says. "Why do I say yes for everything? It worked for a while, but Ryan 3.0 is how I think about myself. I say no to things and that way I can conserve resources."

Ryan admits he's terrified of wasted potential, which drives him to achieve. He also adheres to the four Ws to help get motivated:

What's your why? What propels you forward in your career?

What's your work? What do you do daily to broaden your business?

What's your wall? What are you running from? A place you never want to go back to and will do everything in your power to never be there again? This could be an awful job, a bad relationship, or a time when you couldn't afford to pay your bills.

What's your win? What are you most passionate about? What inspires you to wake up and greet the day? This can't be money, by the way. It's got to be about legacy and what you want to be known for, like we feel about Beekman 1802.[8]

Who knew when we started fifteen years ago that we would be so respected in how we built our brand that Harvard Business Review Press would ask us to write a book about it.

A Buoyant Vessel

A contemporary way of talking about empty, noisy vessels is the concept of "irrational exuberance." This phrase was first uttered by Alan Greenspan, then chairman of the Federal Reserve Board. It was 1996, the dot-com heyday, and the expression was widely considered to be a cautionary tale that the stock market might be inflated.

It's also the name of a book by Yale economics professor Robert J. Shiller, who wrote this: "Irrational exuberance is the psychological basis of a speculative bubble. I define a speculative bubble as a situation in which news of price increases spurs investor enthusiasm, which spreads by psychological contagion from person to person, in the process amplifying stories that might justify the price increases and bringing in a larger and larger class of investors who, despite doubts about the real value of an investment, are drawn to it partly by envy of others' successes and partly through a gamblers' excitement."[9]

We all want something to be too good to be true. Entrepreneurs, the press, consumers—everyone wants the emperor to be clothed in Armani. As businesspeople, you have to remember not to believe your own hype. If you're having success that feels outsized to you, be wary. Because at some point in the cycle of your business, there's going to be a gap between hype and reality. And the last thing you want to do is to believe your own PR. Because believing your own loud noise or hype can prevent you from doing the work needed to sustain a business for the long term.

No one illustrates this point better than Elizabeth Holmes. By now, her story is familiar to nearly everyone on the planet. Her legacy has been written. Because of her portrayals in popular media, the world thinks of her as an evil, psychopathic, almost serial killer.

But let's look at it from a slightly different angle. Holmes was a Stanford dropout who started Theranos at age nineteen. The company was promoting blood tests that could be performed very quickly while only using tiny droplets of blood. Her intentions were sound, there was a demand for the discovery of a technology that could achieve this, and her vision was solid. Luminaries in the business and political worlds—including former US secretaries of state George Schultz and Henry Kissinger and former secretary of defense James Mattis—told her she was brilliant, a revolutionary, sure to change the healthcare landscape. In 2014, when she was thirty, *Forbes* named her the world's youngest self-made woman billionaire, worth a whopping $4.5 billion.[10] She posed on the cover of *Fortune* in a black turtleneck à la Steve Jobs. In fact, *Inc.* dubbed her "The next Steve Jobs."

That's heady stuff no matter how old you are, and it's hard not to buy into it when you're the subject of that kind of praise. And truthfully, all startup tech companies exaggerate their successes and potential all the time. (Puffery!) They raise their hundreds of millions of dollars of investment by being an empty vessel that makes a lot of noise hoping to make enough money to fill it. Silicon Valley's entire business plan is built on the concept of "fake it until you make it." Some fulfill their potential before they're found out. Many others, like Holmes, don't.

We believe there are other, better ways to go about conducting business: "Face it until you ace it." "Be it until you see it." And "Learn it until you earn it." These expressions were all coined by author and entrepreneur Curtis Morley.

They're all valuable lessons: if you're looking at your product and your product isn't living up to the hype or you know it doesn't live up to the hype, you have to ask yourself honestly: Can it ever live up to the hype or is this just a hype product? Once you understand that, then you can plan your business accordingly. Having a buzzy or trendy product or service isn't inherently bad. In fact, it can be great business, but only until the buzz or trend dies out. Forecast the arc of the hype, plan a soft landing, and you'll walk away successful.

It's the difference between exuberance and irrational exuberance. By definition, every entrepreneur should be exuberant. You have to dream big and envision all the possibilities. At the same time, you need to have the humility to know your limits and the patience to do it the right way.

Filling Our Coffers

We took our first investment in November of 2021. It took us twelve years to decide to bring in an outsider even though many had come calling, because we had been so vocal right from the start that we didn't want to take investment dollars. Remember, our company began out of desperation after we lost our jobs due to the irrational debt exuberance and subsequent collapse of the economy in 2008. We had some justifiable PTSD about taking on debt.

But eventually Beekman 1802 got to a size where we couldn't ignore the possibility of bringing on investors. We were getting older, we weren't going to live forever, and we had a significant number of employees who deserved careers that could grow to their fullest potential. By limiting our growth, we were limiting theirs.

Now that we were rolling out into all the Ulta stores, we were suddenly competing against the biggest players in the beauty industry, like L'Oréal, Estée Lauder, and Shiseido. That meant that we had to be able to compete with them on marketing and innovation. Because now that we're sitting alongside them on shelves, the consumer doesn't see us as a little brand. We're just as big as they are, and we have to compete with those guys accordingly.

And while Beekman was successful and profitable, competing with the likes of huge conglomerates meant that for the first time in our history we were spending more money than we were bringing in. We freaked out! We kept trying to figure out how not to take investments. That's why it took us thirteen years to take our first one. We also could have taken out business loans, but we were apprehensive to take on debt.

We interviewed multiple bank partners, and ultimately the decision came down to two things: (1) How much were the fees that bankers would charge for doing this work? (2) Do we like the people we'd be working with at the bank? So, it was both financially and personality driven. To be perfectly honest, to us, personality probably mattered most. It's more important to spend time with someone you like than to save a few extra thousand dollars.

We chose a bank partner who officially started the process of attracting investment suitors. In meeting after meeting with potential investors we found ourselves surrounded by a long table full of men. While they admired our company's growth, they didn't really understand what made the company special . . . and valuable.

It quickly became clear who would and would not be good part-ners for us. The private equity companies that primarily valued buzz and hype when looking for brands quickly fell by the wayside—like that original beauty retailer who spurned us. While it's always disap-pointing to be turned down by potential investors, in hindsight we're grateful they turned up their noses at our slow but steady, hype-less brand.

The potential investment partners who took the time to drive the three-and-a-half hours from New York City to visit our headquarters and farm instinctively knew that the *lack* of hype surrounding our company was our most seductive selling point—especially since we had large revenue numbers despite our low industry profile. When they met us in person, they realized how much we truly had going for us: an enthusiastic employee team, an authentic founding story complete with real live goats, and customers who drove hundreds of miles to visit our flagship store, the Beekman 1802 Kindness Shop, in the "middle of nowhere." It was precisely the huge gap between our lack of hype yet solid success that attracted the best investment partners. To them, that gap signified a much greater potential than the gap between a lot of buzz and lower sales. Smart investors know that a quiet, half-full vessel is ultimately worth more than one that makes a vociferous splash. We ultimately chose to work with an in-vestment fund called Eurazeo Brands, whose two lead investment partners happened to be women and understood the current and fu-ture potential of what we had created.

It wasn't easy to wait as long as we did to bring in investors. It was painful to watch some competitors explode with growth after taking on cheap money. But all business is cyclical, and it's important not to get seduced during boom periods when money's cheap, investors are in search of windfalls, and valuations based on anticipated future growth are high. As a business owner, don't be discouraged if you're seeing other people get all the attention and the hype—and yes, in-vestment dollars—because the actual business odds are that five years from now they'll be gone. But if you've built your business solidly and paced your growth properly, you'll always be moving forward, even when your sexier competitors find themselves retrenching.

In summary, all entrepreneurs should shoot for the moon. But the smartest ones don't build a rocket. They build a ladder. Because if your rocket fails, you've got nothing. But if you don't quite reach the moon with the ladder you've built, at least you're a few feet higher than where you started and you still have a pretty great view of the moon.

 ## CHEW ON THIS

- Ignore both the good publicity and the bad, developing a stance somewhat akin to Buddhist detachment that allows you to honor your core values and build the business you dream of.

- It's OK to have modest ambitions for your business. If you do have bigger dreams, acknowledge the challenges in your path and set more realistic short- and medium-term goals.

- Look for investors and other partners who truly get your business. Find the right partner who brings value added capabilities, the right attitude, alignment with your vision and belief in the path forward and, of course, capital. Don't despair—they're out there!

BECOME A G.O.A.T.:
Reality Checking Your Business

Consider important dimensions of your enterprise—your functional areas, culture, leadership, strategy, processes, business models, talent pool, capacity to innovate, and so on. For each one, assess the reputation that this dimension of your enterprise has on a scale of one to ten. Then think about the actual quality of this dimension, ranking it on a one-to-ten scale. No one but you will see this, so be brutally honest with yourself.

Is your business overhyped or underhyped? In which particular areas does the reality of your business not match the reputation? When you identify gaps, ask yourself whether you might viably close that gap either by making improvements or by attempting to adjust external expectations. It may be that others just won't get your business or particular parts of it—and that's OK.

Don't Kill the Goose That Lays the Golden Egg

How to Find Your Purpose

Have you ever noticed that a lot of timeless sayings mention eggs?

Don't put all your eggs in one basket.

Don't squander your nest egg.

Don't get egg on your face.

And whatever else you do—*never count your chickens before they hatch.*

What's up with all the eggspressions?

Well, an egg is a symbol of creation. Life literally comes from an egg. If you look at the world from that perspective, you can see why the egg is venerated and such a powerful metaphor for people. Because that egg is the most precious thing that you have. And you have to understand how to take care of it.

It should come as no surprise that one of our favorite sayings involves an egg: "Don't Kill the Goose That Lays the Golden Egg." It dates back to ancient Greece and Aesop's fables. As Aesop's story goes, a farmer has a goose that lays precisely one golden egg each day.

But one magnificent egg at a time is not enough for this avaricious farmer—he wants more gold all at once. Imagining that many golden eggs sit already formed inside the goose, he kills the animal and cuts it open to find . . . no golden eggs, just the usual gross innards. The moral of the story, of course, is don't be greedy. Your craving for riches might boomerang on you, leading you to extinguish the source of the wealth you currently do have. That's G.O.A.T. advice for life in general, and an essential guideline for business growth.

The magical "goose" in any business represents the ultimate source of its ability to create value. Usually, that's not a specific product or technology but rather an idea—the core insight, mission, or purpose that gave rise to the business in the first place. As Harvard Business School professor Ranjay Gulati notes in his 2022 book *Deep Purpose*, purpose is nothing less than "the heart and soul of high-performance companies" in that it fulfills a whole number of functions that enable an enterprise's healthy growth and success.[1] That's precisely what we mean when we speak of a golden egg–laying goose (or, in our case, the very rare and valuable egg-laying goat).

If you've got your golden egg, you sometimes do have to rethink what your egg is or how your egg is portrayed or what color it is. Just because it's golden doesn't mean it's a perfectly oval ovum. Nor does it mean it can't, or shouldn't, change. But first you need to identify it.

Hatching a Goal

"Purpose" and "mission" have become fashionable buzzwords of late, but many leaders of small and midsized businesses still don't know what their magical goose really is and, by extension, how best to protect and nourish it. They've got lots of eggs, but they don't know which one is comprised of that dense and precious metal.

For much of our company's history, we didn't either. Since Beekman 1802's inception, we'd focused on running a business that served our Neighbors and gave back to the local community. Although we often told stories about our Neighborly relations in the course of brand-building, we never stopped to think much about what we were doing. Or why. We just did it instinctively.

But who were *we*? We couldn't really say for sure.

By 2019, Beekman 1802 was a fairly sizable company. The two of us had always been front and center in our marketing, advertising, and company leadership. But the company was getting so large that we couldn't be the personification of our brand everywhere all the time. We may have been the golden eggs, but what exactly was our goose? We were so close to our work and business that we needed help to gain a better perspective.

So in 2019 we hired a branding agency named Tether to help us figure out our reason for being. If we were to disappear tomorrow, what would be the continuing purpose for the business? How would the company keep evolving while keeping true to its roots? What was our True North?

As you grow, people need to make hundreds or thousands of decisions every day, and you can't be there making the decisions yourself or telling them what decisions to make. They have to make their decisions based on something, and that's where your brand values or mission statement comes in, so they can make that informed decision. We needed to know: Who were we? What were we all about? What would our mission statement be, if we had to craft one?

We set up an all-day brainstorm with the team at Tether to share the complete history of our company. How we initially took in a Neighboring farmer named John, who was losing his own farm and needed a home for his herd of goats. How we were rooted in our little community of Sharon Springs. How we called our customers "Neighbors" and how as we grew, these Neighbors began forming their own friendships and communities around their love of the brand. We had hundreds of stories from Neighbors who loved our brand, but why? What did they all add up to? We knew that getting a fresh outsider perspective would help us describe the mountain.

Words like "Neighborhood," "artisanal," "community" were being written on white boards around the room. But none of them seemed to completely sum us up.

When we broke for lunch, our office manager brought in the meals, including a homemade pie Josh had whipped up the night before. Someone on their team admired the ceramic serving plates, so we explained that they were made by one of our Neighbors. We told them they were free to take one home if they wanted. Another Tether consultant had a tight deadline for a flight home, so a Beekman team member volunteered to leave early to drive them to the airport. None of this seemed unusual to us or our team. But it inspired the Tether folks.

Before our afternoon branding exploration started, the lead of the Tether team leaned back in his chair and said: "Beekman isn't a brand. It's a behavior."

He must have seen the quizzical looks on all our faces. "You aren't selling beauty products," he continued. "You're selling Kindness."

A giant light flashed in our heads. They had encapsulated exactly what we'd always felt but hadn't yet articulated: we were in business to spread Kindness. Bingo—our magic goose! We were in the business of Kindness.

Our goose was Kindness, and it always had been. But it took someone who wasn't intimately involved with the company, who hadn't evolved with us and been there since our inception, to point it out. This makes sense. Because when you're mid-evolution, you hardly ever see the evolution happening because it goes so slowly. It's like when you see a teenager after a few months, chances are they look like they've sprouted a few inches. But their parents might not notice because they see them all the time.

Now that we knew what our goose was about, we could be much more conscious about nourishing the eggs it laid. We could infuse everything we did with Kindness. Members of our growing team could use this purpose as a valuable guide when making decisions large and small (Is the product we are making Kind to skin? Are the marketing messages we are putting out Kind to our community's self-image and mental health?). We could also hire people who were receptive specifically to the notion of Kindness.

You may not know your golden egg at the beginning of your journey. (Real geese don't even start laying eggs until they're about two years old.) But once you've identified and defined your magic goose, it's vital not to slit its neck in pursuit of growth. You'll almost certainly reach inflection points in which growth threatens to destroy your goose. But it's important to tread carefully, balancing between the imperative to grow and the need to keep the goose alive and waddling.

If you want a sustainable, steadily growing business over the long term, you can't simply make decisions on an economic basis; you must allow other considerations to inform your choices as well. By the same token, you can't simply pursue idealistic ends and deny the possibility of growth. You must take a middle path, aiming for the right kind of growth. Nor can you try to force a purpose on the company, which is how a lot of companies start out: trying to create that purpose instead of actually having one.

Three of the most successfully scaled companies of the last twenty to fortyish years are purpose-driven companies—Burt's Bees, Crocs, Lululemon, and Patagonia. They all managed to find the right balance between staying true to their core identities while building hugely profitable businesses.

Burt's Bees, for example, was cofounded by hippies Burt Shavitz and Roxanne Quimby in the eighties. Shavitz was a back-to-the-land sort of man who lived in a small Maine cabin with no electricity and no running water. A beekeeper, he and his friend Roxanne, who was also living off the grid, began making candles from his leftover beeswax, and sold them at craft fairs. In 1991, they launched what became their ridiculously popular lip balm. Quimby eventually moved the business to North Carolina and, after a rift with Shavitz, bought out his stake in the company for a thirty-seven-acre property (she later gave him an additional $4 million). In 2007, it was sold to Clorox for more than $900 million—and Quimby began snapping up hundreds of thousands of acres of Maine wilderness.[2] In 2016, she donated more than 87,000 acres—about $75 million worth of her holdings—to the National Park Service, and $6 million to other charities.

"I had renounced the pursuit of capital as a radical nineteen-year-old in the 1960s," said Quimby. "I was going to live without money. I didn't need it. I was going to trade and grow stuff and keep my expenses low."

She is still living simply. "I have a theory about really expensive things," she told *Forbes*. "You become a prisoner of them, and you have to lock your doors. Then you lose your key, so I just can't do that."[3]

Craig Koch, the fifty-three-year-old founder and CEO of WAG-A-LOT, which provides daycare, boarding, grooming, and retail products for dogs, is also clear that purpose is necessary in building a business. He created his business more than twenty-five years ago, and it now has three locations in Atlanta. He is adamant that passion and money aren't enough to build a business. "You can't just love something or desire financial success, though both are the most common reasons for starting a business," he says. Rather, when building his business, he tried to answer the question: *How does what I'm creating leave the world and/or life better for others?*

The way he sees it, a great idea or a desire for success, fame, or riches is not enough to make an entrepreneur successful. Neither is a genuine passion. Instead, every business needs a purpose. "Otherwise, you will at some point ask, 'What's it all for?' and either fold or perhaps partially succeed but not reach your full potential or feel completely satisfied in your endeavor," he says. "The world does not need another something to merely satisfy your ego. Anything you put forth should be meaningful, have purpose, and ultimately make the world better on some level regardless of how small." (By leave the world better, he means give more than you take.)

Koch believes he hit the purpose-driven company jackpot in 1999, when he had an epiphany that dogs needed a safe, fun place to burn off their energy during the day while their owners were at work. He wanted to create a place where canines could "embrace their pack mentality, live healthy lives, and reconnect with their parents at the end of the day in a calm state where everyone can enjoy quality time together," he says.

Not only would such a service have an obvious initial purpose, making the lives of pet owners easier and more pleasant, but it would also improve the quality of dogs' lives, allow more people to actually consider being a pet owner, and experience the endless benefits of this magical connection plus provide an outlet for fellow animal lovers to connect. "This was all overwhelmingly gratifying but in retrospect only the tip of the purposeful company iceberg," he says.

In 1999, Atlanta was euthanizing as many as 100,000 dogs a year in its overcrowded shelters. That same year Koch founded WAG-A-LOT, giving birth to one of the nation's very first doggy daycare establishments, providing upscale overnight boarding, professional grooming, and retail. "I quickly ascertained that this mix of services and products was necessary to achieve viability and the short-term and long-term financial goals I had in mind," he says.

Koch also began working with Lifeline Animal Project, which offers shelters, clinics, and adoption services. Atlanta is now a no-kill community that rarely has to euthanize any adoptable pets. "The fact that my business has played a part in this journey is beyond satisfying," he says.[4]

Koch quickly became a major advocate for dog adoption not only as an obvious way to give back to a community that was supporting his business, but also as a genuine extension of WAG-A-LOT's mission: "That all dogs deserve a chance to WAG-A-LOT!"

Caveat: by "purpose," we aren't only talking about doing something altruistic that's good for the world. It could also just be good for the consumer, like Crocs. Crocs are inexpensive, profoundly comfortable shoes that people love. Like any big company, Crocs does support several charities. But that's not what it uses to sell its shoes. Its stated purpose is to "create a more comfortable world."

It's that simple. Like Beekman 1802 spreads Kindness. The true power comes when your purpose also aligns with your product. Croc's shoes, charitable giving, and corporate policies all tie back to "creating a more comfortable world." Just like everything Beekman 1802 does, internally and externally, relates to spreading Kindness.

Apple is another good example. Steve Jobs recognized that consumers' needs weren't satisfied with their PCs. The idea that they wanted something better designed, where all consumer devices could talk to each other, was revolutionary. He was satisfying a need that hadn't been satisfied with a PC. That became Apple's purpose: to create well-designed products that make the consumer's life easier.

Ditto for Walmart or Amazon. Walmart has always been about cheap and convenient. Amazon has been about customer service and delivery. Their purpose has always been their purpose. No more, no less.

Boeing is an opposite story. For decades, the company was known for its excellent quality control and safety record. In fact, there was a common phrase that fliers used: "If it's not Boeing, I'm not going."[5] But, like so many companies, its quality controls were seen as drags on the bottom line. Little by little, it cut back on the protocols that made it famous in the first place. In recent years, after its planes had been involved in several fatal crashes, a six-week FAA audit of Boeing's 737 Max production found dozens of incidents where the company lagged in quality-control practices.[6] By doing so, it effectively killed its golden goose. In March 2024, CEO Dave Calhoun and other top Boeing executives stepped down, and the company is still struggling to right itself.[7]

And then there's Allbirds, the footwear and apparel company. It thought its golden egg was a sustainable shoe.[8] And, at first, it was. Its shoes were spotted on nearly every Silicon Valley exec and celebs like Blake Lively, Jennifer Hudson, and Barack Obama. But its explosive popularity led it to expand too quickly—perhaps not fully understanding the mountain it was standing on. Between trying to reach too many new demographics, and the inevitable quality issues that come with rapid expansion, it lost both its focus and its customers. Like the original Aesop's fable farmer, it cut open its goose in hopes of quickly harvesting more golden eggs. It's still trying to recover from getting egg on its face. (Sorry, we couldn't resist.)

Sometimes the egg will have to morph as the culture and society change. Gap learned this after years of fumbles and, in the first quarter of 2019, a 10 percent decrease in sales of its namesake brand.[9] (Sales tanked by 4 percent across all brands in Gap's portfolio during the same time period.[10]) Ditto for social media platforms that peaked too soon like Clubhouse, Be Real, and Friendster. Each one was praised in the media as the new golden egg. And then the egg cracked.

Then there's the Body Shop. Originally founded in 1976 by Anita Roddick, it was truly a pioneer in purpose-driven brands. It quickly became known not just for its fun scents and bath products, but for its clean ingredients and unwavering commitment to not testing its products or ingredients on animals. It grew a fiercely loyal fan base, opening stores all over the UK and the world. Eventually it was acquired by L'Oréal in 2006. From a marketing perspective, it's tough for a brand with a charitable purpose to navigate being bought by a large international conglomerate. Even though it still honored its commitment never to test on animals, consumers began to question the depth of that commitment since it was now owned by a company that tested thousands of products on animals. And as the rest of the beauty industry caught up by using more clean-ingredient formulations and cruelty-free testing, suddenly the Body Shop's goose wasn't so golden anymore. L'Oréal sold it off first in 2017, and then it was sold again in 2023. In 2024, its US operations filed for bankruptcy.

Growth comes with difficult moments. What matters is how you handle those moments.

Don't Kill the Goat That Makes the Golden Soap

There were two main inflection points in the growth of our company when our golden egg of Kindness was threatened by the hammer of scalability: the source of our goat milk, and the production of our soap bars.

For the first couple of years of Beekman 1802's history all the milk for our soap came from Farmer John's goats on our farm, was handmade by one of our Neighbors down the road, and was wrapped on our dining room table. But as we expanded—particularly as we began to sell our soap wholesale—it became obvious to Beekman Neighbors that there was no way our eighty goats and Neighborhood soap maker could produce tens of thousands (then millions) of suds a year.

There was an easy way that we could have expanded. We could have bought soap directly from a "white label" company that had a catalog of products that anyone could slap their brand on. In fact, that's how most packaged goods companies scale, by finding ever larger and larger manufacturers. But that approach didn't jive with the homegrown story that had made us successful in the first place. Nor did we want to pick some random overseas personal care manufacturer; that wasn't who we were. So we went on a quest to find a way to produce at scale while still spreading the Kindness we were known for.

One of our teammates attended a trade show where there were hundreds of beauty care manufacturers from all around the world. They all had fancy brochures and videos touting their capabilities, but one company, Vanguard Soap, stood apart from the others. Its main production facility was in Tennessee, where it had been founded by a husband and wife, Charles and Evelyn Breazeale in 1943. Their descendants still were leading the business. And even though they had manufacturing facilities and laboratories around the country, they still owned and used the factory and equipment in Memphis, where they had originally made soap for soldiers in World War II, the Korean War, and the Vietnam War.

A married couple who started a company in their hometown during hard times? Hmmm. Sounded familiar.

We signed on with it immediately. Fun fact: our soap is famous for its generous size. But it wasn't a choice we made: the giant dimension was the only size the World War II–era equipment could produce. Soldiers got one bar of soap that could last eight weeks; that's why they were so large. We transparently shared on social media that we were working with this new (but old) manufacturer.

We braced for an onslaught of criticism about "selling out" or "getting too big for our britches." Instead, Beekman Neighbors were thrilled that we were expanding. More than that, we were being true to our mission of spreading Kindness by choosing a partner that shared our same history and values. Consumers aren't stupid. They knew we could have chosen an easier and cheaper expansion path. They were more than happy to reward us with their loyalty knowing that we hadn't.

The same thing happened when our goats' milk production couldn't keep up with the demand for our products. We faced a choice. Buy more goats? Or buy outside milk? We knew firsthand all the difficulties and disadvantageous economic factors that come with trying to scale a farm. (There's a reason the plight of farmers is always talked about in the news.) But at the same time, Beekman Neighbors loved how well we treated our spoiled goats, and believed their milk was the magic ingredient in all of our beauty products.

Additionally, because we were growing to such a large scale, we needed a reliable, dependable source. We decided to look for an outside supplier. There are many suppliers of goat milk in the world. Globally, goat milk is more popular than cow milk.[11] But was any old goat milk as magical as our own?

After months of research, we found a goat milk distributor that purchased from American farmers (check), certified the quality of its milk (check), and only sourced from farms that had certified humane practices. (Ding! Ding! Ding!)

The magic of our products wasn't just milk. It was "Kind" milk. We knew we'd found a purposeful supplier that Beekman Neighbors would love. In fact, there was even more to love. Not only were our Neighbors supporting our small farm, but they could now help support small farms across the country . . . and one day small farms around the globe.

Clinging too closely to your purpose, however, can be a stumbling block for growth. Many founders get very dogmatic and inflexible about their core beliefs. Say you start a toothpaste company where for every tube purchased a second one is donated to an orphanage in Brazil. It's very noble, but it's unscalable. Eventually either you can't survive with the tiny margins, or you run out of orphanages. You can, however, better define your original purpose (charity, children, accessible hygiene) and swivel the execution.

As we've repeated endlessly, there's a middle ground. Grow as big as you can, but never kill your golden goose.

Make no bones about it: millennials and Gen Z are all about purpose and supporting companies with clear purposes.[12] A 2018 Accenture survey of nearly thirty thousand consumers in thirty-five countries—including more than two thousand consumers in the United States—found that 62 percent of consumers prefer companies that have taken a stand on corporate sustainability, transparency, and fair employment practices.[13] A 2024 survey by Deloitte found that purpose can help create profitable outcomes.[14] Sixty-four percent of companies that integrate sustainability into operations see lower logistics and supply-chain costs; 88 percent say they'd buy products from a purpose-driven company.[15]

If that's not enough incentive to change with the times, what is? If you're in it for the long term, you *must* change with the times. If you're an entrepreneur, you must think of your consumer now and down the line.

CHEW ON THIS

- Even if you feel your company is mission-focused or socially responsible, look deeper to try to pinpoint your golden goose. Bring in outsiders who might be able to spot trends that you can't by virtue of your proximity.

- Remember that your company's purpose doesn't have to be rooted in social responsibility. Your purpose can be as simple as most convenient, lowest-cost, or best service. Whatever your goose is, you need to commit to it.

- Scrutinize every growth-related decision to determine if it will somehow compromise the health of your goose.

- Look for creative growth-enhancing options that will also protect and nourish your golden goose.

BECOME A G.O.A.T.:
Scrutinize Your Decision-Making

Take a comprehensive look at your operations, including your HR policies, processes, vendors, and products. Can you identify any decisions you made that leave you feeling a little uneasy, as if you prioritized growth at the expense of other important, non-economic factors? Go back and methodically reconsider those decisions, looking for creative solutions that might allow you to take good care of your golden goose while still supporting profitability and growth. Going forward, how might you revise your decision-making and strategy-making processes to prompt you to think more about your magical goose?

You Can Lead a Horse to Water, but You Can't Make It Drink

How to Exert Influence

The most interesting happenings in TV retail like QVC and HSN aren't on screen. They're behind the scenes at the studio. Since the networks are on air live for twenty hours a day, there is a constant stream of brand guests flowing through the green rooms. From old-school TV retail veterans like entrepreneurs Joy Mangano and Lori Greiner to hopeful founders making their debut, they all have one thing in common: they need to close as many sales as possible in as short a time as they're given.

The art of persuasion is on full display. We've been fortunate enough to learn from the best in the industry, so that now we've become the best in the industry. And for all the hundreds of tips and tricks we've heard over the years, one piece of advice from a longtime TV shopping veteran sticks out above all others.

"There are only three reasons people buy something," he said. "Either they need it, they want it, or they don't want someone else to get it."

When you watch any TV shopping channel or hear any good sales pitch—whether it's at a car dealership or from an influencer on TikTok—you'll notice all three of these tactics on display. There are the rational reasons to purchase something like product benefits and usefulness. There are the emotional reasons, evoking memories, positive feelings, self-validation. And the urgency reasons: "Act now, before that countdown ticker reaches zero!"

We believe that rational reasoning will get you 20 percent of the way to any transaction. Emotional pitching will get you 79 percent of the rest of the way. But a touch of FOMO will 100 percent seal any deal.

If you only concentrate on one approach and ignore the others, well, "You Can Lead a Horse to Water, but You Can't Make It Drink." No matter how thirsty your customers are, at the end of the day it's your job to persuade them to quaff.

This oldie but goodie was first recorded in *Homilies,* written around 1175. "Hwa is thet mei thet hors wettrien the him self nule drinken."[1] If Old English isn't your thing, here's the translation: "Who can give water to the horse that will not drink of its own accord?"

It was also featured in English writer John Heywood's 1546 work, "A Dialogue," a compilation of English proverbs. "A man maie well bring a horse to the water, But he can not make him drinke without he will."[2]

And, of course, it's been a staple in countless songs and books. The saying is sort of the iPhone of maxims, both ubiquitous and functional.

This may be the G.O.A.T.iest of all time G.O.A.T. wisdom, because it's about exerting influence, what works and what doesn't. The horse is anyone you seek to influence: an employee, a potential investor, a Neighbor. The water is whatever solution or idea you want them to embrace.

Sure, you can lead a horse to water by explaining rationally (with "Hi-Ho Silvers" and "giddy-ups" sprinkled at appropriate intervals) and step-by-step why your solution makes sense. But you probably can't close the deal on the basis of reason alone. In order for the horse to actually bend its head and lap up that cool, clear liquid, it has to want to out of its own volition. Invariably, this happens while it's feeling a strong rational or emotional tug that compels it to take action. Which means it needs to feel like you truly understand its needs, and not simply want it to consume your product.

Because if you try to force the horse's head into the water, it could drown. Or kick you.

Think about those TV commercials for St. Jude, the children's hospital. We go through a full box of tissues whenever they come on, especially when we hear weeping parents talk about their sick children, or the kids who are now cured. That's intentional. The ads are designed to do just that. That's how they get viewers to reach into their pockets and make a life-sustaining donation. We become so emotionally invested that we can't not.

One of our company's strengths is that we've always been very good at appealing to emotion. Rather than leading a horse to water and waiting for it to drink, we emotionally prepare it to drink. By the time the horse is at the trough, it's practically begging to drink because we created a story about how beautiful the water is and how sated the horse will feel when its thirst is quenched. Life (and your skin) is better when you stay hydrated.

A logical horse would say, "Hey, I'm really parched, thanks for bringing me to this nice trough." But horses aren't always rational. You'd probably get more of a reaction if you said something like, "We spent all day filling this trough up with water that we lugged from an artisan well five miles down the road. Our arms are exhausted, but we know how much you'd like it and how great you'll feel after drinking some. And oh, by the way, this is the only water for miles around." None of what we say is false. Or even exaggerated. It's simply telling our story as the best, most effective storytellers we can be.

Most business decisions—heck, most decisions, period—are emotional ones. Reason just serves to help people rationalize choices they've already made in their hearts. It gets them over the hump of indecision. Academic research has confirmed the importance that emotions make in decision-making: Gallup has found that 70 percent of decisions are emotional.[3] Harvard Business School professor Gerald Zaltman has upped it, arguing in his book *How Customers Think: Essential Insights into the Mind of the Market* that 95 percent of cognition takes place in consumers' subconscious. Any time they encounter a product, they're carrying their own associations and frames of reference to it.

"Learning that a communications device or even a personal care product invokes deep thoughts and feelings about social bonding can be very helpful to R&D experts," he says. "In the case of a communications device, this suggests that tactile experiences of social bonding be 'engineered in' through the design of how the product is gripped in the hand and in the choice of finish in the device's housing material. In the case of a personal care product, colors and scents known to be evocative of social bonding experiences can be used. In both cases, the basic idea of connection is central to the product's value proposition and becomes a more profound basis for developing marketing strategy than, say, technical superiority or long-lasting benefits. While the latter attributes are important, it is because they serve the deeper needs of connection or social bonding."[4]

So, not to beat a thirsty, dead horse, but you often can't make people drink, despite leading them right to the water fountain, because their emotions—which determine whether they drink or not—aren't fully on board.

Companies often forget this. Consider Weight Watchers, which alienated many customers when it decided to cancel every single one of its meetings in Brooklyn in favor of virtual meetings.[5] Dieters relied on those meetings the way many alcoholics and drug addicts rely on Alcoholics Anonymous or Narcotics Anonymous; they felt that the company cared more about its bottom line than about them. Many had felt similarly when WW began offering weight loss drugs, essentially abandoning its previous promotion of willpower and nutritional education, which it had been touting since its inception in the sixties. Some customers were unsure if they were going to continue with Weight Watchers. They felt angry, abandoned. The company had severed the emotional connection and sense of community. The stock tumbled, not totally because of this, but it didn't help.

Customers like to feel emotionally connected to a brand, a principle our Neighbors keep teaching us.

Reining in Customers

The idea that consumers purchase with their hearts, rather than only their heads, is not a new concept. Just ask someone in advertising, like Josh was. One of the phrases he repeatedly heard when he worked in that industry was that "it's not what you want to say, it's what your customer wants to *hear*." A favorite example of this was a frozen food client. The company had spent years trying to reconfigure its recipe so that it contained 100 percent real cheese, instead of real cheese plus a small amount of cheese flavoring (which helped stabilize the product and increased its profit margin). When it finally achieved its mission, the proud and excited client asked Josh and his agency to create television ads proclaiming that its product "Now Contains 100% Real Cheese!"

Yes, while this had been a goal of the client for many years, Josh pointed out that marketing this presented a problem on several levels. First, the company's most loyal consumers really hadn't ever noticed or cared that it wasn't 100 percent real cheese. Pointing this out after the fact could possibly alienate them. Second, cheese is cheese. Trying to convince someone to buy a cheese product solely because it contains cheese is not a breakthrough pitch.

Instead of saying what the client wanted to say, Josh's company asked potential customers what they wanted to hear. And what they wanted to hear was how easy it was to bring a hot, cheesy meal to the table that their family would praise them for. You could lead the customer to cheese, but they needed the love of their family to buy it.

In our case, we might be really proud of the fact that we're the number one goat milk skin health company in the world. It's a huge achievement. Our team loves bragging about that. Now, in some industries, being number one might be a great selling point to consumers. People like to know that their banks, insurance companies, and medical providers are rock solid and trusted by millions. But do customers really care if they're using the number one goat milk soap instead of the number two goat milk soap? Probably not. They want to know that it cleans well, or feels luxurious, or has a great founder story, or comes from a company that cares about animals, and so on. Being the biggest goat milk soap company is probably pretty far down the list. The trick is knowing what customers want to hear, what their emotional trigger is.

Pinpointing the emotions customers are feeling can, according to an article in *Harvard Business Review*, "provide a better gauge of customers' future value to a firm than any other metric, including brand awareness and customer satisfaction and can be an important new source of growth and profitability."

The authors call these connections that inspire consumers to buy something "emotional motivators," hundreds of which drive consumer behavior. They include things like the desire to "feel a sense of freedom," "stand out from the crowd," "protect the environment," and "be the person I want to be."

But, the authors point out, identifying consumers' emotional motivators is challenging, because customers might not even know that they have them. "These sentiments are typically different from what customers *say* are the reasons they make brand choices and from the terms they use to describe their emotional responses to particular brands," they say.[6]

And yet, for some business owners, recognizing the importance of emotions is difficult. These leaders might be more analytic, data-oriented types who aren't used to moving people emotionally.

We're the opposite: as natural storytellers, we're always cuing into emotions and tend to struggle more with the rational, analytic stuff.

On a fundamental level, branding is about emotion, while operations are about reason. Throughout Beekman 1802's history, our brand-building has consistently outpaced our ability to execute operationally. We recognized that about ourselves early on, so we brought in team leaders who were experts in finance, operations, and forecasting. Traditionally, those are easier expansion hires to justify than adding creative and marketing employees. Conventional corporate wisdom says that the finance department is more indispensable than the creative department, but that's not true. Like individuals, corporations function best when they balance rational proficiency with emotional skills. We may be one of the few companies in which, as founders, we never named ourselves CEOs. Great CEOs have a particular skill set that we freely admit we don't possess. We've had three different CEOs in our history, each chosen for different stages of growth, and each for their skill sets that were needed at the time.

Most companies focus on making rational, hard-sales arguments. In our model, the softer-touch storytelling does all the work. By the time you get around to making a rational pitch, those customers who are liable to persuasion already will be 99 percent convinced. You're just sealing the deal.

The downside of that is that we're always playing catch-up to meet demand for our products and to satisfy our Neighbors. The upside is that we've always had a sixth sense about what will sell and what won't.

We are able to hone this innate talent during our appearances on QVC and HSN, when we're able to communicate with the customer directly and get feedback in real time. We can always tell what's resonating with viewers based on the number of clicks on the website or phone calls coming in. The information lets us know how to modify our sales pitch. We often change the story we highlight about our products based on what's going on in the world. The yarn that may have worked two days ago might not be the same one that works today.

So, you have to know which story to share to get the customer over the finish line. Doesn't matter if it's a $29.99 or $299.99 product—you still have to get the consumer to respond. And the best way to do that is to appeal to their emotions, while still being sure you've ticked all the boxes for their rational left brain.

You have to keep pulling out different stories, different brand attributes, and different product attributes until you find the one where the producer says, "*Yessss*! Stay on that story! Viewers are loving it!"

Once we have refined these story iterations, our field team can put them to use in real life in Ulta stores when they're educating customers. (The circular economy rearing its head!)

Sometimes it's not even words that do the work. It's a visual. When we started in television retail, we made all sorts of mistakes. One that we've become famous for is "overflowing the bowl."

For years, other soap companies on HSN and QVC would demonstrate making lather in a bowl. But when we first started, we would sometimes get distracted and make too many suds. They would overflow and even drip down off the edge of the table. Soon the producers realized that phone lines lit up every time that happened, and eventually we began overflowing the bowl on purpose. (As have our competitors!) We've all seen beer commercials where the head of beer seductively spills over the rim of the glass. Or chocolate commercials where melted chocolate oozes out of ladles. Our overflowing suds worked on that same principle. (It's also how Josh got the nicknames: The Soap Star, The Lather Daddy, and yes, The Sud Stud.)

It's also important to recognize that horses have different triggers on different days. A persuasive tactic that works one day might not work the next. For example, we've learned that every four years, as election season heats up, consumers get tired of all the fighting and negativity. This is when we ramp up messaging of our brand value of Kindness. People are thirsting to connect with a brand that supports community and empathy. Likewise, during the holiday season, we often feature the fact that our products are made in America. We rarely use that in marketing during the rest of the year. But it's the perfect combination of rational and emotional benefit that resonates during a season of homecoming and tradition.

Obviously, people have different strengths. If you struggle to exert emotional influence, you might make extra efforts to immerse yourself in the world of your customers or other stakeholders to grasp what's at stake for them emotionally. You can then experiment with modifying your persuasive efforts.

Now, emotional storytelling may not be as quick a "win" as a deep discount or a FOMO appeal, but it adds greater value over the lifetime of the customer. But by now you already know that we're not about FOMO.

Customer lifetime value (CLV) is critical for building a company with longevity.[7] CLV helps you identify which customer is only a short-term user, and who's going to be a longer-term loyalist. It costs five to ten times more to acquire a new customer than to retain one you already have. And you want those returning customers, because they spend 67 percent more than new ones.[8]

A report by Bain & Company found that boosting retention by just 5 percent can increase profitability from 25 to 95 percent.[9]

Conor Begley, thirty-six, is the cofounder of Tribe Dynamics, a software company that helps people manage personalities on social media. This has become a really big deal. He's the brain behind earned media value, or EMV, the metric that measures an influencer's effectiveness.

"Creating personal connection with your audience and creating commercial value are often at odds," says Begley, who's a find-the-solution kind of guy.

"The sweet spot is when you can create inherently interesting content that also has commercial appeal. It's a difficult balance to find as a creator."[10]

The only way that he knows how to build personal connection is by creating inherently valuable and interesting content consistently that people enjoy and then engaging proactively with your community to build relationships.

You can also create personal connection by aligning yourself with issues important to your customer. It's incredibly risky to align your brand with a political cause. But when a cause is true to your values or purpose, almost nothing can create a stronger emotional connection with your consumer than a common enemy.

As married gay founders, it's only natural that we would pick the side of LGBTQ+ equality in today's culture wars. We're also prepared to lose any customers that would take issue with that. Two of our most successful social media content pieces in our history were connected to LGBTQ+ issues.

First, in 2015, when Mike Pence was governor of Indiana, he signed a bill into law that allowed businesses to choose not to serve LGBTQ+ customers. As gay business owners, we felt that what was good for the goose was good for the gander, so we decided to ban Mike Pence from Beekman 1802. If he could do it, so could we. We did a single Facebook post banning Mike Pence and received tens of thousands of responses. Our ban also got picked up by several press outlets. Out of all those responses, the only negative ones we received were from people who were not our customers (and probably never would have been, regardless of whether we banned Mike Pence).

In 2013, the chairman of the world's largest pasta manufacturer, Barilla, publicly stated that he would never use a gay family in his advertising. This sparked a boycott around the world. Perhaps coincidentally we had also just launched a Beekman 1802 pasta sauce as part of our original food product line. Simply pointing out our sauce as an alternative to Barilla products garnered a lot of attention and was highlighted in several articles about the boycott. Even after we discontinued the rest of our food line, we still produced our pasta sauce for several years since it had consistently stayed among our top-five bestselling SKUs. That's the strength of forging a common cause–related emotional connection with your consumer.

Water on the Brain

While we never know going in whether one tactic will work over another, it's important to have a tool kit and to consider the myriad potential ways you could lead a horse to water and make it drink.

For many years we had a counterintuitive marketing rule inside our company called "Five times telling, one time selling."

The gist is that any content that is released into the ether, whether it's an email, press interview, Instagram post, or blog posts, it purposely doesn't try to sell anything five times. We mentioned products and provided links to purchase, but we didn't give a list of product features, benefits, and price discounts. Usually, however, we showed photos of us baking bread, or taking a walk around the farm, or playing with baby goats. On the sixth time, we went wild. That's when we would give a sneak peek of a new product, or announce a warehouse sale, or launch a new loyalty program. These points of interest allow time for a powerful emotional attachment to percolate, which makes the actual sales pitch, when it comes, more potent.

We are a consumer product brand. But keep in mind, in the business world, the "consumer" (or the "horse") is not always the end user of your product. The consumer is sometimes the banker that you're trying to get a loan from. Or your landlord. Or your glitter maker. Or whatever vendor is manufacturing something. Or even colleagues or bosses you're trying to persuade to your point of view. But the same rule applies: everyone makes at least part of every decision based on emotion. Check in with partners throughout the year on a casual basis, so that when you really need something from them, it won't seemingly come out of the blue.

We've certainly used emotional strategies to get what we wanted with our retail partners as well. When we were trying to decide which brick-and-mortar retailer we were going to go with, we decided to use some psychology.

We'd had plenty of meetings with Ulta and Sephora and laid out business plans and new product strategies; both were nodding their heads and seemed eager to join forces with us. But you can never be too sure; there are millions of brands they want. In fact, they see almost two thousand product pitches a year.

We were pretty sure that at that time our biggest opportunity was with Ulta, and we really wanted to get it across the finish line and sign up with us. We wish we could say it was Ulta's Midwestern values, its unique business model, and the fact that it pursued us that attracted us to them. Plain and simple, it had more stores. It was a better option for us.

Now, the two companies are highly competitive. They're like the Magic Johnson and Larry Bird of cosmetics. And remember: the three reasons people buy something is because they need it, they want it, or they don't want someone else to get it. We tapped into that competitive spirit to create some urgency to close the deal.

We knew that members of Ulta's executive team followed our personal Instagram account. We decided to stoke the fire and put up a very short post: "Where would you like to see Beekman 1802 in Ulta or Sephora?"

Within minutes, our Neighbors began commenting. Thousands of comments began flooding in. They all had opinions.

It was really just a question, arguably an innocent one. Where would they like to see our products? To the Ulta execs, it added more urgency to the decision-making. Within a week, Ulta's CEO came to our farm to seal the deal.

Score!

We understood the emotional mindset and what emotions are likely to kind of trigger them—namely, a good old-fashioned dose of competition. We played on those emotions.

It wasn't manipulative, per se. It was smart business: creating urgency to close a deal. And Ulta was thrilled to see that so many of our existing customers loved Ulta. (Of course, there were many customers who preferred Sephora, so we were especially careful never to burn that bridge.)

Our pal Stephen Brown was equally savvy. Stephen is the founder of the lifestyle company Glitterville, which sells fabulous ornaments and decorations.

Stephen oozes creativity. Talk to him for five minutes, and he'll entrance you with stories about his past life as a costume designer in TV and film, which led to meeting Oprah, a judgeship on the TV show *Craft Wars*, and a stint decorating the White House for Christmas 2023 and 2024. "All those reindeer flying over the grand foyer?" he says. "I made those by hand, by myself, night and day."

It was an enormous job, but Stephen refuses to delegate. "If I hand it off, then it's not me, and I want it to be me," he says. "I'm always behind the eight ball because I'm working night and day. And I love it."

Stephen was born in Rockwood, Tennessee, a tiny town outside Knoxville. After his high school guidance counselor suggested he take a job at the local post office upon graduation, Stephen hightailed it out of town so fast you could see skid marks. He landed in New York with a whopping $80 in his pocket.

Stephen's a lot like Forrest Gump. Not only does he have the accent, but he's sweet and guileless and always assumes things will work out. They usually do. You might think he's lucky, and you'd be right. But he created his luck, usually by appealing to people's emotions (and egos).

"There is not a job in New York that I got that I didn't send a handwritten note saying, 'I'm Stephen from Tennessee, I'd like to work for you,'" he says. "Ninety percent of the time people would respond, and I'd go and work myself to death. Then they'd refer me for other jobs. I always say, 'If you're honest with people, they'll give you a chance.' If you can't make a connection with people, they're never going to embrace what you're doing. Realness and being sincere with people got me where I am."

But not connecting emotionally also impacted him. When Glitterville started in 2008, its Atlanta showroom was painted sky blue, hot pink, and lime green. It looked like a cartoon. Potential clients found it beautiful, but they didn't want to buy anything. The environment was almost too childlike. It screamed "unsophisticated," which wasn't a word anyone wanted to be associated with.

"People said, 'This is the most magical place, but it's not right for me,'" he recalls. "The products don't look like they would live anywhere but in this room. I love it, but it's not for me or my store.' That occurred every day."

One day a stranger came into the showroom—Stephen had no idea who he was—and asked to speak with him privately.

The two men went into the hallway, and the man launched right in. "He said, 'I've been coming into your showroom since you started, and I love it. But people don't know what they can do with it. You need to make it approachable so people can envision the items in their homes.'"

Stephen thanked him. He wasn't upset; he realized that many people felt this way. So he completely redid the showroom, painting everything colors similar to what people would have in their home, like navy and pink.

The next time he had a show, buyers from Anthropologie popped up. They were gobsmacked. "How would we not know you?" they asked. "We couldn't have missed anything this beautiful!"

The products were the same as they had always been, but the environment had changed. In the past, the buyers had walked right by. This time, they connected to it on an emotional level. Anthropologie began selling Stephen's products, and Glitterville was off to the races.

"You have to be willing to listen to people," says Stephen. "If they're all saying the same thing, or feeling the same thing, then they're usually right."[11]

Leading a Horse to Oil

There's probably no more rational transaction than getting your car's oil changed. You don't see a lot of automotive maintenance marketing that tugs at your heartstrings.

On the other hand, beauty product purchases are very rarely rationally driven.

In 2023, we were launching a new facial oil. Facial oils are a very crowded category, so we knew that we would need to pull out all the stops—rational and emotional—to get women to switch from the oil they were currently using to a new one. "How," we wondered "could we get women to change their oil?"

As with any new launch, we were trying to maximize the marketing dollars we had. We wanted to amplify our message with a partner but needed to find one that was surprising enough to get us press that we wouldn't have earned anyway.

One day Brent saw an Instagram post that Jiffy Lube had partnered with the women from the Home Edit, a home-organizing empire, so he deduced that it was targeting a female demographic. What more surprising partnership could there be than a beauty brand and an automotive maintenance company?

He reached out to people at Jiffy Lube and set up a meeting. Our idea was simple. We'd convince women it was time for an "oil change" while they were changing their oil. We pitched the idea of a Beekman 1802 day spa inside a Jiffy Lube location where customers could get a facial, manicure, and hand massage for free while they were waiting for their car. It was a stunt, of course. But it was the perfect one. The connection between a rational brand like Jiffy Lube and an emotional one like Beekman 1802 captured people's imaginations. We received a great deal of press, and a lot of fun responses. We even won a major beauty industry award for the collaboration.

The best part? Jiffy Lube loved the idea so much that it offered to foot the bill.

Why? Because how often does Shell, which owns Jiffy Lube, get the opportunity to sell a feel-good story around oil? To a female customer? Not very.

Saddling Up

A similar thing happened when we finally decided to look for a key investor to fuel our growth.

Over the years, many private equity companies that were interested in investing in the company have approached us. We started getting bids from potential investors and were surprised (and a little disappointed) that their valuations of the company didn't include many of the elements that we knew were most valuable about our brand. They discounted the fact that we had a flagship store in Sharon Springs. (Too tiny. Too remote.) They discounted our popular farm tours and festivals. (Not directly tied to significant revenue.) They discounted the portion of our customer base over fifty-five. (Not a desired demographic.) Meanwhile, we knew that these things were actually the heart of our successful brand. Rationally we understood where they were coming from, but emotionally we knew the truth was different from what could be put on a spreadsheet.

But of course, from a founder standpoint, we wanted to maximize value. We wanted someone willing to pay a premium on what the numbers were not showing. We had a surplus of bidders, but a lack of understanding. We needed to help the bidders forge an emotional connection. And, as we mentioned at the top of this chapter, we also needed a bidder who was afraid of losing to another investor.

So how did we do it?

Well, we immediately cut loose any potential suitor who refused to come meet us at our headquarters in Schenectady. Most private equity firms are based in New York City and haven't been north of Central Park in decades, if ever. We decided that if they weren't willing to venture out of Manhattan, they didn't really understand the appeal of our wholesome brand. We knew we couldn't build an emotional connection over Zoom.

After we met with the handful that came to Schenectady, we decided to do something very foreign to financial bigwigs. We invited them to dinner at our farm.

There was no fancy catering. No valet parking. No bajillion-dollar bottles of wine. Josh cooked. Brent poured rosé. Farmer John passed around baby goats (to play with, not to eat). And we went to the local ice cream stand for dessert.

This was the heart of the brand. Our farm and our values were the real gold. And, as we hoped, word spread around New York City financial circles about these amazing dinners on a small upstate farm.

They became a much sought-after invitation and stoked the bidding competition.

In the end, we found the perfect partner. They had submitted the winning bid because they understood what made our company different and more valuable than just what showed up on our spreadsheets. And we knew that we'd found an investor who had the same kind of vision and values that we had. We're still together today and beating all of the goals we set for ourselves as we sat around our picnic table sipping cheap rosé on a warm summer evening.

Riding into the Sunset

Its prudent to take the time to understand the emotional motivation of anyone you are trying to obtain as a customer or partner. Any time we go into an important meeting, we do our due diligence. We research the hell out of everybody we meet with, which of course includes Googling every news item that has come out about the company in the past three months.

Have any of the people who are going to be in that meeting been quoted in the last few months? We want to know. We might even check out their personal Instagram feed, their Facebook page, to see what's going on in their lives, what seems to be important to them in their lives. Listening to the earnings call of whatever partner you're trying to get is also savvy, because whatever that earnings call is, that's the CEO or the leadership, giving their priorities and their vision and what they need to work on.

This might sound stalkerish, but it's not. It's *smart*. The goal is to walk into that meeting and show how you fit into their vision, so they know that they know they're going to please their boss by working with you.

Always stop to consider emotions when forging a pitch for any product or idea. That means constantly empathizing with those across the table and considering how they see things. We use this tactic when we try to land business partnerships. Rather than have one standard pitch, we modify our pitch slightly to either arouse or squelch the fear or satisfy the desire or fear we sensed on the part of our potential partners. No two people are the same, and neither are any two businesses. Each deserves its own approach.

Josh always says the three most important words in any meeting are "to your point." In this day and age when people are more interested in being seen as experts and leaders, simply acknowledging that you heard what someone else said goes a long way to winning them over to your objectives. Even if you don't fully agree with what they're saying, try to find one thing that you do agree with, and repeat it back to them. If they say, "The sky looks green to me," you can say, "To your point, the sky does appear green sometimes, but I think we can turn it blue together." Chances are they'll be flattered enough that someone finally listened to them and be more willing to listen to what you have to offer.

 ## CHEW ON THIS

- Spend a little more than 80 percent of your persuasive efforts on emotions or storytelling and a bit less than 20 percent on rational argumentation. (Also, don't forget to make your customer or business partner a little bit afraid *not* to transact with you.)

- Make intensive efforts to investigate the emotional space of your customers. Forget the usual focus groups, quantitative surveys, or ethnographic studies. Get creative, even if it means attempting your own version of the popular TV show *Undercover Boss*, in which leaders go undercover to observe frontline operations.

- Make emotional research and empathy a regular part of your pitch process and develop guidelines for people across the company to do it as well.

BECOME A G.O.A.T.:
Craft an Emotional Persuasion Strategy

Think of a problem or issue in your business that's causing you a lot of angst right now. It could be a challenging relationship with an employee, a vendor, or a customer. Or it could be a deal with a prospective partner that you really want or need to land. Focus on the key person or people on the other side of the table.

What baseline emotions are driving their behavior? Is it fear? Desire? Sadness? Hope? Something else? If you struggle to pinpoint it, think of ways you might gather evidence—perhaps by talking to a close colleague of theirs or reviewing their company's annual report to understand their challenges and their potential emotional impact. On the basis of what you conclude, draft a strategy for influencing this person or people emotionally.

The Grass Is Always Greener on the Other Side

How to Use Competitive Intelligence

It was starting to get a little bit ludicrous. The younger women in our office were constantly getting boxes and boxes and boxes delivered full of cosmetics, stickers with cute sayings, multiple samples, pink pouches, and other ephemera. When a box arrived, everyone would huddle around the recipient's desk excitedly to help unpack its treasures immediately. We'd heard about the meteoric rise of Glossier, the company that practically invented Millennial Pink and girl-bossing. But now we were witnessing firsthand our employees' devotion to it. We started comparing everything we did to Glossier. Should we add more samples to our boxes? Should we print up some cute stickers or other little toys? Even though it was a cosmetics company and we were a skin-care company and thus not in direct competition, it did make us a little (OK, a lot) jealous to read headlines like "Glossier Tops Billion Dollar Valuation with Latest Funding" (*Wall Street Journal*). Everything was coming up Glossy.

Soon, though, we started waking up to headlines like "Glossier to Furlough Most of Its Retail Employees" (*Wall Street Journal*) and "What Went Wrong at Glossier?" (*Refinery29*) and "The Complicated Rise and Fall of Glossier" (*Guardian*).[1]

We shouldn't have been surprised. We've fallen victim to "brand envy" many times, only to learn that things weren't always as great as they looked from the outside. You'd think we'd learn. Nope.

Like everyone else, we too are susceptible to the adage "The Grass Is Always Greener on the Other Side," which has adorned so many posters and coffee cups that it's become almost an afterthought. But it's a good, solid maxim, and interesting because it means the opposite of what it's saying: The grass is *not* always greener on the other side. We all tend to think other people or businesses have it better than we do; simply scroll through people's Instagram feeds, or other companies' LinkedIn posts, and it's hard not to feel that way. Everyone seems to be having a rollicking good time. But they aren't. It's an illusion. A well-crafted, heavily curated fantasy.

Mary Giuliani can attest to his. Giuliani, forty-eight, feeds high-level people at high-level events in New York City and the Hamptons. She's around movers and shakers in art, entertainment, fashion, music, media, tech, politics—you name it—on a regular basis, catering about two hundred parties a year.

"I have seen over some great lawns and wonderful hedges and it's only made me appreciate my life more," she says. "There are some people that seemingly have everything, and then they have to keep up with that everything and it seems like an exhausting existence. I've had amazing glimpses into so many lives and the more glimpses I have, the more grateful I become."[2]

Back to the grass and its verdant tint. The phrase dates back to the first century BC and the Greek poet Ovid, who wrote: *Fetrilior segest est alenis semer in agris.*[3] That means: "The harvest is always more fruitful in another man's field." Over time, it morphed into the catchphrase we know today.

God was also aware that humans tend to compare themselves to others. So the good Lord came up with the Tenth Commandment: "You shall not covet your neighbor's house; you shall not covet your neighbor's wife, nor his male servant, nor his female servant, nor his ox, nor his donkey, nor anything that is your neighbor's."[4] While this commandment is technically about envy, God was wise enough to know that it's not good to desire anything your neighbor has, not even his ox, because it's not necessarily better than what you already have. (Beyond that, it can cause big problems, especially if you have a soft spot for your neighbor's spouse.)

We've thought a great deal about this piece of G.O.A.T. wisdom in a business context, precisely because it's such an apt description of animal behavior. When we watch our goats roaming freely on the farm, we always notice how highly attuned they are to the other side of the fence. Never mind that the grass over there is *exactly the same* color and texture as the grass on our side. The goats will spend an entire day trying to figure out how to cross over. If they do gain access, they'll kind of hang out and chow down, convinced that they've hit the pastoral jackpot. But it's the same damn grass they were eating before! They just don't know it.

Humans are animals who are always going to think the grass is greener on the other side. This is a cognitive bias known as the "focusing illusion."[5] The gist is that we all focus on one area of our lives—say, living in a sunny climate—and overlook the other aspects. As economist and Nobel Prize winner Daniel Kahneman, who co-coined the phrase, put it, "Nothing in life is as important as you *think* it is while you are thinking about it."[6] Why? Because you're thinking about it!

In a famous study, Kahneman and professor David A. Schkade surveyed 1,992 students at the University of Michigan, Ohio State, UCLA, and UC Irvine and asked about their satisfaction with their life. You'd think the Californians would be happier: Sun! Sand! Palm trees! Vineyards! Celebrities! Respondents thought they'd be happier, too. So Schkade and Kahneman measured this. Turns out California living wasn't the overall life panacea the Midwesterners thought it would be; the Midwesterners were just as contented as those on the coast. They all had the same life stressors and challenges—work, love, health, relationships—no matter where they lived.

"People are exposed to many messages that encourage them to believe that a change of weight, scent, hair color (or coverage), car, clothes, or many other aspects will produce marked improvements in their happiness," the authors write. "Some of these changes may work for some people (there is evidence that the benefits of some types of cosmetic surgery are long-lasting), but there are probably many more cases in which the messages merely induce and exploit a focusing illusion. Our research suggests a moral, and a warning: nothing that you focus on will make as much difference as you think."[7]

Coveting what your neighbor—or your rivals—appear to have is an extremely powerful instinct, but it usually doesn't leave us better off. In a business context, paying too much attention to the other side of the fence can be hugely damaging.

Still, leaders and teams so often obsess over their competitors, believing that the other teams' products, marketing, and operations are better *even when they're not.* By obsessing too much over competitive analysis and attempting to clone their grass, companies all too often sacrifice what most distinguishes them in the eyes of customers: their uniqueness, originality, and authenticity. If you only fixate on the comparison, then you're not looking at the fundamentals of your own business.

(We're happy to note, however, that Glossier is currently in the midst of a remarkable turnaround and success.)

One of the most important and basic business lessons any of us can learn is to take a balanced approach to competitive analysis, focusing as much on your own fundamentals as on what other market players are doing.

David Stark, the chief creative officer of David Stark Design and Production, an event design and planning outfit in Brooklyn, has been working in the field for thirty years. He produces corporate events, nonprofit fundraisers, and individual social events like weddings and birthday celebrations, with about forty-five full-time employees.

There are a lot of people in the event planning space, and it would be easy to get overwhelmed by the competition. But not David. He doesn't really worry about what other design and event planning companies are doing, because *they're not him*. They do what they do, and David does what he does.

"There's always been an open-endedness in how to do things without really caring about what was deemed acceptable and what was the status quo," he says. "We're really focused on art-making and goals for our clients, and the fact that every client we work with is unique and has specific goals, and they're not necessarily the same as other clients' goals and unique characteristics."

Because his company focuses on the client's individual goals, he doesn't really think about what the competition is up to.

"When I meet with a bride, it's very common for me to say, 'I don't want to see pictures of other people's weddings. I'm less interested in seeing photos you've pinned on Pinterest. What I'm really interested in are things you like—art, films, travel, hotels, books, nature. Things that you're attracted to. The things that make you *you*. I'm not concerned with someone else's wedding. But if you need to show me—I want to see what you didn't like rather than what you like.'"

His reasoning is all part of what makes him *him*. "If we're looking at other people's weddings, we're making a watered-down version of someone else's wedding, which was probably a watered-down version of someone else's wedding," he says. "But if we can focus on how you are as a person or couple and focus on what inspires you, then we can create something that's only been done for you." And only been done by him.[8]

Growing Your Grass

We know full well the dangers of the copycat mentality. By 2018 our creative and marketing team had grown to fifteen people. Because of our outsized success in the beauty category of our business, we'd made the intentional decision to focus more on becoming a beauty company versus a multicategory lifestyle brand. Prior to that shift, we were selling food, home décor, and artisanal items. They were selling fine, but not as well as our beauty products. Ultimately, they became a distraction from our growth engine. It was very emotional to have to change directions; we loved all of these other products. But sometimes you have to kill your darlings.

As we shifted to a single beauty focus, we fell into more direct competition with other beauty companies that had much more experience and much deeper pockets. Our email marketing, digital advertising, product photography, packaging, and so on looked vastly different from these other companies. And while it's always beneficial to be unique, we also weren't having the success with our marketing that we used to have. It wasn't that the marketing was less successful, but it all required a tremendous amount of effort and resources. And because we were putting it all into smaller verticals, we were taking it away from resources that could be used to promote our beauty growth. It was not an efficient use of human and financial capital.

Looking at competitors who are best in class can be a way of learning what they're doing right. Presumably, a larger, more successful company has a deeper team and more research. By seeing what it's doing, you can have access to those resources as well.

Taking a play out of a common management playbook, we created a war room in which we tracked everything that our key competitors were doing—the emails they were sending out, their social media posts, their product launches. Everything. We met as a team once a week and went over everything our competitors were communicating to their customers. This deep competitive analysis showed that while we had the fundamentals right, we were missing some category nuances. We weren't showing photography of the texture of the product. There was a promotional cadence unique to the beauty industry that we were missing out on. We were focusing a bit too much on what made our products great and not enough on what the benefits were of using them—all things that more seasoned beauty marketers built their careers learning.

We talked about ingredients and formulations of the goat milk, but our competitors were doing clinical testing and showing the scientific results. And that's what our customers wanted.

We changed our messaging to lead with the trials, and we also began showing before-and-after pictures. It worked beautifully. With just a few, relatively small tweaks to the messages we were sending out, we saw our sales begin to grow—and then exceed—category growth.

But after about a year, we saw our marketing ROI plateauing. We went back into the war room and began dissecting our competitors even more closely. We pinned up our social media posts and email blasts right next to theirs. Was there something we were missing? We couldn't see it. Ours was exactly the same. And then it hit us . . . . *Ours was exactly the same.*

It was time to go backward a bit. To take all the tools that we learned from our competition but use them to till a more fertile pasture, one that better fit the foundation we'd poured for ourselves over the past decade.

For example, we explained to the customer how our two unique ingredients—goat milk and Kindness—improved the health of their skin, leading to the clinical studies. Acts of Kindness have actually been shown to reduce cortisol levels and increase dopamine, resulting in healthier-looking skin.[9]

It worked. We once again began besting our competition while using all the lessons we'd learned from them.

Getting the balance between learning from competitors and building a unique brand means fighting your best marketing instincts sometimes. Rather than aspiring to some ideal of perfection that your competitor has allegedly attained, it's smarter to take your own essence as the starting point. Yes, learn from others, but lead from your authentic self.

We define authenticity as being completely open *to a degree*, revealing oneself and one's motives to a degree that maybe didn't exist before. These days, that also means not getting caught being inauthentic.

There's so much pressure on all of us, companies and people, to actually be what we say we are. If you're trying to present yourself as an eco-friendly brand, you have to be walk the walk, talk the talk, and sit the sit. It's way too easy for consumers to research you and call you out.

When we were researching investors, one person we talked to challenged us by asking: "Well, can't *anyone* put goat milk in a product and have a goat milk product?"

Of course, anyone could. But they don't have a farm and a doctor founder to explain the science. We did! It would be hard for any goat milk brand birthed in a boardroom to compete with ours, which was birthed in a barn. Our brand reeks of authenticity. (And not just because it was birthed in a barn.)

With every executional detail, ask yourself: *Is our product or branding as uniquely identifiable as our brand?* While you should certainly explore what competitors are doing, looking for elements that you might adapt to your brand's own needs, first and foremost, you must direct your attention inward—to your own, unique purpose. We've always had a test for our team members whenever they present new marketing or products or packaging. If they can put a competitor's logo on your product, ad, or social media post and it still works, then it's not going to work for us.

Sometimes the Grass Is Blue

While you want to be different in business, you don't want to be *too* different. This applies to life, too (just ask any high school student grappling with being an individual but not *too* much of one). You want to do *some* of the same things your competitors are doing, but not the exact same things. You need to "be you" in the best way possible.

When you're competing for consumers who are just entering the marketplace, there will always be consumers who are already loyal to another brand. How do you get them to switch over to you? You always need to position yourself as the "greener grass" that they'll covet over their existing brand. You can be greener by being newer, sexier, more effective, lower-priced, higher-priced, or a million different ways to be different. But you must be different and know how to point that out in a language that the consumer already understands.

One of the ways we strike the balance between being competitively curious and authentically unique is to avoid comparing ourselves to the latest sexy brand on the block. Instead, we look at what brands with *longevity*—in any arena—have done in terms of building an identifiable mark or look or voice. We don't care if they're selling toenail clippers or eggbeaters. In fact, our very company name owes itself to this approach. When we were trying to come up with a name for our yet-to-be company, we made a list of every premium brand that had stood the test of time. Tiffany. Hermès. Mercedes. One of the names we wrote down was Chanel No. 5. It's unique, yet memorable to billions of people over decades of time. It's just someone's name, plus a number.

We knew we wanted to incorporate the name of our farm, which had always been locally called Beekman Farm after William Beekman, who built it in 1802. Someone's name and a number. "Beekman 1802."

We're terrifically proud that even in an industry in which companies are constantly evolving and rebranding, we've never needed to touch our name or logo once in our seventeen-year history. (Thanks, Coco Chanel.)

The Grass Is Greener Where You Water It

Our friend Stephen Brown, whom you met in chapter 7, knows a lot about illusion. Brown grew up in a small town in Tennessee; as a kid, he'd spend his afternoons watching TV and desiring everything he saw on it. He believed the grass was greener on *Happy Days* and

The Waltons, because that's what TV executives wanted him (and all viewers) to believe.

These feelings didn't disappear when he got older.

"It's everyone's immediate thought that someone else has it better and easier," he says. "But the truth is, any time something is beautiful, there's someone who has done a lot of work on it. Everything in life is held up by a group of people working so hard. Behind every company is someone passionate and willing to work longer, harder, and faster than anyone else. The grass may be greener, but that's just because someone is tending it night and day."

Brown practices what he preaches (yet another maxim). He starts working early in the morning and keeps on going until bedtime—which he still does, years into his business. "You can't make someone want to do that," he says. "You can't tell someone if you want a business, you have to work around the clock. Successful businesses exist because people really want to do them. And if you don't have that kind of passion and drive—at least for a creative business—then it won't work."[10]

At the end of the day, every entrepreneur—even those who are constantly referred to as "overnight successes"—knows that no business succeeds without plain old hard work. If the grass at your competitors is actually greener than yours, it's not magic. It's because they tended to it better. It doesn't always mean longer hours or sacrificing life balance. It can result from working more efficiently (see chapter 1) or finding better tools (see chapter 3). Your job is to figure out *how* they have it better or, more specifically, how they got to better.

Josh learned a lot about competitive analysis early in his career when he worked in advertising. Sometimes he learned almost too much. Some advertising practices border on spying.

For instance, there was one advertising agency in New York City in the 1990s that seemed to win almost every new business pitch it competed in. Let's call it "Company Q." When agencies compete for a brand's business, they work up speculative campaigns for the prospective new client and present them in big, secretive presentations.

The client usually views all the competitive presentations within a few days, compares them internally, then awards the business, usually all within a few days.

It seemed impossible that any agency could win as many of these pitch competitions as Company Q did. The other agencies were eager to figure out how it did it; one agency found out by poaching Company Q's head of new business.

"It was simple," he explained. "After we made our presentation and the prospective client needed to head to the next agency's pitch or back to the airport, we'd offer them the use of the agency town car to save them the trouble of getting a cab. What no one realized was that the driver of the town car was an employee of the agency. He would listen to the prospective clients as they debated the merits or problems with the pitch they'd just heard as well as all the competitive pitches. After he reported the discussions back to the agency execs, they could preemptively follow up with the potential client and address their concerns. And even sometimes find subtle ways to undermine the competitors' pitches." That's not the kind of subterfuge that we would ever resort to, but you have to hand it to them for the simple ingenuity of it.

We don't mow our grass that way at Beekman 1802. But we have our own means. If we're trying to find a creative agency for a new ad campaign, we will gather some serious competitive intelligence. We'll scour the web to find a campaign or slogan or design that we like, and then try to find out who was behind it.

When we were creating a new set of products to be sold in Ulta, we needed a new type of packaging. We made a list of the other brands that we thought had exceptional packaged design. We especially liked a brand called Tatcha, so we reached out to the design agency that had done its packaging. We didn't want to look like it, but we did want to achieve the same quality.

Many of the companies that you see profiled in the media are from the sexy industries of tech, fashion, beauty, entertainment. They can be great companies to learn from because they're often pushing boundaries and thinking creatively. But it doesn't necessarily mean they're the "best" business or that they have it all figured out. They're just clickbait in today's click desperate media landscape. As we've mentioned previously, many of the sexy companies that got all the attention over the last decade are struggling or no longer exist. Sometimes the grass looks greener because it's AstroTurf.

Check out other people's yards for ideas and inspiration but do the hard work of tending to your own, and your grass will always be the greenest on the block. Or farm.

Brent is always alerting our team to other people's yards. Brent wakes up early, between 4 and 4:30 a.m. He begins his morning by checking out at least twenty different newsletters across an array of different industries. They include, in no particular order:

> *The Wall Street Journal, the New York Times, Financial Times, the New Happy, Go to Millions by Ari Mayer, Global Cosmetics News, Beauty Matter, Beauty Independent, Business of Fashion, Glossy, Global Wellness Institute, Seeking Alpha: Wall Street Breakfast, CEW Daily, Air Mail, Digiday, Modern Retail, WorkLife, Simon Sinek, From Brené Brown, Chain Store Age, TD Cowen, the Information, Design Milk, Vogue Business, Axios Macro, Axios Markets, Axios What's Next, Axios A.M., Medscape Trending, the Economist, Chief Executive, Digital Commerce 360, Retail News, WWD, Harvard Business Review, the Atlantic, Apple News Trending*

Yes. He reads them all.

When Brent sees something that he thinks is relevant to a team member's job, he'll forward it to them. He doesn't tell them why he's sending it; he wants them to figure out how it applies to their day-to-day work. Employees often get bogged down in the minutiae of whatever they're working on and lose curiosity about what's going on in the larger environment. They don't see the wider world and they most certainly don't have time to see the grass past the fence.

 CHEW ON THIS

- Conduct regular competitive analyses, but always balance your insights with respect for your own business's fundamentals.

- Take your core mission and values as the starting point for your marketing efforts.

- As your company grows, subject your marketing to the copy-cat test. If you swapped in your competitors' logo, would your product or communications still work? If so, you have a problem that needs to be fixed.

BECOME A G.O.A.T.:
How Envious Are You?

Think about what you do on a typical day at your company. How much of your time do you spend thinking about your competition? Are you constantly trying to one-up them or is your approach to competitive analysis more balanced?

Next, consider five lessons you could draw from your competition and five lessons they could learn from you. Disseminating this analysis among your team members can remind them to keep one eye on competitors but to lean into your company's own fundamentals. The mission, values, and executional approaches that make you unique and valuable are paramount.

An Ounce of Prevention Is Worth a Pound of Cure

How to Mitigate Risk

Many entrepreneurs focus on taking big risks rather than on proceeding carefully to preempt risks that eventually can and will materialize. Contemplating potential risks seems counterproductive and, frankly, boring. Better, they think, to simply grow as fast as they can in the present and handle challenges in the future if and when they materialize.

That approach might work if you aspire to build a unicorn—that's industry jargon for a company with a billion-dollar valuation—and then quickly get out. The odds of success at this, however, are very slim. If instead you want to create an enduring business, you have to think more carefully about risk. The reality is that the challenges your business faces might be much more damaging and even catastrophic if left unchecked. As we've found it's far better to stay alert to risk and take preventative action early on, even if it bogs you down a little bit, than to find yourself putting out massive fires later. A more measured, realistic approach to risk isn't sexy, but it really does work.

Preventative Prevention

We were proactive and cautious from the beginning of our entrepreneurial adventure. Instead of going all in financially, we decided that one of us (Josh) would continue to work freelance in advertising for at least a few years to help us get off the ground. It would have been great to have him working full-time on the business, but we anticipated the possibility that we would struggle at first and wanted to mitigate that risk (and wanted health insurance).

We believed then and still believe now that "An Ounce of Prevention Is Worth a Pound of Cure," another gem from ye olde founding father, Benjamin Franklin.

There are other ways of saying this: "Plan ahead." "Try to cut off problems before they occur." "Always be ready, because you never know what's coming." "Have tough talks sooner rather than later."

In embroidered pillow talk: "A stitch in time saves nine."

In Joshland? "Assume the worst, but plan for the best."

As we saw it, an ounce of prevention—in the form of Josh taking freelance work—would prevent us from having to come up with a pound of cure, perhaps in the form of both of us having to give up our new dream and go back to our former careers. It was a wise decision. But once we got Beekman going, we continued to focus on risk mitigation whenever we could.

Early on, for instance, we understood that we would need to find outside partners to help us scale up production. We were sourcing all of our product from Deb, our Neighbor who operated out of a barn on her property and made soaps using traditional, artisan methods. (You've heard us mention her before.)

Deb is a hard worker and smart businessperson, and she was perfectly content with the size of the business she'd grown—not just making our soaps, but her own soaps as well. Her goal wasn't to buy more equipment, hire a bigger team, and spend time organizing and overseeing others.

We made and sold thousands of bars of soap with Deb through our website, but as we looked to expand into the independent retail market, we knew Deb wouldn't be able to produce the tens of thousands we would need.

Because we're cautious by nature, we knew we needed a backup plan. We could've just signed up new independent retail partners and put the pressure on Deb to scale up her operations. And Deb is the sort of lovely human who would have done her best to make us happy. But in the end, we knew that neither of us would be satisfied. So, as you read earlier, we found a larger soap maker who not only could handle our growth goals but could also produce the same quality of soap our Neighbors had come to expect from us.

But once we found them, we sought to mitigate the risk of any Neighbor backlash by selling both types of soap for the next five years. We also wanted to make sure Deb didn't lose a source of income. Planning ahead to find this new manufacturer turned out to be a doubly wise move. Shortly after we began working with our new soap partner to service our growing independent retail accounts, we landed our first TV retail partner. Suddenly we didn't need tens of thousands of bars. We needed millions. Even if we'd been able to convince Deb to scale up to reach those first goals, she never would've been able or happy to accomplish these new ones.

Having open and early discussions about what Deb wanted from her work allowed us the time to find the right partner to scale with. We avoided years of growth headaches and built a runway that allowed us to take off long before we even knew for sure where we were going.

Just by conscientiously planning for future issues, we, at best, avoided a lot of bumps in the road and, at worst, averted manufacturing limitations that would have forced us to turn down large retail partners when they came calling.

An Ounce of Cure

As you've no doubt gathered by now, we've always been very conservative in every part of our business, whether that's hiring, manufacturing, or projecting revenues. So many companies dig themselves into a hole because they over-project, over-hire, or overinvest to reach a goal. And then, if they don't achieve what they promised, they're even further behind than where they started.

As we explained earlier, Beekman 1802 began as a full lifestyle brand that produced and sold products in many different categories. Artisanal home goods. Food products. Garden wares. Books and magazines. From the beginning we had some success in most of these areas. A more intrepid entrepreneur than we were probably would've doubled down and hired different sales managers to grow each of these categories. But we've always been conservative and only hired new team members when we had already grown the revenue enough ourselves to pay for a new salary. Could we have succeeded in all of these different categories if we'd gone for broke and speculatively hired multiple category managers? Perhaps. But we also could've gone broke. We believe that our conservative approach turned out to be the perfect strategic method to slowly winnow out less productive categories and ultimately identify that the beauty category was our winning gambit. (Actually, it wasn't a gambit at all since we never gambled; we slowly built instead.)

One preventative measure that you can take as a leader is to have very realistic projections about your business. As we've mentioned before, when we started Beekman, Josh went back to freelancing in the city so that we would have at least one paycheck guaranteed to come on a predictable schedule. Looking back now, the early numbers show that Beekman probably would've survived and grown at roughly the same pace whether or not we did have Josh's backup income.

But what if it hadn't? What if we'd optimistically projected much higher revenues than the lower ones that led us to believe we needed Josh's Plan B? Then we would've run the risk that Brent also would have had to go back to work to tide us over, which would have taken more time and attention away from our new company. Or worse, caused us to give up on it completely. With Josh as our cushion, we were able to keep going with our business without risking much at all. Instead, we took a pound of cure into consideration and planned properly.

Of course, every business owner must walk a fine line between being risk averse and playing it too safe.

"Playing it safe is a risk. Playing it safe is not mitigation. Incorporating risk into your strategy is risk mitigation," says Sally Hogshead, a highly sought-after public speaker and author of the New York Times bestseller *Fascinate: How to Make Your Brand Impossible to Resist.* "Marketing is not about risk mitigation. It's about opportunity enhancement."[1]

We agree with Sally. Risk is essential. And planning for the right amount of risk today gives you the freedom to take more and bigger risks tomorrow.

Curing Expectations

Everyone wants to go to the board meeting and announce with confidence that they're going to hit double-digit growth, or double revenues, or double EBITDA, or double anything. But if you don't try to be a little bit realistic, you'll likely wind up with double the times of disappointment. "Realistic" means just that. It means that the odds are more in favor of something happening than not.

As with everything in life, you need to strike a balance. We're big fans of setting both reasonable goals and stretch goals. You get all the inspiration for overachievement with none of the demoralizing effects of missing a goal. If you reach your stretch goals, everyone is pleasantly surprised and, more importantly, everybody's a winner.

In order to do this, though, you have to *understand* what's a realistic goal and what's a stretch. Take baby steps, set short-term goals, and pick the lowest-hanging fruit. This way, you're setting yourself up for success, and you don't give up if you fail. If you set the goal too high, it can become self-defeating.

When we were struggling to get the business up and running, and we wanted to know what it would take so Josh did not have to go into the city and freelance, we decided that we needed $1 million for him to do that (roughly the price of our outstanding mortgage). We realized that worrying about meeting a mortgage payment was the stumbling block that made us fearful to invest more in the company. Having a steady paycheck made us more comfortable placing more bets on ourselves.

Now, Brent has always been more of a magical thinker than Josh. He's the one with the big dreams and goals, who truly believes that everything he envisions is destined to happen. It's a powerful trait. It allows him to take huge risks, and coupled with his skill sets and work ethic, it pays off more often than it doesn't.

Josh has always been more of a pessimist. If there's a fraction of an iota of a decimal point of a percentage that something can go wrong, he believes it will. Not surprisingly, he's been treated for clinical anxiety for most of his life. But while deep-seated anxiety can be crushing, Josh also feels it's his superpower. Josh can see every potential defeat coming from every possible angle, like a military leader. There's never been a strategic business threat that can hide from Josh.

Anxiety gets a bad rap in the culture, but as Josh can attest, it's actually quite normal. Anxiety can even have benefits.[2] As Tracy Dennis-Tiwary notes in her book *Future Tense: Why Anxiety Is Good for You (Even Though It Feels Bad)*, "In terms of information, anxiety tells us there's this uncertainty, but it's priming us to navigate that uncertainty, to avert disaster, to make the positive possibilities into reality. That's what it actually primes us to do. So it can be protective, but it's also highly productive."[3]

That's because anxiety is a motivating emotion. "It's one that doesn't just trigger fight-or-flight, it also increases oxytocin, the social bonding hormone," she says. "What you find is that especially with moderate levels of anxiety—not necessarily full-blown panic—you actually increase levels of oxytocin, which primes us to seek out social connection and support. So it's almost like a fractal beauty that within anxiety it contains some of its own solutions."[4]

Adrianne Shapira, fifty-three, is a private equity investor in New York who invested in Beekman in 2021. As a woman in a male-dominated industry, she knows all about risk-taking. And yet, she is very measured in her approach to her career.

When she graduated from Columbia Business School in 1999, the business world was focused on dot-coms. Everybody had a business plan, and buckets of money were being throw at smart (and not-so-smart) ideas.

Adrianne was on the cusp of launching a startup with a friend. They had a deck and a business model and met with venture capitalists. "We were drinking our own Kool-Aid," she says. She was all in. Almost.

As it happens, at the same time she had an offer from Goldman Sachs. She was leaning toward the startup, but her husband, an entrepreneur who runs a few businesses, felt differently.

"He was so adamant," she says. "'You've got an offer from Goldman Sachs versus this startup? Is this really even a choice?'"

So she listened to him and took the Goldman Sachs job. The dot-com bubble burst soon after. She was at Goldman for thirteen years.[5]

One benefit from two of us having such opposite risk appetites is that on the rare occasions when Josh does believe something will be a runaway success, it is almost guaranteed to be. So when Beekman had an opportunity to partner with Nestlé Toll House to create a limited-edition line of chocolate chip cookie–scented bath and body products (see chapter 2), Josh listened to all the reasons his colleagues thought it would be a failure (not a traditional bath product scent, not aspirational enough, too "silly") and debunked the risks one by one in his head. As unlikely as the pairing might be, Josh thought that at the end of the day, everyone likes the scent of chocolate chip cookies baking, and everyone likes a bubble bath. And on the day the line finally launched, it sold over $1 million in product in the first hour.

And likewise, when Brent talks himself out of something, it's invariably a true crisis averted. During one product development meeting that Brent was leading, he was initially excited by the idea of a new CBD-infused skin-care product. It seemed to be right on trend: it had an ingredient that was being widely searched for and the price point was perfect. But a few weeks into development, Brent cooled on it. He couldn't see the longevity in it. It felt like it was so on trend that it risked being a fad. We halted development. Sure enough, the following year, one of our competitors launched something similar. And while we don't have its sales numbers, we did notice that it was dropped from retailers' shelves within a year.

Whenever we're coming up with marketing strategy—as we mentioned earlier—we have our zero-dollar spend. When we're first strategizing, we'll ask, "What can we accomplish with zero dollars, through our connections or already existing platforms?" Zero dollars is zero risk, which is the ultimate prevention.

What the zero-dollar rule really does is force the rest of the team to be creative. Sometimes we actually do find a zero-dollar idea. More often, just by searching for one, we find an idea that's truly worth putting extra money behind. This has happened with every product launch and pretty much everything we've done.

Our way of thinking is similar to that of Jonathan Anderson, a visionary in fashion and lifestyle branding who heads up his own brand as well as the ultra-luxury Loewe label. He acknowledges that when his back is against a wall, that's when he becomes more creative.

"I work better when there is no option," he said in an interview with Imran Amed, founder of the fashion media company Business of Fashion. By literally forcing himself to be creative, he's minimizing risk.

He also spoke about the risk of irrelevancy, especially as a creative. "I think 360," he says. "I want my team to think 360 on what we're putting out there. And sometimes you have to make the decision that you may have to give the audience what they don't want—to annoy them. Because there's nothing better when people are annoyed, because then they think. . . . The minute a brand becomes formulaic the clock starts clicking."[6]

One of the things we've done, and still do, is make a list of the biggest threats to our business. We think of it as the opposite of a vision board. It's a nightmare board!

Josh has been known to dissect Brent's ambitions and then elucidate, in impeccable detail, the potential issues with each scenario. This goal is not to stomp all over Brent's dreams, but to answer the ultimate question: *Is the risk worth the possible reward?*

This really speaks to the importance of getting multiple voices and opinions, and not surrounding yourself with people who will simply reiterate your viewpoints. (We delve into this further in chapter 11 on partnerships.)

Calculated Risks

The beauty industry is highly competitive. You always have to come up with something new, because the customer is all about the next big thing.

We launch two to three major new products per year. In 2022, one of our big bets was an under-eye serum that used a proprietary new blend of mushroom ingredients. We put it through our internal channels of safety testing, as did the agency we hired to do the industry-regulated testing—and the product was green-lit to go into production. We were planning to ship thirty thousand batches to Ulta stores around the country.

Of course, whenever we come out with a new product, everyone in the office is excited to get their hands on it. When the first shipment arrived at the office, we passed out samples. By the next morning, we got an email from one of our team members.

"Just FYI, I got some little red bumps under my eye after applying it," it read.

Hmm. This was interesting (in a not good kind of interesting way). Then Josh tried the product again. His skin didn't turn red, but he

LEARN FROM A G.O.A.T.:

Wisdom from Sharks

Few things have been as influential to entrepreneurs than Shark Tank. *Here are some of our favorite insights, straight from the Sharks' mouth.*

- "Treat your customers like they own you—because they do." —Mark Cuban[7]

- "Oh, I'm all about small business. I think what we've learned from big business and big Wall Street is that unchecked greed and the creation of false value gets us all in trouble. If we look at the American economy, who's really creating value? It's the small businesses." —Robert Herjavec[8]

- "The joy is in the getting there. The beginning years of starting your business, the camaraderie when you're in the pit together, are the best years of your life. So rather than being so focused on when you get big and powerful, if you can just get the juice out of that . . . don't miss it." —Barbara Corcoran[9]

definitely felt a slight tingle that he didn't remember when the product was in its prototype phase.

So we decided to have everyone in the company—all 130 employees—test out the product to see how their skin reacted. About 60 percent of them had some irritation, ranging from a minor tingle to full-blown redness. There was no universe in which we could release that product. So we pulled it all from distribution.

It was an enormous loss—about $800,000 in immediate revenue potential, and even down-the-line ramifications for our retail partners—but we had to suck it up. Sixty percent of negative reviews would have had an even greater negative impact on us. After a few weeks, it was determined that one of the ingredients was reacting to skin differently when the batches were scaled up to production quantities from prototype quantities. It's rare, but that sometimes happens. It's similar to what can happen when you double or qua-

- "I prefer to like the people I invest in, but it's not an absolute necessity, as long as they have a good mind and I know they'll do whatever it takes to be successful." –Lori Greiner[10]
- "I'd rather invest in an entrepreneur who has failed before than one who assumes success from day one." –Kevin O'Leary[11]
- "Always look to do business with people you would happily invite to Christmas dinner!" –Kevin Harrington[12]
- "Mentors don't have to be the Daymond Johns or the Mark Cubans. A person running a successful bodega or a tax firm in your community for the last twenty years, that person is working just as much as the individual who's running General Mills." –Daymond John[13]

druple a food recipe. Sometimes increasing proportions equally impacts the final result disproportionally.

But for us, the experience begged an interesting question: If we were a larger company, would we have risked it? After all, no one was dying or being rushed to the emergency room. Many larger companies would have pushed it out, read the negative reviews, fixed the problem, and produced new batches as if nothing had ever happened. It would've been a risk they would've been willing to take. But because we were a new brand, we knew that this product might be the first Beekman product many people might be trying. And if 60 percent of the people had a bad experience, we knew they wouldn't come back for any other Beekman product.

We had a similar situation with a product called our Little Black Mask, a charcoal face mask that was named for the proverbial "little black dress" that's a staple in so many closets.

We were launching it on both HSN and QVC, and like all new products, its marketing strategy had been planned out for months. But right around the time we were set to launch, then Virginia governor Ralph Northam was caught in a yearbook photo in which one person was dressed in blackface and another was wearing the Ku Klux Klan's white robes.[14] Canadian prime minister Justin Trudeau had a similar situation, as did the editor-in-chief of *Bon Appétit* magazine.[15] Given that our product clearly didn't have any sort of racial intention behind it, many people on our team as well as at the retailer encouraged us to launch it anyway.

We weighed the risks. If we delayed the launch until the media storm abated, we would surely miss our quarterly goal. If we went ahead and launched, we would likely hit our goals and could potentially best them. But any resulting bad publicity might possibly tank the entire company for, well, ever. At the very least, just having our team and PR agency on continuous high alert for the launch would expend resources and cause distraction.

We refused to launch.

While we took a bit of a financial hit on inventory, we simply wound up launching a year later and never received a single negative customer reference to the scandals that dominated the airwaves just one year earlier.

Stopping Workplace Risks

Brent still reads every single customer service email that comes in. (We have five Neighbor services people, and they're each responsible for responding to a fraction of our email. But Brent reads through everything.) By doing this, he can spot a trend of complaints and figure out where they're coming from and how to address them before issues arise.

About three years ago, we launched a new type of deodorant with a proprietary formula that works with the body's microbiome to control odor. It's such a new concept in deodorant that no one had produced it. It was an immediate success on a functional level, but there were other problems. We didn't know that in the summer months, when it's sitting in a hot mailbox, some of the ingredients can separate and start leaking out the bottom of the container. It wasn't a huge issue. Not every package was delivered to a hot mailbox. And since the complaints were divided among several of our Neighbor services reps, no one rep got enough complaints to elevate the issue. But because Brent reads all of these emails, he quickly identified that this was a larger issue, and we were able to craft a way to respond to customers who wrote in to tell us what had happened. We swiftly sent them a new product and explained that we were aware of the issue and were addressing it. It's really a question of just being very detail oriented and being very thoughtful every step of the way. It's that simple.

Risk Attuned

There are a number of practices you can adopt to stay attuned to risk and address it proactively. Many entrepreneurs rely on gut feel to gauge how their company is performing, but we believe that even the smallest companies should adopt the same process as giant ones by using key performance indicators (KPIs) or metrics to spot performance issues early and to validate their gut. This is especially true when monitoring risks involved with individual employee performance.

When we first hire someone or give an annual review, we make sure there are as many concrete numbers on the page as possible. Simply saying that an employee needs to "focus on revenue growth" or "reduce out-of-stock issues" leads to far more frustration with both our team members and their managers than saying, "Needs to grow revenue by 15 percent" or "Reduce inventory issues by 10 percent." By monitoring the numbers on a regular basis, and by giving our team members the tools to monitor their progress regularly, we are calculating their risks for failure (and success) in real time against real metrics. And if necessary, they can make adjustments that benefit everyone.

You should also push yourself to address performance issues quickly, even if it means having potentially uncomfortable conversations with employees. You should take a detail-oriented approach to your business, asking yourself whether every part of the offering to customers (the price, the product, and so on) is on target. Finally, you should find ways to stay in intimate contact with customers, as doing so will allow you to spot potential risks or challenges that had previously gone unnoticed.

Your personal risks as an entrepreneur evolve over time as well. Remember how, in the beginning, Josh took on freelance work to mitigate risk of personal finance issues while building the company? Eventually we grew large enough so that risk wasn't a threat anymore. But we still were investing everything Beekman made right back into the company. ("In business," one of Josh's mentors used to say, "if you're not growing, you're shrinking. There is no status quo.") Sure, we were paying the mortgage and car payment, but we were also heading into our fifties. All of our assets were tied up in Beekman. And no matter how much you're worth on paper, you can't pay for your retirement with paper. Which is part of the reason we decided to take on an investment partner, one that aligned with our goals and shared our temperature for risk-taking.

 CHEW ON THIS

- Identify a blue-sky thinker (Brent) and a nail-biting thinker (Josh) as either a counterpoint or mentor. Or train yourself to always look at both sides of the coin.

- Stay alert to cultural sensitivities and the risks these might pose to your business. When it's possible to mitigate these risks in relatively painless ways, be sure to do that.

- Adopt KPIs or other quantitative metrics to spot performance issues early on.

- Move aggressively to address HR issues early, even if this means having difficult conversations.

BECOME A G.O.A.T.:
Create a Nightmare Board

Entrepreneurs often create vision boards that convey their hopes for the future. Your job here is to create a "nightmare board," capturing everything that could go wrong in your business in the months and years ahead. Challenge yourself to list twenty-five to thirty risks that your business could conceivably face. These should be big and small. It's important to stretch for a long list, because if you really make yourself consider every potential outcome to get to twenty-five or thirty, then you're truly likely to think about the risk in every way possible.

Once you've compiled this list, consider those that you would do well to address in the short term.

Look in particular for risks of any size that seem likely to materialize and risks that are unlikely to materialize but that would be catastrophic if they did. What might you do right now to forestall or protect against those risks?

Many Hands Make Light Work

How to Care for Your Employees

We're not bragging when we say that people genuinely love Beekman 1802. Our Neighbors are emotionally attached to the brand, and fiercely loyal. We've cultivated this loyalty by treating all of our Neighbors with Kindness. This also extends to our staff.

We never wanted to work in an unpleasant, dictatorial environment, where owners had the ultimate say and employees were treated as if they were dispensable. We've worked at plenty of companies where it's easy to win by someone else losing or being exploited. That was unacceptable to us. We wanted to create a company that could be successful and profitable, where customers *and* employees were happy.

Employees need to feel valued, appreciated, and honored, and that their input matters. Because it does. Each and every job counts in an organization. So does each and every person. Nothing kills a business faster than low employee morale.

We decided to try to quantify the relationship between Kindness and happiness in the workplace. So in 2022, we commissioned a study with Kindness.org, a global nonprofit whose mission is to educate people about Kindness.

With our support, and working with researchers at Oxford University, Kindness.org developed a questionnaire that would measure a workplace's "Kindness Quotient." The survey asked participants to answer questions about eighteen acts they'd do for a colleague. The researchers also asked which acts they'd expect a colleague to do for them. Most people said that they would perform most of the acts on the list for their colleagues and expected their colleagues to reciprocate.

Not surprisingly, we found that general workplace Kindness is a significant predictor of workplace happiness. We found that Kindness *to* one's boss is an additional predictor of workplace happiness and general workplace Kindness. Feeling valued as a person at work and finding your work purposeful also predicts workplace happiness and general workplace Kindness.

We didn't just commission this research to be "Kind." As we said earlier, every aspect of your business should have a KPI. And if your company's entire purpose is Kindness, we figured we needed a way to accurately measure it—especially internally. "If you can measure it, you can manage it," the old business adage goes. And before our research, there was no way to measure Kindness and, more importantly, tie those measurements to the bottom line. If a company works to make itself Kinder, will it also make itself more profitable?

To improve on something, you need the tools to do it. So we became the first consumer packaged goods company to partner with KindWorks.AI, a platform that encourages and enables Kindness habits. The enterprise platform has an AI agent called "Beni" that connects through Slack, WhatsApp, and Teams to enable and promote Kindness. We found that it increased the amount of connectivity, noticed an increase in feeling appreciated, while also showing an increase in sales revenue for those who have sales data.

Traditionally, American corporations have cared more about the bottom line than employee satisfaction. That's no secret. A sure way for companies to boost bottom-line performance is to cut overhead (employees) and drop the savings to the bottom line. The remaining employees simply work harder and longer (and often for less). This strategy works when the overall economy is relatively well balanced, but once there's a stressor to that system—like a pandemic or recession or rising inflation—the corporation has nowhere further to cut because it has already worn its main asset, its team. down to the bone.

Research has noted how companies can benefit from Kindness. Employees are 13 percent more productive when they're happy.[1] A meta-analysis of more than two hundred studies showed that "altruism, courtesy, conscientiousness, civic virtue, and sportsmanship" are not just associated with company productivity and profit, but also with happiness at work.[2]

More salient for you, the owner: *leaders* are especially critical for fostering Kind companies and employee well-being.[3]

A 2022 survey by McKinsey Health polled fifteen thousand workers in fifteen countries and found that a quarter of them have experienced burnout symptoms.[4] This matters: seventy-six percent of respondents in a Mental Health America and FlexJobs study agreed that workplace stress affects their mental health.[5] Not only is burnout bad for one's physical and psychological well-being, but it negatively impacts business, too, with absenteeism and job dissatisfaction.[6]

So it behooves every business owner to pay sufficient attention to the workforce, to listen to employees' needs and respond proactively rather than wait for a crisis to emerge. It's also why employees have to feel emotionally connected to the brand they're working for. It can't just be about a paycheck, or everyone is miserable.

James Timpson, CEO of the Timpson Group, a family-owned shoe-repair, key-cutting, engraving, and dry-cleaning outfit in the UK, has gained accolades for his approach to employee well-being. Every year, Timpson, who's the author of *The Happy Index: Lessons in Upside-Down Management*, sends his employees a "happiness index" comprising one question: "On a scale of one to ten, how happy are you with your boss or team leader?" In 2023, 86 percent of employees responded with an average happiness score of 9.1 out of 10. Pretty good for a company that has about twenty-one thousand stores.

When Timpson took over the company, which was founded by his great grandfather in 1865, he wanted to learn what to do and what not to do. He spent two years reading about businesses, and then he started writing to business leaders in the UK, Europe, Australia, and the United States and asked to spend a day with them. He wanted to find out what was the magic ingredient to their success.

He and his father, James, then created something called "upside-down management," which works on the principles to trust. It can be summed up in one sentence: "We trust our colleagues because we think they're fantastic."

The Timpson Group has two rules for employees: you put your money in the cash register, and you keep the shop and your appearance tidy. Other than that, you can charge what you want, offer the discounts and deals you want, and go on break when you want. If you feel moved to paint your shop pink, as one employee did, go for it.[7]

To Timpson, this is common sense that makes for good business acumen. "The more you are trusted, the more you can innovate and the more you can be yourself," he says. "The more people are trusted, the happier they are. The happier they are, the better they serve customers, the more likely they are to stay, and they are better at selling and being part of our culture."[8] (He also has a director of happiness on staff to make sure everything's in working order.) In other words, don't focus on money. Focus on keeping your workforce happy, which will translate into greater sales.

Beyond trust, companies must make sure to get Kindness right. Every week, Timpson Group employees can receive a £90 sales commission. They get an extra day off on their birthday, a day off when their kids have their first day of school, and a week off when they get married. He even offers pet bereavement days! He estimates that the company spends 1 million British pounds "making dreams come true" for employees. So when one employee became a grandfather and refused to smile at his grandchild because he was embarrassed by his teeth, they paid for new teeth for him (the employee, not the grandchild). They paid for someone's garden, and even sent a colleague to Disneyland.

But for this to happen, leaders need to know and understand their employees. Timpson is so passionate about this that he tests his team leaders annually on how well they know their people. If they score less than 80 percent, there's an issue.

This is all well and good. But, as Timpson points out, it only works with the right employees. It should come as no surprise that Timpson has thoughts on this, too.

When hiring, he ignores CVs and instead focuses on personality. Interviews are just a chat. "We want people who are fun, interesting, sparky, a bit eccentric," he says. "We are looking for nine or ten out of ten. An eight has opportunity to improve."

Timpson also looks for talent in unique places. Twenty years ago, he was invited to a prison. His mother had been a foster parent, and he grew up surrounded by people from all walks of life. As he walked around the prison, he got into a conversation with an inmate named Matthew who took him on a tour. Timpson was impressed with him—his personality was a definite ten—and at the end of the afternoon, he slipped him his card.

"When you get out, call me," Timpson said.

Six months later, Timpson got a phone call from Matthew's mother. Her son was unable to find work; would Timpson take him on?

Timpson would and did. Twenty years on, Matthew is still with the company. So are six hundred other ex-offenders.

"They're really good, they're honest, they work really hard and they're ambitious," Timpson says of his workforce. The Timpson Group has since opened up training academies in prisons so that inmates can leave with confidence, knowing that they'll have work when they get out.[9]

At Beekman 1802, we've instinctively done these sorts of things from the start. That's one of the reasons we've never used the word "employee" to describe the people who work for us. It's been "Team Beekman" from day one. An individual employee is a "member of Team Beekman," or a "Team Beekman member." And whether in the early days when we had three employees or now when we have hundreds, we never said that any single Beekman Teammate worked "for" us. Everyone at Beekman 1802 works "with" everyone else, not "for" the next person up the org chart.

Part of the reason we do this is to build camaraderie. But it's also so that everybody knows that they're never siloed in their own job responsibilities.

Everybody must chop the company's wood; everyone is responsible for everyone else (as discussed in chapter 1). In that sense, we've always been a collective effort, sort of like a kibbutz. We want people to think about their job at the company as if they're just one member of the village. We don't distinguish between the different kinds of hands.

In G.O.A.T. lingo: "Many Hands Make Light Work."

Lightening the Load

The maxim has been circulating since at least the early 1300s, when it appeared in a middle English knightly romance called "Sir Bevis of Hampton."[10] It then made an appearance in English playwright John Heywood's book *Proverbs*, which was published in 1546.

On one level, the phrase seems to affirm the basic importance of a team: if we bring in people to help us, we can lighten the burden on us. But we take it a step further, interpreting it as a call for us as leaders to take care of the "many hands" we rely on to serve our Neighbors.

There are three dimensions to caring for employees that are especially important. The first is to instill a democratic ethos, the second is to learn as much as possible about what drives each individual team member to do their best, and the third is to know when it's the right time and manner for them and us to go our separate ways. (Yes, all employment comes to an end sometimes. The hard part is acknowledging when it's the best time for both parties, since it's rarely the case that it's mutually agreeable.) Since all employees matter to us, it's up to company leadership to seek out and honor everyone's perspectives, including those of frontline employees.

The year 2018 marked one of the most significant expansions in Beekman 1802's history. We acquired a company in Orlando, Florida, that we'd contracted with for the majority of our logistics, warehousing, and major product development. We'd begun working with it three years earlier, and Beekman 1802 had grown to become such a sizable percentage of its business that it made mutual sense to join forces. We immediately wanted to fly down to Orlando and introduce ourselves to the new team members, which consisted of about seventy-five people.

Everybody thought we were going to go in, introduce ourselves in an hourlong town hall, lead a couple of faux team-building cheers, and continue on our merry way. Instead, we structured the first four hours of the day to meet with executives and management; for the second four hours, we worked in the warehouse, packing boxes and assembling product. This was actually the most important part of the day for us. We completed the full afternoon shift on the packing line so that we could understand the employees' everyday experience. Most everyone was shocked; no one expected these two New York guys that they had watched on QVC to stand beside them and join them on the front lines. But it afforded us an invaluable opportunity. We got a good feeling for the morale of our new teammates. We needed to know if folks were enthused about the newly merged company, or if we were on the verge of a mass exodus. We witnessed the ebb and flow of the warehouse and got a first feel for where any efficiencies were to be gained. (Remember: Chop Your Own Wood!)

And while our assembly line teammates were initially wary of our presence, by the end of the day we knew not only their names but the names of their spouses and children. (And we even got an amazing empanada recipe that we still use at home.)

Consistency is key. For many years we continued the tradition of putting in time on the assembly line each holiday season, so that everyone understands how important that time of year is to the company's success and future.

You don't just show up and snap a photo for Instagram. It can't be performative. It has to be real. You must help everyone get their orders out.

As the boss, you can alleviate some of their stress and help them with their workload. Setting a goal is important: "I'm not leaving until I've sent out X number of orders." This is one of the ways we stay in tune with our workers. It's part of our Team Beekman ethos, where no employee is more valuable than another. Clearly, each employee has varying levels of skill, seniority, and influence. But we still strive to maintain the spirit of a small village, in which everyone matters, and everyone pitches in when needed, from the top on down.

One of our biggest marketing investments for the first ten years of our company was an annual Harvest Festival that we sponsored and managed in Sharon Springs. It was a giant celebration of autumn, Neighbors, community, agriculture and . . . goats! (People also came into the Kindness Shop, so we moved a lot of product.) By the final, tenth anniversary festival, over twenty thousand Beekman Neighbors arrived in our little hamlet, contributing millions of dollars to the regional economy.

This was a huge undertaking for us; we were a packaged goods business, not an event company. But back in the early days, there was no possibility of hiring an event organizer. When we realized the camaraderie that developed when our team had to be "all hands on deck" for that weekend each year, we continued managing the event with only Team Beekman, even after we could have afforded outside help. There was something magical about seeing the CEO parking cars in the school parking lot, and the CMO emptying trash bins, and the creative director giving tours of the farm that signaled to everyone that we really do believe that winning is a team sport. (The festival ended during the pandemic, but not a year goes by when employees don't ask if we can start up again. Never mind that they had to sacrifice a weekend to host it.)

We've never really thought of ourselves as experts at running a company; we're in constant learning mode. When you continue to learn new things, you learn new ways to use your own hands, and you are in effect creating more hands. Think of yourself as an octopus.

We've always solicited advice from people, right from Beekman's early days. When we first moved to Sharon Springs, we were complete outsiders to this rural community. We were city slickers with big ideas; we didn't want people to think we were going to barge in like know-it-alls. When we wanted to raise chickens, we asked a Neighbor how to do it. Same with when we wanted to raise pigs. We called on our Neighbors as experts. Any time you acknowledge someone else's expertise, you make them feel wanted. That really ingratiated us to the community. They *were* the experts. We needed them for our farm. It also helped us win friends.

This is a good time to mention our internal quarterly, *Voice of the Customer* report. Each section of the company is responsible for submitting its data to the VOC report.

As we noted before, we look at all the messages that come through Neighbor services, but we also read all the reviews that are on all our retailer sites and our social media. We want to know what people are saying about the brand naturally; even things that are overheard about us in places like Ulta go in the report. This enables us to make sure we don't have our heads in the sand and are really listening to what the customer says. It also enables us to lean in and find out what's important to the customer. What do they like about us? Why don't they like? Because we do listen to those messages—and they know we do—they feel more loyal to us.

It's such common business advice, but so many companies fail at this. We give everyone in the company the chance to contribute thoughts and ideas. When we started our careers in New York City, the people at the top of companies held all of the information (and power). There were very few outlets in which all of that information could be dispersed either internally or externally. The world of media was so massive, and media outlets were so few, that marketing messages had to be crafted to appeal to the widest possible audiences. The CMO (often an affluent white male) approved marketing messages that naturally appealed to him. By the time we started Beekman 1802, media was beginning to fragment. Due to the proliferation of social media and other digital media channels, consumers were falling into ever more niche categories. Suddenly having one CMO making marketing decisions based on their personal preference became a terrible idea. The way we saw things, there were two solutions: hire a slew of communications agencies to cover all the bases or reach into our own diverse Team Beekman to bring more voices into our marketing strategies.

It's a lot less expensive to utilize the resources already under your own roof than pay to outsource. Not only does listening to people from all strata in your company make them feel more connected and valued; it's strategically smarter for the company as well. And that method doesn't only apply to marketing; it applies to all departments. Today's junior bookkeeper is just as likely to discover a new accounting app as the CFO. An HR intern is as apt to discover new management techniques by listening to a podcast as the head of HR is to learn from an industry convention. Your consumer is more diverse and connected than ever, so it pays to mirror that with a diverse workforce that has broad interconnectedness within your organization.

In their book *Open Strategy*, Warwick Business School professor of strategic management Christian Stadler and his colleagues lobby for—you guessed it—"open strategy," a concept in which leaders invite others inside and outside the company to help them form strategy.

"Open strategy offers leadership teams access to diverse sources of external knowledge they wouldn't otherwise have, while also making individual leaders aware of their biases and helping them build the buy-in needed to speed up execution," the authors write. "Opening up the strategy-making process can help your company avoid the pitfalls that lead to isomorphous, unimaginative, and biased strategies."[11]

Consider Barclays, the retail bank. In 2012, the company asked groups of senior staff and frontline employees what the bank should look like in eight years. After a two-week "strategy jam" that all thirty thousand staff members took part in, the group came up with radical ideas. For instance, if Domino's Pizza could track customer orders, why couldn't Barclays keep borrowers appraised with the progress of their loans? The idea helped usher in new digital products and platforms.

Kinari Webb, cofounder of a nonprofit called Alam Sehat Lestari, asked Indonesian villagers for ideas on how to help combat illegal logging in Borneo.[12] Their solution? If they had more access to affordable health care, they wouldn't have to resort to illegal activities to pay their medical bills. Of *course!*

Every time we talk with a team member, we're always wondering: *What can we learn from them? What can they learn from us? How can we learn from each other?*

Our team holds open strategy sessions through our Slack channel. Anytime a new challenge, question, or problem arises, someone generally puts it out to the entire company on a Slack channel and invites their contributions. Solutions come from every level of every department in the company.

During our virtual town hall meetings, the chat feature on Zoom becomes a running side conversation in which team members from across the company react to what they're hearing and can submit ideas in real time. We and our leadership team tune in to the chat throughout these meetings, taking in this valuable flow of information and frequently using it to improve how we operate, often changing course in real time.

One of our greatest "look within" successes came from the same Florida warehouse where we put in that initial assembly line shift after we merged with them. Many of the workers in the warehouse were South American immigrants who had taken the first and only jobs available to them after getting their legal work status in America. The majority spoke little to no English.

During our first meeting there, when we worked on the factory line, we tried to talk to as many different people as possible, using other teammates as interpreters. We asked them about their life before coming to the States. It was sobering. Many of them were political refugees who had to flee their countries when unstable and dangerous new political leaders took over. Several of them had high-level jobs that they'd been forced to abandon to come to the United States. One had been the former head of HR for the Bank of Venezuela. Another employee from Argentina had been the lead merchandiser for a large department store there.

At the time, Beekman was growing very quickly, and our inventory system was a hodgepodge of solutions we'd cobbled together over the years. We had all sorts of inventory and inventory management issues and sometimes completely lost track of products once they came into the warehouse. One day, a man named Luis who was working on the packing line approached the COO as the COO was touring the warehouse. The man had arrived in the United States on an asylum visa from Venezuela. He explained that he worked in the IT department of one of the largest financial institutions there. He said that he knew how to code, and he could code a customized inventory system specifically for our needs.

Aha! Within six months he'd solved most of our major inventory problems, saving the company over hundreds of thousands of dollars per year. Naturally, he was promoted to a management position where he could continue to contribute his expertise.

Another employee, Pete, a retired dairy farmer, rose through our ranks to become the head of shipping for our Sharon Springs warehouse based on his dedication to Beekman Neighbor satisfaction, and was able to excel no matter where in the company he went.

A third employee who started on the warehouse floor is now vice president of operations and purchasing for all of Beekman 1802. This story illustrates another way we care for our many hands: by offering them unusual opportunities for job advancement. We've always aspired to not just be a strong company, but also a training ground for great talent and creativity.

We see ourselves as parents, nurturing our offspring before sending them off into the world to fly on their own. We take pride in their successes as if they're our own. A lot of our entry-level employees in the warehouse still come from first-generation Americans. Long ago, we decided that if any employee wanted to take English classes, we would pay for it. We didn't want them to lose anything in translation. We also understood that if we emboldened employees with this extra credential, there was more of a chance that they would leave us. Our actions were both selfish (we'd get more out of them) and selfless (they would leave us one day to do something else). We send them off with jazz hands and spirit fingers.

We always tell our employees that when they leave our company, we're still rooting for them to be successful, especially if their résumé cites Beekman as a former employer. When team members do well, Beekman does well. It's always surprising to us how small the world is, especially when it comes to business connections. If word gets out that your former employer helped you get a new job or supported your passion, it circulates throughout the industry and reflects well on us. And if a former team member is impressive in a new workplace, it might one day influence a star employee from that place to move over to us.

One of our young team members desperately wanted to go to law school, but she was afraid to tell us that she wanted to leave. She thought we'd be angry with her and would force her to leave before she got all her applications in. When her plans accidentally came to our attention via another employee's slip of the tongue, we approached her and said, "Let us help you. This is your passion, it's what you're supposed to be doing, and someday we're going to need a head counsel here at Beekman." It turned out that we had a connection at the lead school she was considering, and we wrote her a killer letter of recommendation. She got in. As she's risen through the early stages of her new career, she's always one of the first to comment positively on our social media posts and share favorable stories about Beekman 1802.

Another example was the head of our email marketing campaigns. She was a star at Beekman and wore many hats. She was always working late into the night and was highly dedicated to the company's success. She was also beloved by her teammates. So when we heard she was leaving, we were devastated. The thought of replacing her was daunting.

But then we learned that she was leaving for an important role at one of the breakout companies in our industry, e.l.f. Cosmetics. e.l.f.'s revenues and stock price have soared over the last several years, and while we're not in direct competition with anything it's doing (we're a David to its Goliath) it's still one of the most major players in our industry. If she did well at e.l.f., the right people would know that she started her career at Beekman 1802. And that raises our own profile in the industry in a way that can't be bought. Since she's left, several more from our team have headed over to e.l.f. And while some companies would be mad at this, we're thrilled. Over time, we've become good friends with both e.l.f.'s CEO and CMO, and our connection has served us well at industry events.

It has also served us well when these highly respected leaders mention Beekman 1802 in their presentations, or if they comment on our company LinkedIn page. This signals that we're a significant presence in this space.

The obvious question is whether we worry about not being able to find good people to replace those who are leaving. The answer is an emphatic *no*. First off, if an employee isn't satisfied, you're going to lose them anyway. We would rather support them and help them follow their dreams rather than waste time and energy on an unfulfilled team member. Nor will we make a counteroffer if we think the job they're going to is better than the one they have. If they've decided a new job opportunity is better for them, that's their call to make. And if we trusted their judgment while they were working for us, what would it say about us if we stopped trusting them when they saw a better option?

This applies to hiring, too. In his 2016 book *Superbosses: How Exceptional Leaders Master the Flow of Talent*, Dartmouth management professor Sydney Finkelstein explores the value of looking at the whole person and their potential when hiring, rather than sticking narrowly to what appears on their résumés.

"Resist the urge to automatically eliminate prospective hires solely on the basis of their past credentials and experience—remembering that in doing so, you may be weeding out the very best, most creative candidates," he says. "Don't eliminate job descriptions, but at the same time, don't slavishly follow them by hiring only those prospects who allow you to check off every last criterion. Don't throw out the format of the formal interview, but feel free to loosen it up and incorporate new elements, such as holding the interview in an unusual venue."[13]

For us, the most important criteria for working at Beekman 1802 is how badly you want to work there. When a job listing is posted online, it's common practice for prospective applicants to tailor, and sometimes twist, their résumés to fit the posting. Many HR departments consider this an annoyance. We consider the possibilities. If you're willing to apply for a job that might not be the best fit for you because you love the company that much, we'll remember you when we have a job that does fit.

We've been fortunate enough to attract some exceptional talent just based on our company's values of Kindness and inclusion. Shortly after we launched in Ulta stores, and employees in those stores were trained about Beekman 1802's products and mission, several Ulta employees decided to join Team Beekman. One relocated from Ohio all the way to upstate New York just so she could work in our Sharon Springs store. Another Ulta employee moved from Texas to Orlando and helps coordinate our TV retail business.

As Adam Grant notes, "Narcissistic leaders are threatened by talent. They want to be the smartest person in the room. Humble leaders are drawn to talent. They surround themselves with people who make them smarter. Great leaders grow talent. They strive to make everyone in the room smarter."[14]

Our current CEO, Jill Scalamandre, was global president of Shiseido Americas and many other beauty brands in New York City. She's also a leader in the Cosmetic Executive Women, an international organization of 10,000 individual members representing a cross section of beauty and related businesses. She comes up from New York City three days a week to work in the Schenectady office in person. One of the biggest beauty CEOs is coming to Schenectady to work with our team. How crazy is that? With her past career, Jill could have had any job she wanted in the industry, but she wanted to be at an organization that reflected her beliefs, passions, and values—the exact reason we built Beekman 1802 after our own corporate lives. Not only are we honored to have her, but just think of how her presence expands the potential career opportunities of the younger Team Beekman members in upstate New York, far away from the beauty capitals of the world. It's a winning formula for all of us.

Another way we care for employees is by staying closely attuned to their evolving needs. We've became a conduit for the American dream, where people can start with very little and, through their own interest, talent, curiosity, and initiative, can soar to great heights.

Remember Luis, who took the initiative to let us know that he could write code? Well, he left the company this year. He went from seeking asylum in America, to a $13 an hour packing job in our warehouse, to a managing position in our IT department to an over $100,000 a year salary at his new company. All in under five years. This is exactly the kind of person we want to talk about his days working at Beekman 1802 for the rest of his life.

In addition to caring so deeply about our own teammates, we also help them care for others outside of work. We give paid days off for employees to do acts of Kindness in their community. Employees can bring children and pets to work. These aren't rules we have in a handbook. These are just ways we try to address the needs of individual employees.

During the pandemic, we avoided furloughing or laying off our retail store team members. Recognizing that many Beekman Neighbors contacting our call centers were hurting from isolation and loneliness, we wound up reassigning team members from our shuttered brick-and-mortar store to our Neighbor services department. While most customer service departments measure their success by minimizing the amount of time they are kept on the phone, we knew that our success during the pandemic could be boosted by how long we could keep Beekman Neighbors on the phone. We told our Neighbors that if they were feeling scared or lonely, they could call just to talk, even if they didn't want to buy a product. So not only were these team members able to keep their jobs, but they were also able to live up to our mission of Kindness in a powerful new way that built more loyalty with our Neighbors. Our team members felt wanted and needed because they *were*.

As we mentioned earlier, no employment lasts forever. "Layoffs," "terminations," and "separations" are all just euphemisms. Anyone who has ever had those words spoken to them (including ourselves) hears the same thing: "You're fired."

Terminations are the hardest thing that any responsible employer has to deal with. For us, there's no greater feeling of guilt than bringing someone onto the team, someone whose skills we've tried to develop, but for whatever reason they didn't work out. It's even harder if it's someone whom we genuinely like who truly loves the brand. We take it personally when we bring someone in and they don't thrive. Some of the lengthiest internal discussions we have are about how to handle an employee who isn't performing well.

Brent is actually incapable of terminating anyone. The minute someone cries, he joins in. So Josh is in charge of layoffs, and he's very good at it.

"I learned to do it respectfully," he says, noting that he'd been through two major recessions in the ad industry, so he understood firsthand how important it is to be Kind. "You just keep it short and to the point and do it as quickly as possible. It will never be good, so it might as well be quick. The best tip I ever got was that the minute the person you are laying off walks in, say, 'This is going to be a difficult conversation.'"

Perhaps the most important thing we've learned about terminations is that they need to happen before either side grows toxic. Delay is the worst strategy. We've never terminated anyone who didn't find a job later that fit them better. By delaying the inevitable, you're actually *preventing* their (and your) happiness. That should be your motivation, not fear of ill will.

We often say that it's not always nice to be nice. The nice thing to do would be to keep people employed beyond their effectiveness. The Kind thing to do is to release them and their teammates from an untenable situation. There's a huge competitive strategy to being a Kind company and having that be your brand value. Consumers love it. It works internally. But when it's mistaken for being nice, all kinds of problems arise.

All Hands on Deck!

Many hands make light work, but the work is even lighter if those hands have what they need to be happy. So you have to know the difference between your employees' wants and needs. Obviously, if you anonymously asked American workers how many days a week they want to work, most would answer "zero." But what people *want* is different from what they *need*. Studies have shown that a healthy career and workplace lead to a more fulfilled life. So a person's want of a zero-workday week isn't exactly what they need.

Nothing brought this into higher relief than the pandemic. American workers had been telling us for a long time that their quality of life was not where they wanted it to be. They were fed up before the pandemic; postpandemic they're no longer willing to sacrifice their lives for their work. Many of them disliked the work they were in because it was unfulfilling or sapped so much of their emotional energy that they didn't have anything left to nourish their family or inner lives. The reward balance wasn't there for them.

Now, millions of workers do double duty by working and taking care of their families. Many employees got used to working at home, especially when their kids returned to school. They didn't want to return to the office full-time when the pandemic ended. So companies across the country had a kneejerk reaction and initiated shorter workweeks and fewer (or no) days in the office.

According to Gallup, in 2023, 20 percent of remote-capable employees spent their week working fully on-site, down from 60 percent in 2019. Today, 29 percent of remote-capable employees are fully remote, compared to only 8 percent in 2019.[15] Our company was no different. We'd gone from being 100 percent on-site to 100 percent remote with no discernable hit to our productivity.

You can find arguments claiming that work from home has stifled creativity, and arguments against this idea.[16] In our personal ideal world, all Beekman team members would be on-site. Why? (1) Because that's how we like to work, and (2) We really like to hang out with our team. But, of course, we acknowledge that people work in different ways; some people are better working alone, and others thrive in groups.

We could have done what other companies did and proclaimed sweeping mandates about shorter workweeks, or permanently

LEARN FROM A G.O.A.T.:
Deepak Chopra

Deepak Chopra became a G.O.A.T. after becoming a top New Age prophet, bestselling author, entrepreneur, and alternative medicine advocate. He counts several celebrities, including Madonna, the Dalai Lama, and Alicia Keys (he officiated at her wedding), among his fans.

Please tell us your favorite saying or piece of homespun wisdom, the one that has meant the most to you personally or professionally.

My favorite saying is simple but profound: "Take it easy." It's a reminder that life, in its essence, is meant to flow with ease, and when we allow ourselves to relax into the present moment, we open ourselves to boundless possibilities.

How did you first discover or learn of this maxim?

I first discovered the wisdom of "take it easy" early in my medical career when the pressures of success and achievement overshadowed my inner peace. In seeking balance, I realized that the more I resisted and strained, the further I moved from harmony. This phrase became my anchor.

Why is this maxim so wise and valuable in business and beyond?

The wisdom of "take it easy" lies in its simplicity. It reminds us to trust the natural rhythm of life. In business, as in life, when

reverted to being fully remote. But because we are so close to our team members, we knew that no all-encompassing solution would be a good idea. The media was spewing articles every day about how younger employees wanted to never come back into an office. But we noticed that it was actually our younger team members—not the ones more advanced in their careers—who were sneaking back into the office more and more. And then we remembered how much we we approach challenges with ease rather than tension, we tap into our creativity, intuition, and inner guidance. It fosters clarity and helps us make better decisions without the noise of stress.

Does this maxim have any special relevance given what's currently going on in the world?

Given the uncertainty and upheaval in today's world, "take it easy" is more relevant than ever. Amid global stress and anxiety, we must remind ourselves that we can only respond effectively when we are centered and calm. By taking things easy, we create space for wisdom and compassion to guide our actions.

How has this maxim contributed to your own success? Any particular stories come to mind?

"Take it easy" has been a guiding principle in my life, especially during moments of uncertainty. One particular story comes to mind: The pressure to succeed was immense when I was transitioning from medicine to writing and public speaking. But when I embraced the idea of ease, opportunities unfolded naturally. It wasn't about forcing success but allowing it to emerge through presence and openness.[17]

liked being part of a "work gang" when we were younger. That's who we socialized with. It's where we found people to date.

We decided to create individualized plans. Which departments were more productive when working in person? The creative department people certainly drew inspiration from each other by being together. The finance department folks, however, got even more done remotely when they were relieved of excessive meetings and office disturbances. We also created a system to monitor productivity and check in with employees. As we said, what employees want isn't always what they need. They may *want* to be home with their family full-time, but they may *need* some on-site work as an excuse to have a different focus for their own mental well-being. The only rule coming out of such a period where all rules were smashed to pieces was that individualized rules—based on the needs of and connections with our team—was the most productive way forward into this new work world.

There's No "I" in Team—or Beekman

We didn't realize it, but we aging Gen Xers have a Gen Z approach to work. We're a lot like Ziad Ahmed, the twenty-five-year-old founder and CEO of JUV Consulting, a Gen Z marketing agency. JUV caters to clients who are trying to better understand and connect with diverse young audiences; the company, which was recently sold to the talent agency UTA, is staffed mainly by Gen Zers.

Ziad was born in Princeton, New Jersey. The son of Muslim immigrants from Bangladesh, in the eighth grade he started a nonprofit built around social justice and social equality. President Barack Obama mentioned him in a speech. He was invited to the White House.

No one was more astounded than Ziad. "My mom was so effusive with her love that she gaslit me into believing I deserved it all," he says. "My takeaway was not 'I don't belong.' It was, 'So many *more* of us belong.' These rooms and spaces needed to have diverse young people in them if we were going to do our jobs well and push society forward."

He launched JUV as a high school junior. "This company has always been about the hands of the many," he says. He wanted to empower the young employees to publicly take ownership of the company. That meant letting young people lead important accounts and inviting them to give talks to CEOs at major conferences.

"You can pass the microphone if you can't pass the equity," he says. He wants his employees to be thought leaders, and so he encourages them to post on social media.

He also encourages them to tell him what they think of *him*, "a culture where they can call me out," he says. "My team has been instrumental in challenging me. It is beautiful and dynamic and inspiring. But, my God, it is exhausting! I'm told every day the ways in which I'm not measuring up." Still, he wouldn't have it any other way.

In early 2024, he sold his company to UTA, one of the world's largest talent agencies. At the time, he had twenty-four employees. Every single one got a cut of the deal.

"We take a very human approach to being flexible in terms of people's mental health, physical health, many things humans go through that require flexibility," he says. "The kindest thing anyone ever said about JUV was from an intern who spent a summer with us. They said, 'JUV is what he hopes the workplace is like in fifty years.'"[18]

We take a similar approach at Beekman. At our quarterly town hall, we share the company's most current financial report so that everyone, from senior VPs to packagers on the warehouse floor, will know exactly to the penny how we're reaching our goals. Or missing them. Maybe sharing gross profit margins with every single team member is excessive. But we believe it puts everybody on a level playing field, which is important to us. Also, if people don't hit the company's overall growth goals for the year, everyone's bonuses will be less than they expected. If everyone knows what's happening day to day, everyone can have an impact on making it better.

CHEW ON THIS

- Nurture a democratic ethos, connecting with frontline employees and giving these employees a voice when it comes to company strategy.

- Turn your company into a training ground for talent by creating diverse and unusual career paths and helping employees to leave your company when they're ready.

- Stay in touch with the needs of your team members rather than responding to generic trends. When possible, take extraordinary steps to help your employees address the challenges they face and thrive.

- Make a list of your employees, and when you hear them say something random about something they enjoy doing, surprise them with a moment of Kindness when you find something you think they will like. You'll be amazed at what a powerful community builder that will be.

- Rewarding employees doesn't always have to cost money. Josh trades French recipes with one teammate who loves to cook as much as he does. The CEO loves historical dramas, and so they trade recommendations. Josh sends another teammate articles about adventure travel, which they have in common. As in any relationship, sometimes the small things are the big things.

BECOME A G.O.A.T.:
Conduct an Employee Deep Dive

Think of the last three high-potential people who left your company. Why did they elect to leave? Did they simply outgrow the company and the opportunities you could offer? Or did you fail to care for them in the three ways discussed in this chapter (creating a democratic environment in which they feel valued, turning your company into a talent training ground, and staying proactively attuned to employees' evolving needs).

How did you handle these departures? Did you support and encourage employees to take the next important step in their careers and lives, or did you resent them for leaving or attempt to anxiously cling to them? If you're not caring for your many hands as well as you might be, now's an ideal time to start.

A Brief History of Kindness

2009: Josh published his bestselling memoir, *The Bucolic Plague*, which documented the story of Kindness that began at Beekman 1802.

2013: Brent and Josh won *The Amazing Race* by—you guessed it!—being Kind to everyone they met, even the other contestants. After winning, we created a yearlong program with Target that helped other small farms pay off the mortgages.

2015: We sent out our first shipment of Beekman 1802 face and body wipes to help firefighters and those displaced by wildfires in the western part of the United States. This was the start of a giveback program that has sent wipes as a moment of Kindness and luxury to natural disaster areas around the country.

2011: *The Fabulous Beekman Boys* premiered on Discovery's Planet Green Network, becoming the first reality show in history focused on a gay couple. The show and the way it portrayed our Neighbors turned Sharon Springs into "the Kindest little village in America."

2007: Our original act of Kindness: taking in Farmer John and a herd of homeless goats.

2007   2008   2009   2010   2011   2012   2013   2014   2015   2016

2008: We sold our first bar of soap, which we called "Soap for Sensitive People" because it was so Kind and gentle on the skin.

2016: Brent published the first edition of *The Precious Little Snowflake*, which teaches that by working together, we can truly create a Kinder and more beautiful world. Each year, a new artist at the start of their career is chosen to illustrate that year's version.

2012: We created the Rural Artist Collective to support small artisans and American craftsmanship. These artists received widespread public recognition by the likes of the *Wall Street Journal, New York Times, Vanity Fair, Vogue, House Beautiful, Country Living, Food & Wine,* and more.

2010: We created the first Harvest Festival in Sharon Springs, New York, as a way to bring tourism into the small, downtrodden rural village (population 547) and to help support the local farmers. Over the next ten years, the festival grew to 20,000 attendees and brought millions of dollars into the economy.

2014: We rehabilitated a historic building on Main Street in Sharon Springs to become the flagship Beekman 1802 Kindness Shop, which welcomes thousands of people each year from around the world.

2018: Beekman 1802 formalized its commitment to Kindness by creating a Kindness curriculum that would teach all of our employees how to treat themselves, each other, and our Neighbors with Kindness. The curriculum was so successful that it eventually became a Kindness class that Neighbors could travel to Sharon Springs to take.

2017: Goatie, the global ambassador for Kindness, made his first appearance as an emoji on a tote bag for Beekman 1802. (He didn't yet have the name "Goatie.")

2019: We published the first 365 Days of Kindness calendar with little reminders of how to spread Kindness each day of the year.

2021: We installed *The Rainbow Cathedral* by artist Tom Fruin on a hilltop at our farm and allowed people whose weddings had been canceled because of the pandemic to get married there free of charge in a twenty-four-hour wedding marathon.

2023:
- Beekman 1802 partnered with Kindness.org and researchers from Oxford and Harvard universities to create the first scientifically validated measurement of Kindness in the workplace. Companies can now use this Kindness quotient to encourage Kindness and empathy in the workplace. Companies can now use this Kindness and empathy among their own employees.
- We rang the opening bell at the Nasdaq to celebrate World Kindness Day.

2017   2018   2019   2020   2021   2022   2023   2024

2020:
- We launched our Clinically Kind skin care with Ulta Beauty.
- We worked with small mom-and-pop bakeries around the country that were suffering from pandemic shutdowns to send cookies to each Ulta store.
- We opened up Beekman 1802 farm to create "the world's largest restaurant," which allowed restaurants in upstate New York to use our property to serve guests in an outdoor setting permissible by pandemic guidelines. This kept many of these restaurants afloat during the worst of the pandemic.
- We sent out 20,000 bottles of Beekman 1802 hand wash and hand lotion to frontline healthcare workers around the country to honor their heroic efforts during the pandemic.

2024:
- We created our Kindness Coaches program, allowing our Neighbors free thirty-minute sessions with our life coaches to learn tools for bringing more Kindness into their lives.
- We became one of the first companies in the world to use AI as a way to encourage, monitor, and amplify Kindness in the workplace.
- We partnered once more with Kindness.org to fund a study looking at the role of Kindness and mental health in the social sphere.
- We also partnered with the American Red Cross for World Kindness Day to encourage people to give the gift of life, the ultimate act of Kindness.

2022:
- The second Beekman 1802 Kindness Shop opened in the Delta terminal at LaGuardia Airport.
- We gave out our first Kindness grants to small communities around the United States to demonstrate how one small action can ripple throughout the community.
- We partnered with the American Nursing Association to raise funds for nursing education by working with nurses to create a special ceramide barrier-protecting hand cream. Each nurse spreads Kindness to approximately forty people a day in their community. Then each of those people has the chance to spread that Kindness to others, creating a profound ripple effect.

Two Heads Are Better Than One

How to Be a Partner

When we began training for *The Amazing Race*, one thing was abundantly clear from the get-go: physically, we were never going to be the strongest team.

We were both in our mid-forties when we heard we'd been cast on the show. Brent is 5'8' and weighs 140 pounds, and Josh is 5'11" and weighs 155. While we both kept pretty fit from farm chores, we were not on any short list for decathlon medalists.

If you recall, initially we didn't focus on winning. Our goal in doing the show was mainly to promote Beekman 1802. But we also didn't want to humiliate ourselves in front of millions of viewers. As part of our prep, we watched as many past seasons as we could, just to get an understanding of how previous racers strategized their approaches.

While there has always been an element of luck in *The Amazing Race*, we noticed that the people who won weren't necessarily the strongest or fastest, and the people who lost weren't always the weakest or slowest. For both groups, it was about communication. The latter group stumbled when their partnership broke down. Once they started fighting with each other, they stopped communicating and were no longer able to get the task done. But the winners? They communicated seamlessly.

So, we decided we had to make some decisions. We knew we had one concrete advantage: since we'd been in a relationship for years and had started a business together, we had a super-solid connection and partnership. We needed to use that bond to ensure that we were constantly communicating with one another during the process.

Our understanding of each other was our muscle. Josh knew that Brent approached tough tasks (like building a massive scale from heavy timber in Bangladesh or escaping from a straitjacket while dangling upside down eight stories in the air in the Brooklyn Navy Yard) with grit-like determination. Any form of fake enthusiasm and cheerleading rubbed him the wrong way and made him shut down. Josh always stifled the urge to shout "Way to go! You got this!" like most of the other contestants did with their partners. Likewise, Brent knew that Josh could outwit anyone in puzzle-like challenges (like finding keys for dozens of locks on a bridge in Russia, or deciphering instructions on how to repair a massive windmill in Mallorca) as long as Josh was able to keep his natural anxiety in check. So Brent helped Josh keep his cool even when everyone around them was losing theirs.

Ultimately, while we never once finished first in any of the first eleven legs of the race, the strength of our partnership kept us from coming in last and getting eliminated along the way. On the final leg, when the other two finalist teams were exhausted and falling apart, the strength of our communication allowed us to pull ahead and take home first prize. And there are great lessons in this, for racing and for business.

Dynamic Duos

Batman and Robin. Sonny and Cher. Bill and Ted. We've been told all our lives that partnership matters when pursuing a goal—that "two heads are better than one." Generations of our ancestors have been bandying that G.O.A.T. wisdom around since biblical times. Here it is in Ecclesiastes 4:9–12:

Two are better than one, because they have a good reward for their toil. For if they fall, one will lift up the other; but woe to one who is alone and falls and does not have another to help. Again, if two lie together, they keep warm; but how can one keep warm alone?[1]

This resonates with us on two levels. Since we're business partners, we want a good reward for our toil. But we're life partners, too, and we literally need each other to stay warm (especially in subzero Sharon Springs winters).

We've discovered that we're somewhat of an anomaly. An emphasis on partnership often seems absent in business contexts, particularly entrepreneurial ones. We understand this: it requires an enormous amount of ego for a founder to get a new business off the ground and then grow it. Entrepreneurs often have visions that others don't see, and they take risks that others may consider crazy. (*Really, Mark? You want to drop out of Harvard and start a company based on likes?*) A kind of independence of spirit can take hold that crowds out or subverts partnership and collaboration.

We're not saying that strong partnerships don't exist in businesses of all sizes. Just ask ice cream gurus Ben Cohen and Jerry Greenfield, creators of Ben & Jerry's; Microsoft cofounders Paul Allen and Bill Gates; brothers-in-law William Procter and James Gamble, who launched manufacturing behemoth Procter & Gamble; and the Steves, Wozniak and Jobs, of Apple fame. Nor are we saying that entrepreneurs can't thrive by going it alone.

What we *are* saying is that partnerships can confer huge advantages for leaders of small and medium-sized companies, and that all too often, those advantages go partially or entirely untapped.

You can achieve so much more and have more fun doing it, if you off-load at least some of the responsibility and burden to someone else. As bestselling author, speaker, and the Optimism Company founder Simon Sinek puts it, "It's too difficult to do difficult things alone. We're just not that good. And starting a business is exactly the same."[2]

Business is indeed a race—sometimes (often!) grueling, sometimes amazing. Often it is the best partnership, not the most talented lone genius, that wins in the end.

Defining "Partner"

Business partnerships come in all shapes and sizes—legal, emotional, financial, and so on. For the purposes of this book, we're defining "partnership" as a special, ongoing relationship of any length that helps you carry the burden of running a business. Partnerships in this general sense can be formal equity arrangements (coinciding, in our case, with a romantic relationship), but they can also be much more informal, lower-impact arrangements that involve less commitment.

A partner is someone who, at the very least, is a fellow traveler in some way. Who has shared vision. If you cannot find someone to share that vision, you're not going to have a successful business.

Tank Sinatra is a social media entrepreneur and the guy behind the Instagram accounts "Tank Sinatra," "Influencers in the Wild," and "Tank's Good News," which have 5 million followers.

Like most entrepreneurs, Tank has taken a long and twisty ride to get where he is, with lots of stops and starts. Back in 2003, he launched a blog called *Insight Is Never 20/20*. He was convinced it would put him on the map. It didn't even put him in a city.

A website called "Happy Is the New Rich" followed, which he turned into a video blog with a whopping twenty watchers. Then he made "Ifoundmoney.com." He would leave $5 a day around New York City. That won a Webby award in 2012. He was thrilled. But it got expensive, and he stopped.

Within the next year, he landed a gig with a dating app, and he quit his day job at a fence company. He was supposed to post weekly dating memes. It was liberating. "Once I freed up my brain from a fence company, I had an extra multiple hours per day to think of other things I wanted to do that year," he says. The dating app was not one of them.

"Tanks Good News" was born at the end of 2017. It hit 100,000 viewers in the first week. "Influencers in the Wild" followed, which hit 1 million within its first three weeks.

He decided to turn the latter into a board game because, why not? "I thought it would be fun and funny," he says. He linked up with two buddies to start it, but he discovered that they didn't care about it as much as he did. Why would they? They had different goals. And also Tank had 70 percent of equity, and the other two men got 15 percent each. They weren't motivated the way he was.

Tank then talked to another partner about doing pop up events for an existing Instagram site. They, too, had different goals. "By the time we got to equity talks, I felt like I was doing *him* a favor," he says. Tank offered him a fifty-fifty split, but the other guy wanted 90 percent. "The feeling I got was 'ewwww,'" Tank recalls.

In May 2023, Tank went on *Shark Tank* to pitch his board game. None of the sharks bit—they accused him of fabricating its $5 million valuation—but it wasn't all for naught. Something Canadian businessman and *Shark Tank* star O'Leary said stuck with him: "I never made money until I created equal partnership with people."[3]

This came to mind when Tank started a true crime podcast, *Psychopedia*, and wanted to bring on a partner. He found one in his best friend's wife, Brooke Slater (aka "Investigator Slater"). But this time he learned from his mistakes.

"We're equal partners, fifty-fifty," he says. "She's doing all the work; I'm promoting it. There is something spiritual to having people be equally involved.

"I don't think there will be anything I do that's not fifty-fifty," he continues. "I don't want to make anyone feel smaller or less than in a partnership. I really believe that's the only way to launch something."[4]

A partner doesn't have to be an actual part of the business. You might be independent-minded or an introvert, much more of a lone ranger. In that case, you can take as your partner a mentor or coach in whom you confide on a regular basis. Or you can treat a small group of confidants as your partnership team, debriefing them about business challenges and seeking their wisdom and help. Or you can join up with an especially trusted member of your leadership team— someone you can rely on to communicate on your behalf, perhaps, and challenge your thinking. Maybe it's a best friend or someone you went to school with, or even a family member. The important thing is not to direct your business entirely alone.

One of the reasons partnerships are so powerful is because we know how damaging echo chambers can be. When you're a solo practitioner, you become an echo chamber for your own ideas and thought processes. Having a partner can help you get outside the reverberation of your own voice, your own perspective, and help give you a different perspective on what's happening with your business.

Partnerships can also last different amounts of time. For example, Evine, the TV shopping company whom we talked about in chapter 1, was a great partner for us when we first started selling on TV. It was less than one-fifth the size of QVC or HSN, so we could learn the ropes of TV retail without taking on too much inventory risk. It, like us, believed that the best sales tactic was good storytelling. And it thought it was a brilliant idea to bring live goats—with all their unpredictability—onto live TV.

But a few years in, its management changed, and we were no longer ideal partners. More focus was put on discounting, and less on brand-building. Since we were completely new to the TV retail business, we'd signed a not-so-great contract that locked us into an exclusive partnership with it as long as certain goals were met. Because we'd so quickly become the number one brand at the network, QVC and HSN reached out to us to see if we would join them instead. But even though Evine's overall revenues were plummeting, Beekman easily hit our goals year after year, so our contract was automatically re-newed. We were locked in. What started out as a perfect partnership had turned into one in which we were tied to a sinking ship. We'd made the mistake of thinking a great partner early on would be a great partner forever. (We eventually did find a mutual way out of the contract and left on good terms with our reputation intact. How you leave a partnership is as important as how you start one.)

Often, your clients become your partners, which is what Kim Wahlberg discovered. Kim, sixty-seven, is the founder of Kimberly Wahlberg Company, one of the country's largest sales groups with over 40 territory consultants representing nationally branded companies, including Beekman 1802. The company partners with both the brands and specialty retail partners across the United States to build and support distribution and growth—often for decades.

Kim's brand partner selection process prioritizes relationships built on Kindness and respect.

In fact, Kindness is baked into her mission statement on the company's website: "Our goal is to establish lasting and successful partnerships with our manufacturers, customers, and salespeople. Additionally, we pride ourselves on adhering to the highest ethical standards, always striving to do the right thing."[5]

Kim will always discuss which brand partners are good with her territory consultants. Because they have daily interaction with the vendors, they can provide intimate feedback on how they manage and support the KW team and retail partners. Kim would take this information and work on a solution—or, in some cases, stop working with the brand altogether if the brand partner is not in alignment with those values.

Her company has grown by leaps and bounds directly because of this kind of partnership. Both the brands and employees can trust that she is honorable, ethical, and professional—and that she has their backs. It works because she sees herself as a true extension of the brand she represents, and the brand sees her team as a real extension of themselves.

"That's what separated us from every other agency in the country—we got down to the details and the brands saw this," she says. "It became a partnership with the vendors, which made it better for the retailers. In our business, it's still very personal."[6]

Divide and Conquer

In any relationship, both parties are constantly growing in different ways. So how do you make sure that you're growing together, especially (and specifically) in terms of the business?

You have to make sure you inspire each other. And to check in continuously to make sure your goals are always aligned. Until 2020, we still hadn't met our original goal of having $5 million in the bank and all of our debts paid off. Sure, our gross revenue was many, many multiples of that figure, but you can't retire on numbers in a ledger. So, we were still working toward that goal. That kept us going.

If we'd hit that goal after, say, year five of Beekman, would we have still continued with the business as we are now? Probably, because we're constantly moving the goalpost. Once we meet a goal, we move onto another one. But there always needs to be a mutually agreed-on goal. As one of our investment partners, Jill Granoff, puts it: "Start with the exit in mind."

You must refresh your goals periodically *as a partnership*. We're not talking about your company goals, but your partnership goals. And we do. Now our goal is to build Beekman 1802 to the point that it can continue as a brand forever without us. If we reach the point where every Beekman Neighbor loves the brand and products without having any idea of who "Josh and Brent" are, we'll know we built something enduring.

We didn't enter our relationship thinking we would start a business together one day. We'd both been raised to be fairly conservative with our personal finances and career plans. When we first met in 2000, Josh was well down the path of his advertising career, and Brent was finishing his medical education and beginning his MBA studies. Being entrepreneurs was nothing we'd ever really considered, let alone dreamed of. But we were both very good at seizing opportunity. So when our careers hit a major speed bump during the 2008 Great Recession, we looked at our "hobby farm" as a potential path out of hard times. Entrepreneurship wasn't a goal—or even a passion—for either of us, but it turned out to be the smartest plan for us to move forward. Our personal partnership wasn't based on starting a business together someday in the future. Starting our business together was based on our history as personal partners.

Being a married couple was a key part of our early company branding, a core part of our particular story from the very beginning. We knew that our life on the farm was aspirational to many people. Having a good marriage is also a great aspiration. It all tied together, and was portrayed on our website, social media, and TV appearances. If you loved our life, then naturally you'd love our products. Of course, pinning a brand story to a marriage comes with some risk. Even the most solid couples sometimes drift apart. But our personal relationship was a powerful tool in our marketing toolbox, which resonated deeply with Beekman Neighbors.

Usually if a business has two founders, one person is more visible and out front, while the other takes a back seat. We can't all be Bono, or Mick Jagger, or Springsteen.

Many founders don't mind this dynamic; not everyone has the same level of extroversion or likes being in the spotlight. But sometimes it is a problem, especially since founders typically have egos, which is key to what makes them build a company in the first place.

Then the question becomes: If one person is the face of the company, how does the other person get equal recognition? It's unfair, but typically the front person gets all the credit for the company or brand. So, how does the other person get validated for their contributions?

The most important aspect, we've realized, is for each partner to get the validation and respect from the audience they most value. Some people value the respect of their internal team most; others want to be lauded by their industry peers. Some people want applause from their customers; others just want to be sure their contribution is recognized when it comes to divvying up profits. Knowing what kind of validation is important to your partner—not just yourself—is the first step in ensuring that you help your partner get it.

Different Styles

Brent can be, shall we say, a hot head sometimes. As a result of his medical training, he has been conditioned to analyze things quickly and be decisive and confident about his decisions. He can get very passionate during disagreements and isn't afraid of arguing fervently for his points of view. He believes that it's always best to hash things out on the spot, no matter how many feathers get ruffled. To outsiders, Josh appears a bit more passive. At friction points with colleagues, he first considers the "long game" to see if: (a) the present disagreement will really impact the trajectory that dramatically; or (b) there's a different route to his end game than an argument. We immensely respect each other's approaches and often turn to each other for advice when we recognize that our respective personal styles aren't achieving what we want them to. We also allow each other to step in to diffuse a tense situation or provoke one that needs swifter resolution.

This is a big part of our dynamic. We cover for each other. We have each other's backs, which is the best part of a partnership. When we're doing live TV, sometimes we're talking for six or seven hours at a time in a twenty-four-hour period. We'll get to a point where we're mentally exhausted and physically exhausted. Because we know each other so well, we can tell when the other is flaming out. Sometimes Josh will be so tired he's in the middle of a thought and can't complete it. Josh just gives Brent a certain glance and Brent knows that's his cue to step in and finish the thought for him. So he does.

We also often split our roles. When going into meetings when we know there will be disagreements or negotiations, we aren't afraid to stake out differing positions because, well, we both sincerely hold differing positions. Sometimes our actions in solving a problem between ourselves serve as modeling behavior for the rest of the room to come to an agreement. Other times we'll take on natural "good cop/bad cop" roles. Brent argues passionately, with Josh interjecting only at the most fraught moments. And there are times we play the nuclear option: hotheaded Brent plays the good cop, and pensive Josh comes out swinging. That's when people know things are serious.

We're always together in public, but internally, we each take the lead on different things. Our division of labor has never been about work roles, but about disposition and personality. We like to always focus on our strengths and passions and then delegate responsibilities based on them. but understanding the limits allows you to step in and support them.

This led to what we call our "51 percent rule."

While we're always fifty-fifty partners on everything work and personal, if we each had one vote on every decision that needed to be made, well, let's just say we'd still be deciding on a restaurant for our first date.

In the early days of starting our business, our arguments were legendary. We fought about everything from packaging designs to hiring decisions. More than once in those first few years, we'd been driving home together from work and one of us demanded to be let out of the car to find their own way home. Seriously.

Eventually, we organically realized that the arguments were a worse impediment to success than any resolutions that came from them. Hence our 51 percent rule. It's simple: no matter the disagreement, no matter that we each technically have an equal vote, no matter that we are often equally talented in so many similar areas . . . at the end of the day, there will always be one difference in any disagreement: one of us is truly more passionate about the subject at hand. Even if just by 1 percent. So our rule is that that person ultimately has the deciding vote.

It's not often easy to give up that 1 percent, but we've learned over time that the return on that 1 percent is far greater than its number.

We believe in the 51 percent rule and our ability to discern each other's passions so strongly that we've often surprised high-powered lawyers and bankers. We're frequently presented with contracts or documents that require joint signatures. And most institutions strongly recommend that legal mechanisms be put into writing that will break any fifty-fifty stalemate between us. We've never once agreed to do that, and it's never once been a problem.

Sometimes our decision-making is more sixty-forty. Or eighty-twenty. This relates to our different styles. Josh, for example, often feels more comfortable (and valuable) in the background. He'll sometimes listen to Brent's Zoom calls without being officially on them. Even though he sometimes has to bite his tongue to not interject, in the end his quiet observation often leads to broader recommendations. Being an audience member allows for different observations than being a player on the stage.

Conversely, on certain projects that require a lot of detail, Brent will step aside almost completely until the end. Josh operates best if he has complete, 100 percent focus on reaching a complicated end goal, and Brent knows that any interjections along the way will throw him off his game.

Tomei Thomas came to Beekman when he was twenty-three years old. He did anything that needed to be done. By the time he was twenty-eight, he had worked his way up to CEO. Tomei knows exactly how we operate. We asked him for his thoughts. Here's what he said: "On any issue, whether it's shall we invest in a new branding or logo, Brent and Josh would choose who would be more passionate," he says. "You were always only partnering with one of them on those serious issues. One would be quiet and the other would be leading the conversation. It could totally vary on the day, depending on the issue. They would never argue in front of us about those decisions. Whoever had the more passion would lead. This made it extremely easy for a business to operate."[7]

The Gottman Institute, in Seattle, offers resources and tools for people wanting to improve their partnerships—not just romantic ones, but any relationship. It was founded in 1996 by psychologists John Gottman and his wife Julie Schwartz Gottman. Communication is one of their areas of expertise.

In the 1970s John Gottman and a researcher named Robert Levenson asked couples to resolve a dispute they'd been having. The couples were allotted fifteen minutes during which the two men recorded their interactions. Nine years later, Gottman and Levenson reached back out to them. The researchers were able to predict with 90 percent accuracy who would divorce and who would stay married.

Tolstoy aside, the difference between happy and unhappy couples, they found, was the ratio of negative exchanges to positive exchanges during conflict. A happy union had at least five positive interactions (holding hands with your partner, expressing affection verbally and physically, apologizing) for every negative one (being emotionally dismissive or critical or becoming defensive, along with eye-rolling). They called this the "magic ratio."

A broken relationship, conversely, has more negative interactions than positive. If the positive-to-negative ratio during a fight is one-to-one or smaller, then that couple has a pretty good chance of divorcing, the researchers found.

"When the masters of marriage are talking about something important, they may be arguing, but they are also laughing and teasing and there are signs of affection because they have made emotional connections," says Gottman.[8]

One of the ways we ensure the five-to-one rule is to give a quick compliment at the end of any joint work task. "You did really well on that call." "Your energy really helped me in that meeting." "I wouldn't have thought of that solution." Even the smallest compliment is money in the emotional partnership bank for a future disagreement.

The married founders of NEST fragrances, Laura and Harry Slatkin, take a similar approach. The couple got into the fragrance business in 1992, the same year they married, through Harry's brother, Howard, a high-end interior designer. Howard was famous for creating lovely scents for his clients after completing a job. They quit their Wall Street careers and joined him in his business, Slatkin & Co., one of the first luxury home fragrance brands on the market.[9]

This was pretty radical at the time. "When we all got together to determine a business plan, we came up with the idea of launching a home fragrance company at a time when home fragrance just wasn't a thing," she says.[10]

In 2005, Limited Brands bought Slatkin & Co. Laura had a non-compete clause, so she spent the next three years working for over one hundred brands—among them Jonathan Adler, Calvin Klein, NARS, Tory Burch, Laura Mercier, and Ralph Lauren.[11] She was developing home fragrance extension brands for them.

But they didn't take off. "The consumer didn't want a fashion brand candle or a department store candle; they wanted one from a fragrance company," she said. "People want to buy something that has integrity, authority, and is from an expert in the space." So, she did it herself, founding NEST in 2008, which now has over two hundred scented products for the home, body, and bath.

Laura and Harry are different people and have different roles. "Harry is a caring, brilliant individual," she told the *New York Times*. "He's a positive, glass half-full; I'm half-empty. He's fanatically neat; I'm a slob. I'm cautious and methodical; he's impulsive and a risk-taker. I'm the sensible one, which can be exhausting. But if he weren't the way he is, everything would be chaos. We've found the right balance. Our whole marriage is based on friendship and pure partnership. It's our bedrock."

She says she learned to let "the stupid things" go and accept him for who he is. "One time we got into an argument and I got very upset," she says. "Harry told me to put everything that's good on one side of the scale, and what just happened on the other. He was right. When you look at it that way, we have so much that works, so much goodness. Doing that puts everything in perspective."[12]

Equal Partners

Business partnerships don't just refer to romantic couples, obviously. Alejandro Velez and Nikhil Arora founded Back to the Roots to help people grow their own mushrooms.[13] The duo met in 2009 during their senior year at UC Berkeley. They were sitting in a business ethics class when their professor made a casual remark about sustainability and growing mushrooms on used coffee grounds. They were both intrigued.[14]

After successfully growing their own crop of mushrooms in Alejandro's fraternity during their last semester in college, they got a $5,000 grant from the chancellor of UCLA and bailed on their postgraduation plans in corporate America to become full-time urban mushroom farmers in Oakland, California. The garden quickly became a hit, and the mission to inspire people to grow their own food was born and led them to develop products like a cereal brand and work with major retailers like Target and Home Depot.

Nikhil credits their partnership as the foundation of everything they've achieved.[15] A big help is that they share the same goals.[16] This was evident from the get-go, when they each did double-duty as mushroom farmers and brand ambassadors. Every weekday, they would drive to the office building; every weekend, they would be at farmers' markets selling what they grew. They credit that time with customers for the innovation that would see the Back to the Roots product line expand from a pack of mushrooms to a wide range of do-it-yourself organic growing kits. In 2022 they raised more than $50 million in funding and have doubled business every year for the past four years.[17] That's a lot of fungus.

"There's got to be such a deep level of alignment in your values and your intent," says Nikhil. "And I say 'intent' both personally and with the business—why are we doing this, and where are we trying to take it?"

Their shared long-term goals allow the two to communicate openly. "That creates such an amazing place where you can be vulnerable and debate ideas really hard because you are never debating the intent," he says. These conversations can seem intense to other people on the team, but even though they appear this way from the outside, it's this intensity that drives Back to the Roots forward.[18]

We are intimately acquainted with intense conversations. Mutually assured destruction helps resolve conflict. Several times we got into such incredible fights that if we hadn't been married, we would have dissolved the business. But we were married, and the business depended on the fact that we were married, because we were out in the world as a couple. We couldn't divorce, even if we wanted to (we didn't). We couldn't separate, and we couldn't stop doing the business, because that's all we had as a couple.

Since we're married, we use a shorthand to communicate with each other. Privately, we can sometimes be curt and unprofessional, but we learned pretty early on that we couldn't do that in front of our team. Because even though they might understand that dynamic with their parents, they don't understand it with their bosses. We are supposed to be the ones leading the company forward so that they can succeed in their careers and reap the rewards. If we disagree about the way forward, it raises doubt, confusion, and fear in those we're supposed to be leading. We quickly learned that disagreeing or criticizing each other in front of our team was one of the most toxic things we could do.

The point is that you have to put on a common front, at least with your employees. Transparency is always important, but it should take a back seat when it unduly threatens the morale and confidence level of employees. The level of disagreement between us that we allow ourselves to display increases with the level of the colleague. Our executive team has seen some real heavy-weight championship arguments between us. But hopefully what we demonstrate for our executive team is that even though we might fight for a particular idea or our particular opinion on an idea, after we've come to the conclusion, then we're back to zero and can move on. They can feel confident in our ability to come to a resolution in any circumstance. Even more importantly, they see that we are both OK with giving in—or even being wrong—which leads to more confident decision-making on their part.

Just as Josh says that the most powerful words in any meeting are "to your point," Brent thinks that a sincere apology when wrong is like a "nuclear Kind bomb." It disarms everyone in the room and makes everyone more receptive to negotiation and moving forward. "Apologies are so rare," he says, "they blow up the room."

Josh agrees (that Brent's apologies are rare).

Maintaining a united front is also critical because some people will start splitting you when they see a fissure.[19] Similarly to how many of us would play our parents off each other as kids ("Mom said we should ask you if it was OK for us to light fireworks in the garage"), when employees see leaders disagreeing, some see it as their big break to become a power broker. This needs to be avoided at all costs, since it inevitably expands and can split an entire organization in two.

How to Forge Strong Partnerships

Partnerships are messy. They just are. And what works for one kind of partnership doesn't always work for another. But generally, there are the four main tips we've found that work more often than not.

1. Partnerships need to be complementary but have a common goal

As with romantic partners, it's important that partners in business have complementary talents and personalities, but also that they share common values and goals. We were lucky—we were romantic partners before we went into business together, so we already knew that each of us was intensely goal-oriented and that our goals and values aligned. Our clarity about and commitment to shared goals and values have made it much easier for our roles to grow and evolve as our business has required. We're less attached to the specific roles we play at any given time—in our minds, it's the end goal that matters, as well as the values that determine how we pursue that goal. This kind of flexibility has allowed us to adapt what we do and help Beekman come out ahead.

2. Adopt a clear method or rule for resolving disputes and assigning authority

Accept that arguing is a natural part of collaboration. If you really want something to succeed, you're going to argue about it. If you're worried about something failing, you'll argue about it.

Partnerships can decay when one or the other partner seems to be taking on too much decision-making power, crowding out the other person. During Beekman's early days, the two of us often had major disagreements, particularly when it came to our finances, which were then in pretty rough shape. We obsessed over the numbers every day, and we both felt stressed out about it. We were both trying to weigh in equally on everything. We got nowhere except angry.

One day, after a huge, knock-down drag-out fight, we were sitting in our truck and had an epiphany: there was no reason we both had to be miserable worrying about money. We had different strengths and thoughts. Josh was more invested in (worried about) the financial part of the business, so why not let him handle that? Brent could focus on other important areas, such as operations of our retail store. Letting go of equity in decision-making can be as mutually productive as exercising it.

We adhere to another slogan, too: "He who wakes up last must make the bed." This is for those times when, for whatever reason, one of us was slacking. Maybe we were tired. Maybe we had something else we wanted to do more. Maybe we just weren't interested. Whatever the reason, the other one of us had to do all the work. In those times, you forfeit not just your 1 percent right to complain or disagree. You forfeit it all. (And yes, whichever of us wakes up last literally does have to make the bed. Bed-making score: Josh = 9,125 times. Brent = 1.)

3. Be deliberate in how to present the relationship

Recognize that people react to conflict differently, but almost no one reacts to conflict positively. If you need to disagree in front of others, do so in a way that doesn't threaten their goals, doesn't allow them to divide and conquer you, and models the type of interactive behavior that you want them to practice in your organization.

4. Partnerships always need to have a project

Josh's great uncle, Arthur Russell, used to swear by this advice in his personal life, and he was right. He and his partner, Bob, met in France during World War II, and lived together there and in Switzerland for nearly sixty years before they each passed away. Whether it was renovating a rundown medieval house or starting a "French New Wave" antiques business, they always had a project they worked on together.

When business partnerships—or any other relationship, for that matter—lack a purpose, they tend to wither and die. For many years, we had a clear project: not just to build Beekman, but to achieve a level of financial security that would allow us to satisfy our shared curiosity about the world and travel widely during retirement. For the most part, we've now reached that goal, building out our management team and taking on outside investment. Some couples might take that as a sign to pull back the reins, but not us. Rather than allowing ourselves to languish, we've taken on new projects like, oh, writing a business book.

Strong partnerships represent a significant investment of time and energy over time. It would be a shame to waste that investment once an initial project has come to a natural conclusion. Instead, devise new ways to put the strengths of your partnership to use.

We've built an amazing management team, so we no longer have to do a lot of the tasks that filled our eighteen-hour days. So now we have more time to focus on the next project. It's a really wonderful way of thinking about longevity.

Temporary Arrangements

We've been privileged to have collaborated with some amazing companies that were much larger than ours, among them MacKenzie-Childs, Sony and Mister Rogers, *Schitt's Creek*, Netflix and

Bridgerton, the American Nurses Association, Nestlé, Universal Studios and *Wicked,* and the American Red Cross. We were able to do this because of our philosophy of making sure that you can bring something beneficial to partners that they might not be able to create or accomplish themselves. We always go into these collaborations with the mindset of "How are we creating something bigger together and helping us both out?" That's the ultimate partnership: what's good for me will be good for you.

In the immortal words of motivational speaker and author Zig Ziglar, "You can get everything you want in life if you just help enough other people get what they want."

 CHEW ON THIS

- When considering whether to embark on a partnership, vet your potential partner carefully to ensure that your goals and values align. Make sure that you both have skin in the game and that it isn't easy to exit.

- Devise a clear division of responsibility and stick to it.

- Conduct your partnership carefully, being deliberate about the dimensions of your relationship that you show to others.

- Think of the last negative interaction you had in your company. Sit down *right now* and think of five positive things you're going to have to do counter the negativity.

BECOME A G.O.A.T.:
Embark on a Relationship Challenge

The Amazing Race was an incredibly clarifying experience for us—an intense, twenty-one-day journey that tested our relationship like never before. We emerged stronger and became much more knowledgeable about each other's strengths and weaknesses.

As a check-in on an existing partnership you might be involved with, create a short, bounded challenge for you and your partner to complete. Maybe it's developing a new product or hunting down a new piece of business. Maybe it's something outside the business—running a half-marathon or raising a certain amount of money for charity. Tackle this challenge together, working closely and in a committed way to get it done.

Afterward, debrief together. What is the general quality of your relationship? Is it strong or do you have work to do? What did each of you learn about the other and how you work together? How might you take this knowledge to tighten your partnership inside the business?

Love Thy Neighbor

How to Market Kindly

When people ask us how we've grown Beekman 1802, we have a really simple answer: Neighbor by Neighbor by Neighbor.

That phrase echoes through every phase of our history, and it rang as true when we crossed $100 million in annual sales as it did when we had our first $100 day.

In those first years after we moved to Sharon Springs, when Beekman 1802 was in its infancy, one of our primary goals was to build a business that worked not just for us, but also for our community. Sharon Springs had seen much better days before the twenty-first century. Before the twentieth century, actually. It once was a famous spa town that hosted ninety thousand visitors every summer. Now the population was 547.

Like most rural areas, the local economy was practically nonexistent. The few dollars in everyone's pockets circulated around to other Neighbors' nearly empty pockets. Very few outside dollars found their way into town, and as a result, the population's finances and tax base had been shrinking for decades. We knew that the most valuable thing that Beekman 1802 could contribute locally was attracting customers and commerce from outside the region.

One of our first ideas was to put on a village-wide Harvest Festival, an annual event where we could celebrate the natural beauty and agricultural roots of Sharon Springs, which attracted us two city slickers to fall in love with it in the first place. Of course we needed permission for a village-wide event, so we went to the village board meeting and explained what we wanted to do.

They listened. They nodded their heads. And promptly . . . shot it down. Why? Because they had already tried something like this, and it failed.

In the 1970s.

Throughout Sharon Springs's history, there had been several types of festivals, but over time, like the population, they'd all dwindled and disappeared. It was only natural that the village board members didn't want to put the energy or resources behind another potential failure. They honestly believed that they were doing us a favor by stopping us.

But we are not ones to be deterred. We convinced them that we would do all the work, and it would cost the village zero tax dollars. When we have a hunch about something, we'll take on all the risk.

We ended up throwing that first two-day Harvest Festival in 2010. To attract people, we posted endless notices leading up to the event on our social media, in hopes that our city-slicker friends—many of whom we hadn't seen since the Recession banished us from the city—might be intrigued enough to spend a weekend in the country. We posted profiles of local farmers and volunteers. We shared interviews with the mayor and other local notables who talked about how amazing their little hidden village was. On the morning of the first day of the event, Josh dressed up as William Beekman, the man who built our farm in 1802. He stood on the highway at the top of the village with a bell and waved people in the direction of the downtown festivities. We'd convinced a few dozen local craftspeople and farmers to set up tables in the village park, and a few other Neighbors to help park cars and pick up trash. It was a beautiful autumn day, and everyone felt a spirit of accomplishment and local pride.

About five hundred people showed up, which we thought was pretty amazing. We'd effectively doubled the local population. And more importantly, they were outsiders bringing outside dollars. And they were experiencing Sharon Springs in its best finery and good spirits.

Around this same time, we'd started shooting the docu-series about our transition to country life, *The Fabulous Beekman Boys*. We had no experience in TV and no inkling about whether it might be successful once it aired. So the tiny crew of people with cameras and microphones following us around during that inaugural festival was more a curiosity to us and others than a brush with Hollywood spotlights. The production team filmed every aspect of our tiny group of volunteers trying to get the festival off the ground, and then the actual event.

The episode about our fledgling little festival aired a few months later. Most of our Neighbors never even got to see it since the local cable company didn't carry that channel. By the time the second annual Harvest Festival rolled around, we'd nearly forgotten that the episode had ever aired at all.

So early on the morning of the second annual Harvest Festival, when we got in our truck to head down to the village to help set up tables and traffic cones, we at first thought there must have been an accident. The traffic was backed up for miles. When we finally got to the lone traffic light in town, we discovered that the county road department had already wheeled out a large flashing sign that repeated: "Caution: Harvest Festival" . . . "Caution: Harvest Festival!"

Roughly three thousand people had decided to find their way to Sharon Springs for the festival, most of whom had seen that TV episode about the first Harvest Festival and wanted to be part of something so authentic and simple that harkened back to a time when communities worked together.

Of course, this was fantastic! Except for one minor detail: by noon of the first day, every scrap of food in town was gone. We only had one café and gas station that served food, and they'd planned for six hundred or seven hundred visitors at most, not thousands of raven-ous mouths. What started as a triumph was quickly turning into a disaster.

So we were surprised when shortly after noon we saw festival-goers milling about with hamburgers and hot dogs. Where had they gotten them? We presumed that a new vendor had somehow miracu-lously appeared to feed the masses.

Nope. A local family set up a grill on their front lawn and gave away food. We were thrilled. All these people had come from every corner of the country to little Sharon Springs, and they were fam-ished. That wasn't acceptable. The family took it upon themselves to go to the grocery store about twenty miles away and buy hot dogs, hamburgers, and buns to cook up—and *give* away. Not sell. Give away.

When we first got the opportunity to film the TV show, it was during a time when there were other shows about rural lifestyles, like *Swamp People* and *Duck Dynasty*. When we first pitched the idea, we wanted to be very clear that we didn't want to make fun of coun-try people. Our Neighbors were our survival mechanism, and we loved them. We were very cognizant of the fact that despite the title being about us, we wanted to make celebrities out of all our Neigh-bors, too, and not just ourselves. That's ultimately why Harvest Fes-tival became so successful. People drove long distances to see Mayor Doug and Farmer John and Soap Maker Deb. Upstate Mayberry.

It was lovely, and exactly the kind of community spirit that the vis-itors had seen on our TV episode. But more than that, it was smart. Because this family knew that that kind of hospitality—that kind of *community*—was going to motivate people to return to the Sharon Springs Harvest Festival year after year after year. And they did. By the tenth anniversary of the festival, 22,000 visitors were traipsing to our little village with little to no marketing spend—just "Neighbor by Neighbor by Neighbor."

The festival infused money into the local economy, giving it a much-needed jolt. An informal study by our marketing officer commissioned by Cornell University estimated that between lodging, food, and retail purchases, over its history, the Harvest Festival had brought in over $8 million to the regional economy. It was also a great way to ingratiate ourselves with our Sharon Springs Neighbors, none of whom we knew when we first moved in. And we very much wanted to be part of the fiber of the community. That was one of the impetuses for our moving to a small town in the first place.

Most people who live and work in New York—or any large city— are wedded to their careers. They go to work at 7 or 8 a.m. and come home at 9 p.m., and they rarely get to know the people in their building. We lived in our New York City apartment for seven years, and we were only on a first-name basis with one other tenant. That's it. One person out of sixty-four apartments.

This happens in the suburbs, too, of course. So many people don't know the person two doors down from them. It's a genuine loss. When you have money, that's your safety net. When you don't have money, your community and your Neighbors are your safety net. And sometimes, when communities and Neighbors work together to save themselves, 22,000 other people show up to help.

The People in Your Neighborhood

"Love thy Neighbor" is not only the simplest and most profound G.O.A.T. saying, it's also one of the most universal. A central teaching in the Judeo-Christian tradition, the idea of treating your Neighbor as you would yourself appears in the ancient Hindu book the Mahābhārata, the Muslim Qur'an, the Taoist T'ai Shang Kan Ying P'ien, and the Baha'I faith's Baha'u'llah.

Interestingly, even in their original languages, the word "Neighbor" is very specific. It's not "love humankind" or "love the world" or "love everybody." It's love your *Neighbor*, and it's there for a reason. No one of us can make a dent in the problems of the whole world. They are too many and too big. But every one of us can make a difference in the people closest to us. And if every person helped their Neighbor, who helped their Neighbor, who helped their Neighbor . . . eventually the problems of the world would be taken care of.

Most people think loving thy Neighbor is about being "nice." It's not. It's finding the people that are closest to you and your values and sensibilities and forming your closest bond with those who are closest to you. The word is "Kind," and there's a big difference between "nice" and "Kind."

If you're Kind, you want someone to live their best life. You want to listen to them and find out what's going to make them happy. It all trickles down to our purpose. That's where a lot of purpose-driven companies fail. The company or the corporation has a purpose, but that purpose doesn't necessarily translate down through the entire rank and file of the company.

Jaclyn Lindsey, forty-one, is the coauthor of *Be Kind* and the cofounder and CEO of Kindness.org, whose mission is to educate and inspire people to choose Kindness. (Beekman commissioned the Kindness research with it that you read about in chapter 10.)

Jaclyn grew up in South Florida, in a home in which Kindness was paramount. As a kid, she was driven and ambitious. "I thought I might be the first woman president," she says. "I was a natural leader. My mom loves telling how she'd be out gardening and as a five-year-old I'd greet everyone in the Neighborhood. I had this natural ability in my little self to connect and care and want to learn more about people."

But things shifted in her teenage years when she experienced serious bullying. "There were a lot of different ways it showed up," she says. One of her first memories was being in an art class in middle school. One of the popular kids said, "You're pretty."

Jaclyn couldn't believe it. What a compliment! But then he continued: "Pretty ugly." And he walked away. She was devastated.

"It is the first memory I have of my worth being tied to what I looked like," she says.

She had no prom date. "I was seen as very undesirable," she says. "I wish I could say I had the tools to navigate it, but I didn't." She went from captain of the soccer team and president of various clubs to drugs and alcohol, and getting expelled from school at eighteen. That precocious and passionate kid had disappeared.

Jaclyn discovered faith as a Christian, got clean in her twenties, and pursued a career in the nonprofit space. She married an "extraordinary man," and together they have two sons. But she never forgot where she came from, or what she experienced. This ultimately led her to found Kindness.org.

"I believe Kindness is humanity's greatest asset, and Unkindness its greatest adversary," she says. "Imagine a world if Kindness was at the forefront of all of our choices?" She distinguishes between nice and Kind: "Nice is when you don't tell someone they have food in their teeth, and Kind is telling them the food is there," she says. "Nice is polite. Kind is intentional."[1]

As we've noted earlier, we became involved with the science of Kindness after Brent read an article mentioning Dr. Oliver Curry at Oxford University and the work he was doing with Kindness.[2] Then Brent discovered that Curry was working with Kindness.org, and we linked up with them. We have since funded two major studies on Kindness (in the workforce and within the social influencer sphere) with Curry, and Brent has joined the board of Kindness.org.

What we've learned from our business is that you can't take care of the whole world. You can't love the whole world. You can't love all of humanity. But if you love your Neighbor and that Neighbor loves their Neighbor and that Neighbor loves their Neighbor, then the bigger goal gets accomplished. ("Neighbor by Neighbor by Neighbor.")

It's so obvious, yet modern business often tends to neglect this teaching, particularly with regard to marketing. Leaders think of customers as opponents—or worse, enemies they seek to conquer. The majority of the business world thinks of its day-to-day as an us-versus-them dyad: *we're* the business, and *they're* the customer. The relationship is purely transactional and temporary.

Marketing is rife with military language—"target" audiences, "boot camps," "war rooms," "postmortems," "campaigns"—as if companies were armies fighting wars. Thinking of commerce as a zero-sum game, marketers spend most of their time devising techniques to squeeze the maximum amount of value from customers, often doing this under the guise of building meaningful "relationships." Rhetoric aside, the business and its bottom line remain paramount in their minds. Only secondarily do they think about what might be in customers' best interests.

This is a totally counterproductive way of thinking, a foolproof recipe for failure. As a company, we actively want to improve the lives of our Neighbors, starting with the health of their skin but also to let that moment of self-Kindness start a ripple effect as they walk out the door.

We grew our company organically by being fair with our Neighbors, by valuing them, and more importantly, by *showing* them that we valued them. They returned the feeling in spades.

One of the ways we've made them feel so treasured is by treating them as individuals. *Any* interaction between two people is a personal relationship. The folks buying your products aren't mere customers, they're *people*, just as the people at the other end of the phone line aren't just customer support. They're people doing the best they can to get by, like we all are. You can sign on endless dotted lines, but until AI takes over, there's still a person signing above or below you. There should be no discernible difference between business relationships and personal relationships. (Actually, as of this writing, everyone's talking about how AI is going to change the workforce. But so far, one of the things AI can't do is be socially fluent. Or Kind!)

The relationship must be genuine. Think of the sentence, "The customer's always right." It still has that othering aspect to it. When business owners say the customer's always right, the sentiment is really, "I hate to do this, but I'm going to have to because the customer's always right." There's wisdom in it, but it's also a hard and fast rule that prevents you from actually thinking about who the customer is and building a real relationship with them, and what their motivation or stage of need is.

Because guess what? Sometimes, the customer *isn't* right. Maybe they misunderstood you. Or maybe they made a wrong calculation. If you don't treat customers like adversaries, one of you doesn't have to be right or wrong. You're both always on the same side. You want them to be happy, and they want you to succeed. Especially if you succeed in making them happy.

One of our favorite sayings when it comes to customer service issues is, "Don't just make it better. Make it better than better." We've instilled this ethos in our Neighbor services department, every one of whom are emboldened and empowered to enhance any situation. An example we use is if you borrowed a cake stand from a Neighbor, then accidentally broke it, you wouldn't just replace the cake stand, right? You'd replace it *and* return it with a cake too.

So many business leaders believe they built the business. They're wrong. The *customer* builds the business. But leaders lose sight of that.

Once again, our ultimate piece of G.O.A.T. wisdom: everybody who works at Beekman understands that the purpose of the company is to spread Kindness, and their purpose specifically is to utilize their job to spread Kindness either within the company or outside the company. Our Neighbor services team is always on the lookout for special circumstances, which they'll highlight for us if we happen to miss them.

One Neighbor sent an email telling us that her house had burned down and she'd lost everything. She reached out to us because she had recently placed an order that she needed to cancel. Because of the fire, she couldn't accept packages at her address. Our Neighbor services representatives have developed relationships with our best customers and keep detailed notes on their profiles. The rep looked back through all of that Neighbor's orders for the past two years, realized that she had been a very loyal Neighbor, and decided to reship everything that she'd lost for free. She didn't need to ask permission to do this. She immediately realized that this Neighbor would more than repay the favor when she got back on her feet. And she has.

More than that, we're certain she's told dozens of people about "the company that replaced two years' worth of orders." ("Neighbor by Neighbor by Neighbor.")

Several years ago, a new independent wholesale Neighbor near Atlanta was opening up his first gift shop and had placed a $20,000 order from Beekman. The day his shop was to open, there was a huge flood in his town and his entire store was inundated. He had invested almost everything he had in this new venture and everything washed away. He reached out to the Beekman sales rep with whom he initially ordered to order a replacement (who had once worked for Kimberly Wahlberg; see chapter 11). He apologized that it couldn't be as large as the first order, given what the flood had done to his financial position. The rep elevated the story to us, and we concluded that anyone who apologized for placing a smaller order after such a devasting loss was exactly the type of Kind person who would succeed with his new business, given the chance. And his success would help our success. It was too large an order to replace completely for free, and he did have some insurance, so instead we replaced all of the items at cost and told him he didn't need to pay us for them until they had sold and he needed to place a replenishment order.

A few years later, he heard that we were going to give a talk at the Atlanta gift market. People were waiting to chat with us and snap photos. We noticed a middle-aged man in a denim shirt and khakis leaning against a wall. After everyone left, he approached us.

"I don't know if you remember me, but you helped me out after my store had a big flood," he began.

We knew exactly who he was. He went on to tell us that when he was able to reopen, he directed every single customer to the Beekman 1802 display and told them how we'd replaced everything he lost at cost and deferred payment. Not surprisingly, we became the bestselling brand in his store, and his replenishment orders have long since made up for any loss we took on pricing. ("Neighbor by Neighbor by Neighbor.")

Being Neighborly goes both ways at Beekman 1802. Though we don't have hard data, we're pretty certain Beekman Neighbors are more Kind to us than most brands' customers. Even when we receive a bad review on a product, it often begins with "I'm really sorry to have to say this, but . . . " And when customers call in with complaints, they'll start by apologizing to our Neighbor services representative. This, in turn, helps our team be nicer to them. And the virtuous circle continues.

Studies back up the idea that Kindness is contagious. A 2010 study found that Kindness tends to beget more Kindness. Researchers set up a game in which players would typically benefit more if they behaved selfishly than if they cooperated with others. Researchers found that when participants behaved generously in one round of the game, other players tended to mimic that same behavior, behaving generously themselves in subsequent rounds.[3]

That's all the more reason to be Kind. A 2022 study in the *Journal of Positive Psychology* randomly assigned 122 people with symptoms of depression and anxiety to do something Kind, engage in a social activity, or write in their journal for five weeks. The Kindness group saw the greatest benefits to their well-being.[4]

In her 2024 book *New Happy: Getting Happiness Right in a World That's Got It Wrong*, researcher Stephanie Harrison argues that helping others—not material things—is the secret to true happiness. Those who are part of the "new happy" make working together and asking for help a priority.

"Helping other people is one of our needs," says Harrison. "It's just like a need for connection or for love or for self-esteem, we need to go beyond ourselves and feel like we matter and we're making a difference. The easiest way to do that is through these actions of helping, and at the same time, we also need other people to help us to have our needs satisfied."[5]

Think about your own community. If you shovel your Neighbor's driveway during a big storm, chances are they'll help you out in return—maybe by baking you an apple pie, maybe by shoveling your driveway next time. Neighborliness is a reciprocal relationship rooted in mutual trust, Kindness, caring, and responsibility. If you can learn to approach marketing as the building of direct, reciprocal relationships rather than as a series of abstract—even adversarial—transactions, you'll find that customers feel responsible for you and will take action on your behalf. In our own world, without Farmer John, without our Neighbors helping us wrap those original bars of soap at our dining room table when we had that big order from Anthropologie, without the local volunteers at those first Harvest Festivals, we would never have gotten off the ground. And one of the questions we are asked the most when we tell our story is: "So whatever happened to Farmer John?" Well, he still lives on the farm, with his goats, under the same handshake agreement we forged the first day we met.

Every month, we get tons of cards and handwritten thank-you notes about how our products and message of Kindness have impacted people's lives. Once a month, we go live on social media and read the letters aloud. We feel that the letter is not just to us, but to all the people in the Neighborhood.

We share what they've sent in: candles, fudge, toys for our dog, homemade vanilla extract, homemade blankets, potholders, bookmarks . . . the list is endless. We have a whole Christmas-tree of ornaments made by Neighbors, from hand-painted ceramic goats, to crocheted snowflakes, to miniature bars of soap.

Creating and nurturing this virtual Neighborhood helps us extend beyond the typical brand-customer relationship and further our mission of spreading Kindness as far and wide as possible. In this way Beekman Neighbors become an extension of Team Beekman. Whenever there is some sort of national disaster, we know that there's a pretty good likelihood that a Beekman Neighbor lives nearby. We also know that our cleansing wipes are a godsend to people who've lost power, or water, or sometimes their entire homes. So rather than simply send a check to the Red Cross or another large national organization, we reach out on social media to find a Neighbor who lives in the affected area. Once we locate them, we ask them to find a local charity that they know has boots on the ground and is making a difference. Then we'll ship a palette of our wipes directly to that charity. Or if that's impossible, we've even shipped boxes of wipes directly to an individual Beekman Neighbor to distribute to those in need. ("Neighbor by Neighbor by Neighbor.")

Building a Coalition

One of the things we've come to realize is that we are in the hospitality business. If you think about it, all businesses are about hospitality. Whether you're a dentist or plumber or software engineer, you have to be hospitable to your customer. So, all the rules of hospitality have to apply to your business.

Neighborliness on our part has led to the creation of passionate brand advocates who love Beekman and will go to unusual lengths to help the company grow. Many companies hire influencers, but advocates who feel grateful and deeply loyal to us for being good Neighbors are much more valuable. There's actually a business concept about this, called the Pareto principle. The principle asserts that 80 percent of your profits come from 20 percent of your customers. Those 20 percent typically become your advocates. So it's beneficial for a company to focus on the 20 percent of clients who are responsible for 80 percent of revenues.[6]

Not only do these folks generate legions of new customers for us and send us mountains of handmade holiday gifts each year; they also help our company in our times of need.

We didn't get our first meeting with Ulta Beauty because it read a bunch of news stories about us or we had new investors. We got into Ulta because one of our Neighbors worked there. She loved us and convinced the relevant C-suite people to take a closer look at our brand.

We trained our Neighbor services to understand that customer perspective ("Do unto others as you would have them do unto you"). It's fine to outsource customer service to foreign companies, which can generally help you. But when there is friction, a chatbot or helper from another culture isn't going to be able to understand the same way an informed employee will. They won't be able to explain or diffuse the emotions.

Our Beekman Neighbors really came through for us when we launched that capsule food line in Target in 2017. One of the first things we noticed post-launch was that the displays were disorganized and missing items (which is completely normal in big-box stores with hundreds of thousands of SKUs). As mentioned, we didn't know that most companies in big-box stores hire external teams of people to go in and make sure that their shelves are straight and properly stocked. We didn't have resources to do that, so we sent out a plea to all Beekman Neighbors to visit their local Target and snap a picture of themselves in front of the Beekman display. At the time, we were in about 1,800 Target stores, and we probably received 800 photos of people. We called them . . . "shelfies."

Our Beekman Neighbors came through for us. Through their shelfies, we were able to identify which regions and which stores had the biggest problems with stock and displays. We even noticed one specific issue that saved us tens of thousands of dollars.

Every week we received sales reports, and one of the data points showed that our blueberry pie filling had zero sales. Zero. We knew this was impossible. In 1,800 stores, surely *someone* liked blueberry pie. Target is so huge that it naturally makes its order decisions based on pure data. Having a big zero in its reports meant no reorders, and even worse, the probability that we would have to take all of the inventory back at our own cost.

But we could see when reviewing all of the Neighbor shelfies that the pie filling wasn't on a single shelf anywhere across the country. After doing a little digging, we discovered that all of the inventory was held up in a distribution center somewhere in the Midwest. Once we were able to get those jars to the shelves, they sold at a healthy productivity rate, which averted a financial disaster for us. All thanks to Beekman Neighbors, who took time out of their day to do a favor for us.

Beekman Neighbors came through for us again when we launched in Ulta Beauty in 2020. We had negotiated a full end cap of Beekman products in four hundred Ulta stores, which was a massive inventory expenditure for us. The launch had to be successful. We'd done everything the experts told us to do. We spent most of our budget on creating an amazing display that would tell our story of Kindness. We sent hundreds of "education boxes" to Ulta Beauty employees with video screens inside featuring a video of us on the farm telling them our founding story and commitment to Kindness. We had everything in place to launch and then . . . there was a global pandemic.

Even in the stores that remained open, Ulta prohibited brands' usual practice of sending in sales teams to educate the Ulta staff and customers. All of our beautiful informative displays? No one would see them. The closest anyone would get would be curbside delivery. We had a new product that no one knew about, and no way to educate either customers or staff.

So, of course, the first thing we did was put out a Neighbor call on social media asking them to "adopt" one of the first four hundred stores we were in. We knew that nobody knew and loved Beekman products better than our Neighbors, and therefore no one would be better able to educate the Ulta team. It worked. Our Neighbors visited the stores that were open or, in stores that were closed, chatted with them on social media. They identified themselves as Neighbors and shared a little topline story about our company. While other brands were struggling to be seen during the pandemic, our Neighbors made sure we were visible.

The second thing we did was something that Ulta Beauty and employees still talk about and use as an example for other brands today. We knew that the only way we were going to explain to the Ulta store teams that this new skin-care brand appearing in their stores was rooted in Kindness was not to tell them about it. It was to show them.

They were getting a new brand that was based in milk . . . so we sent them cookies. But not just any old cookies. Cookies from their Neighbors.

Everyone remembers in those early pandemic days how small mom-and-pop businesses around the country were suffering from being shuttered. We wanted to do something that would illustrate the core values of Beekman 1802. So we went to the Retail Bakers of America website and identified small bakeries near each of the four hundred Ulta stores in which we were launching. We called each one individually and placed orders for freshly baked cookies to be hand-delivered to their local Ulta Beauty store from "that new goat milk brand."

This accomplished so much for us. It got us noticed both in Ulta's C-suite and, more importantly, with their employees in the stores. It showed those store employees that we cared about their Neighborhood businesses. And it got Ulta stores—as well as the bakeries we contracted with—to post hundreds of social media posts about this "new goat milk brand that sent them cookies in the middle of a pandemic!"

We didn't need to explain that Beekman 1802 was a brand about Kindness. We showed it. All along, as we were growing our company and talking about our ideals and Kindness practices, industry veterans would tell us, "You can do that as a small company, but you'll never be able to scale that idea."

No matter what business you're in, you're always going to have experts tell you that whatever you're doing now, you won't be able to continue doing it as you grow. When we went into Ulta Beauty, the experts said that we wouldn't be successful because so much of our success to date came from being able to tell our story in person on television. When we succeeded in Ulta Beauty, people said that we'd never be able to be successful on Amazon since we didn't have the brand awareness of the giant conglomerate brands. We did it. Ignore those people. The only people you need to listen to about success are the people who made you successful in the first place. Namely, your customers. We discovered that wherever our Neighbors shopped, they would buy us. That's the power of customer loyalty advocacy.

Beekman 1802 advocates happen to be people who overflow with empathy. But yours might not be. You might run a tech company or a small coffee shop, and you'll still have advocates, just a different type.

If you're a financial bro and you're selling macro loans, your business partners will be the people who share the same values, interests, and knowledge base. That's who you cultivate relationships with, and that's who become your best customers.

Building a reciprocal relationship also means that you have to take personal responsibility for your customers' welfare. This means that an advocate is most likely not going to be someone you dislike. We've never had a good business relationship with someone we don't like. Beekman will never be a beauty brand for cool, trendy "mean girls" (or boys). That's not our scene. That's another piece of business advice—if, as entrepreneurs you don't like or admire a customer or a retail partner, if you can't feel as if they're your Neighbor, you probably won't have a good business relationship with them. Trust your gut.

We're also very accessible. Beekman 1802 has its own social media accounts, but we still control our personal social media handles ourselves. Our Neighbors and biggest advocates know how to find us personally on social media. And they know we will respond to them when something goes really wrong. Or really right.

If we recognize a name that we've seen multiple times on Facebook or Instagram or wherever, and we read that they're going through a tough time, we send them a handwritten note. Just as any Neighbor would do.

One of our happiest moments is when we're walking through an airport and someone comes up to us and introduces themselves with a hearty, "Hi, Neighbor!" Not only is it nice to meet someone who likes our products, it's even nicer to know that they feel comfortable enough to come up and say hello to two strangers. Except we're not strangers to them. We're Neighbors.

One of our favorite Neighbors is a developmentally disabled man named Chip, who first visited our store in Sharon Springs with his parents. He lives in Pennsylvania, about a six-hour commute. Chip has that fun, unique talent that if you tell him your birth date, he can tell you which day of the week it was. So, when Josh told him that he was born on August 28, 1969, Chip knew that was a Wednesday. And even more special, Chip always remembers.

Every year without fail, we both get cards on our birthdays with $1 inside it. And of course, every year, we send Chip a birthday card with a dollar in it. Not long ago, Chip sent us an invitation to his fiftieth birthday party. We sent him $50 in his birthday card so he could go out and celebrate. In our hearts we knew that Chip would take that fifty and spread it around among his friends. Through Beekman, we've made so many friends like Chip. They've changed our lives much more than any P&L statement or gross margin improvement ever could.

The Big(gest) Picture

By now, you got it: Kindness is one of Beekman's most important values. We've already talked about it a bunch. But it's especially important when it comes to our relationship with our Neighbors. So we want to leave you with our favorite story, which to us is the greatest example of successfully fulfilling our mission of spreading Kindness around the world, Neighbor by Neighbor by Neighbor.

For many years, we sold a subscription Bounty Box, filled with products that referenced the seasonality of life on the farm. If you subscribed, every three months, at the start of a new season, you'd get another box with a new fragrance representing that new season. We sold it on TV for several years, and it was hugely popular.

One year, while we were on air selling the start of the new year's Bounty Box subscription, a Neighbor named Diane called in. The producers patched her through, so her voice was heard live on air and over the airwaves. Diane explained how every year her husband had bought her the annual subscription as a birthday gift. This past year, however, he had unexpectedly died shortly after signing up again.

Diane explained how much every single shipment of the Bounty Box meant to her that year. She explained that each time it arrived, she could pretend her husband was still alive and had sent it to her. She was in tears. The host was in tears. We were in tears. And we were sure that everyone watching was in tears.

When we got off air after that show, we checked in on our social media as we usually did.

There were hundreds of posts from Beekman Neighbors about Diane and her late husband. Beekman Neighbors everywhere were moved by her story. So much so that dozens and dozens of them wanted to purchase a new subscription for Diane themselves, on behalf of her late husband.

These were complete strangers to Diane. But as Beekman Neighbors, they felt compelled to take care of one of their own. It wasn't just us doling out Kindness anymore. It was the entire Beekman 1802 Neighborhood.

Our mission to spread Kindness in the world has worked better than in our wildest imaginations. We encourage you to adopt "Love Thy Neighbor" as a core business principle—not just because of any religious or moral imperative, as important as those may be for you, but because over the long term, good Neighborliness really is the basis for a deeper approach to marketing and a strong, enduring business. We spend so much of our lives tending to our businesses, especially as entrepreneurs. A lot of you will spend as many actual hours thinking about your customers as you do about your friends and family. We don't see that as a bad thing. We see that as working to make a positive impact on as many human beings as you can. And using your business as a tool to help create the kind of world you ultimately want to live in . . . Neighbor by Neighbor by Neighbor.

CHEW ON THIS

- Remember, no matter what business you're in, you're in the hospitality business.

- With every business challenge involving customers, start by asking: What are their goals? How can they benefit? Connect your answers to these questions to your own goals, making decisions that benefit both equally.

- Care for your Neighbors and help them in their times of need, without thinking of receiving benefits in turn.

- Disseminate the ethic of loving your Neighbor internally as part of employee training (we do this via something we call our "Kindness Curriculum").

BECOME A G.O.A.T.:
Learn to Be More Neighborly

Consider your customer base. Who are your core customers—the ones who not only buy your product or service, but align most closely with your values? Who are the ones who depend most on your offerings and who find them most meaningful? If you struggle to pin this down, think of the five or six biggest advocates from among your customers. Call them and ask them why they love your company so much. Do you notice any patterns?

Once you've identified this group, consider the nature of your relationship with them. Are you doing everything possible to nurture a Neighborly bond? Is the relationship between you and these advocates reciprocal and balanced? How might you support, help, connect with, or recognize these advocates more than you currently do? Make sure you do this exercise yourself—don't call in a marketing firm. You need to establish a direct and personal relationship with your closest customers that then can radiate outward.

One Last Thing

Go back to that first statement you wrote, the first piece of advice you ever received. Now that you've read *G.O.A.T. Wisdom*, what additional knowledge can you get from these words of wisdom? We hope you've learned to extract more from these words of wisdom than mere platitudes . . . and will be able to utilize them wherever life takes you.

Becoming G.O.A.T. Wise

We've spent all this time talking about what we've learned from G.O.A.T.s, but what about actual goats? Turns out, we've digested a lot of wisdom from observing them, too.

Let Us Share Our G.O.A.T. Wisdom with You

Over the years, we've been invited to speak to the employees of many other companies, including Wells Fargo, PwC, Hallmark, Google, Meta, Pinterest, Nestlé, and various trade organizations. In addition to cute pictures of goats, the best-reviewed part of our talks is always the lessons we share that we learned from our actual goats, so we summarize them here.

If Everyone Is Running in the Same Direction, Join Them

Goats are very skittish creatures. Often, when they're out in the field, one will hear a sound, like a twig breaking, and start hightailing it back to the barn for no reason. The others join the stampede without even knowing why. Entrepreneurs are often exhorted to be brave and do their own thing regardless of potential consequences. But sometimes, there actually is a real threat. In the presence of overwhelming consensus, it's better to join in a mass exodus and reevaluate later than to get eaten by a coyote.

A Certain Level of Bullshit (or Goat Poop) Is Helpful

In the winter, farmers typically clean out the barn less frequently, not only because snowy weather makes it more difficult, but because leaving some decomposing manure in the barn actually helps heat it. We believe a certain amount of hot air in business helps as well. In challenging times, some cheerleading puffery can help motivate teams internally. And externally, spinning moderate successes into earth-shattering victories can help attract more positive attention and relationships.

Taste Everything (You Can Always Spit It Out Later)

The idea that goats eat anything—even tin cans—is an old wives' tale. The truth is that they are very curious animals and explore the world around them through their sense of taste. They'll quickly spit out anything they don't like. We agree that the best business practice is to explore any and all opportunities. We're often too quick to say things like "That's not how we do it," or "That's not what everybody else does." That might be true, but if you don't at least investigate alternatives, you'll miss out on all sorts of innovative, disruptive breakthroughs.

Hard Decisions Today Make for Easier Tomorrows

As soon as a new kid is born on the farm, Farmer John begins using its mother's milk to bottle-feed it. Many times, people will ask, "Wouldn't it be nicer just to let it feed directly from its mother?" Yes, that might be easier, but as we said before, goats are very skittish. Ensuring that the kids imprint on John first means that for the rest of their lives, they won't be stressed out at milking time each day. It's the same for business decisions. Delaying tough decisions, or trying to smooth things over, takes away from the productivity that only comes after ripping Band-Aids off and moving on.

Constantly Revisit Your Organization's Organization

Goats have a herd mentality. Also, like chickens, they have a "pecking order." The herd runs smoothly when all the goats know where they are in it. Problems arise, however, if a few goats wander off further afield or if some go outside, while the others stay inside. As soon as they are all together again, they invariably start head-butting to reestablish their own mysterious (to us) org chart. The same holds true for human herds. Just because everyone agreed to an org chart three years ago doesn't mean it's the best org chart for today. Keep your org flow flexible, so your teams don't start butting heads (or noses).

If you'd like us to speak to your employees, please reach out to NeighborServices@beekman1802.com.

EPILOGUE

You've always had the power, my dear,
you just had to learn it for yourself.

−Glinda, the Good Witch, *The Wizard of Oz*

If you've made it to the end of this book, and even done a few of the exercises, we'd like to congratulate you . . . and ourselves. Attention spans are very short in today's world, and to be able to command attention shows that we are continuing to develop and evolve our own skills in business. Your ability to focus for an entire book demonstrates your commitment to building your business or career. There's no better sign that you are ready to begin your entrepreneurial journey than that.

It's important for us to say this, because so often what keeps people from pursuing an idea is a feeling of inadequacy. We think we can't do it, so we don't.

We are both woefully overeducated: Josh with his BS in English and an advanced degree in advertising communications, and Brent with his BS in public health, his medical degree, and his MBA. While formal education is important and can help with valuable connections, insights, and analytical skills, if you have the drive and desire, you can do *all* of these things on your own.

You've always had the power.

When we first had the concept for this book, we wanted to call it *Tried and Truisms*. Our publisher and agent thought we could come up with something better (and we did). The intent is the same. There's basically no piece of advice that you have read in this book that you have not heard before. Every bit of G.O.A.T. wisdom (and there's much more of it out there if you look for it) has been tried and is true.

As we are finishing up this manuscript, it seems like a new era of business is beginning. A revolution in AI is going to change the workforce in ways that none of us can really imagine completely at the moment. At the other end of the spectrum, there's an increased demand for those who are skilled in the trades. None other than the *Wall Street Journal* predicted that the next wave of American millionaires would come from skilled-trade empire builders.[1] Interestingly, neither of these movements is going to require a college degree to make your mark in the world.

No matter what type of business you want to create, just remember, you have all the G.O.A.T. wisdom you have ever been told. Now take it away!

RECOMMENDED READING

Rutger Bergman, *Humankind: A Hopeful History* (Little, Brown and Company, November 16, 2021)

Brené Brown, *Atlas of the Heart: Mapping Meaningful Connection and the Language of Human Experience* (Random House, November 30, 2021)

Brené Brown, *Dare to Lead: Brave Work. Tough Conversations. Whole Hearts* (Random House, October 9, 2018)

Dale Carnegie, *How to Win Friends and Influence People: Updated for the Next Generation of Leaders* (Dale Carnegie Books, May 17, 2022)

Scott Galloway, *The Algebra of Happiness: Notes on the Pursuit of Success, Love, and Meaning* (Portfolio, May 14, 2019)

Scott Galloway, *The Algebra of Wealth: A Simple Formula for Financial Security* (Portfolio, April 23, 2024)

Malcolm Gladwell, *The Revenge of the Tipping Point: Overstories, Superspreaders, and the Rise of Social Engineering* (Little, Brown and Company, October 1, 2024)

Adam Grant, *Originals; Think Again: The Power of Knowing What You Don't Know* (Viking, February 2, 2021)

Sally Hogshead, *Fascinate: Your 7 Triggers to Persuasion and Captivation* (HarperBusiness, February 9, 2010)

Brad Stone, *The Everything Store: Jeff Bezos and the Age of Amazon* (Little, Brown and Company, October 15, 2013)

NOTES

Preface

1. "Workers Who Jumped Ship during Covid Are Now Regretting It," The Conference Board, May 6, 2024, https://www.conference-board.org/press /job-satisfaction-2024; Alex Koller, "U.S. Workers Are Less Satisfied with Nearly Every Aspect of Their Jobs Than They Were a Year Ago, Survey Finds," *CNBC Make It*, May 29, 2024, https://www.cnbc.com/2024/05/29/us-workers-are-less -satisfied-with-nearly-every-aspect-of-their-jobs-survey-finds.html.

2. Kennedy Hayes, "Majority of Gen Zers Want to Become Entrepreneurs, Report Finds," Fox Business, June 12, 2024, https://www.foxbusiness.com /fox-news-education/majority-gen-zers-want-become-entrepreneurs-report-finds.

PRINCIPLE #1

1. Samuel S. Marquis, *Henry Ford: An Interpretation* (Detroit, MI: Wayne State University Press, 2007), 38; Harvey Whipple, "Mid-Winter Hiking," *Illustrated Outdoor World and Recreation* 54, no. 1 (January 1916): 13; "Henry Ford's Dream as Barefoot Lad Comes True: $2,000,000 Estate Built Where Schoolboy Roamed," *St. Louis Post-Dispatch*, May 21, 1916.

2. Henry David Thoreau, *Walden: or, Life in the Woods* (Boston: Ticknor and Fields, 1854).

3. Embroker Team, "106 Must-Know Startup Statistics for 2024," Embroker, September 19, 2024, https://www.embroker.com/blog/startup-statistics/.

4. Toddi Gutner, "Is It Time to Outsource Human Resources?," *Entrepreneur*, January 14, 2011, https://www.entrepreneur.com/business-news/is-it-time-to-outsource-human-resources/217866.

5. D. Christopher Kayes and Anna B. Kayes, "Experiential Learning and Education in Management," *Oxford Research Encyclopedia of Business and Management*, February 23, 2021, https://doi.org/10.1093/acrefore/9780190224851 .013.294.

6. Maria Ho, "New Research Shows Investing in Experiential Learning for Leaders Pays Off," Association for Talent Development, May 11, 2016, https:// www.td.org/insights/new-research-shows-investing-in-experiential-learning-for -leaders-pays-off.

7. "What Is Experiential Learning and Why It Is the Future of Learning," *Kiwi* (blog), https://startkiwi.com/blog/what-is-experiential-learning-and-why-it -is-the-future-of-learning/.

8. SB Staff, "Kolb's Model for Experiential Learning: A Theory of How People Learn Effectively," *Sounding Board* (blog), https://www.sounding-boardinc.com/blog/kolbs-model-experiential-learning-effectively/.

9. "About," *Undercover Boss*, Paramount Press Express, https://www.paramountpressexpress.com/cbs-entertainment/shows/undercover-boss/about/.

10. Joyce Lee, "Todd Ricketts, Chicago Cubs Co-Owner, Goes Incognito on 'Undercover Boss,'" CBS News, November 8, 2010, https://www.cbsnews.com/news/todd-ricketts-chicago-cubs-co-owner-goes-incognito-on-undercover-boss/.

11. Yankee Candle Company, Inc., "Yankee Candle CEO Harlan Kent to Appear on CBS's 'Undercover Boss,' Friday, March 30th," PR Newswire, March 20, 2012, https://www.prnewswire.com/news-releases/yankee-candle-ceo-harlan-kent-to-appear-on-cbss-undercover-boss-friday-march-30th-143468196.html.

12. "Episodes," *Undercover Boss*, Paramount Press Express, https://www.paramountpressexpress.com/cbs-entertainment/shows/undercover-boss/episodes/.

13. Annie Pilon, "One-Third of Small Businesses Start with Less Than $5,000," *Small Business Trends*, January 9, 2019, https://smallbiztrends.com/startup-funding-statistics/.

14. Martha Stewart, in discussion with authors.

15. Deb McGillicuddy, in discussion with authors.

16. Qurate Retail Group, "QVC and HSN Launch Livestream Video Shopping Experiences on Amazon Freevee," PR Newswire, June 29, 2023, https://www.prnewswire.com/news-releases/qvc-and-hsn-launch-livestream-video-shopping-experiences-on-amazon-freevee-301867259.html; "QVC Named to Newsweek's Most Trustworthy Companies in America 2023 List," QVC, May 10, 2023, https://corporate.qvc.com/newsroom/pressrelease/qvc-named-to-newsweeks-most-trustworthy-companies-in-america-2023-list/.

17. Sangeeta Bharadwaj Badal and Bryant Ott, "Delegating: A Huge Management Challenge for Entrepreneurs," Gallup News, April 14, 2015, https://news.gallup.com/businessjournal/182414/delegating-huge-management-challenge-entrepreneurs.aspx; Leigh Buchanan, "Inside the Mind of the Entrepreneur: Groundbreaking New Research Shows What Sets Inc. 500 CEOs Apart from the Pack," *Inc.*, September 2014, https://www.inc.com/magazine/201409/leigh-buchanan/inc.500-introduction-to-the-2014-winners.html.

18. Steven Satterfield, in discussion with authors.

PRINCIPLE #2

1. "Poor Richard, 1746," Founders Online, National Archives, https://founders.archives.gov/documents/Franklin/01-03-02-0025.

2. "Frugal Innovation: Why Low Cost Doesn't Have to Mean Low Impact," *Nature* 624, no. 8 (2023), https://doi.org/10.1038/d41586-023-03816-7.

3. Helga Dittmar et al., "The Relationship between Materialism and Personal Well-Being: A Meta-analysis," *Journal of Personality and Social Psychology* 107, no. 5 (2014), https://doi.org/10.1037/a0037409.

4. Emily Brown Weida et al., "Financial Health as a Measurable Social Determinant of Health," *PLoS One* 15, no. 5 (May 18, 2020), https://doi.org/10.1371/journal.pone.0233359.

5. Atalay Atasu, Céline Dumas, and Luk N. Van Wassenhove, "The Circular Business Model," *Harvard Business Review*, July–August 2021, https://hbr.org/2021/07/the-circular-business-model.

6. Atasu et al., "The Circular Business Model."

7. Rogelo Oliva and James Quinn, "Interface's Evergreen Services Agreement," Harvard Business School Case 603-112, February 2003 (revised June 2003), https://www.hbs.edu/faculty/Pages/item.aspx?num=29680.

8. Oliva and Quinn, "Interface's Evergreen Services Agreement."

9. Bethenny Frankel, in discussion with authors.

10. Brendan Ballou, "When Private-Equity Firms Bankrupt Their Own Companies," *The Atlantic*, May 1, 2023, https://www.theatlantic.com/ideas/archive/2023/05/private-equity-firms-bankruptcies-plunder-book/673896/.

PRINCIPLE #3

1. University at Buffalo, "Humility Key to Effective Leadership," *ScienceDaily*, December 9, 2011, https://www.sciencedaily.com/releases/2011/12/111208173643.htm.

2. Jia Hu et al., "Leader Humility and Team Creativity: The Role of Team Information Sharing, Psychological Safety, and Power Distance," *Journal of Applied Psychology* 103, no. 3 (2018): 313–323, https://doi.org/10.1037/apl0000277.

3. "Five Ways Your Business Can Improve by Admitting to Mistakes," *Peoria Magazine*, 2013, https://www.peoriamagazine.com/archive/ibi_article/2013/five-ways-your-business-can-improve-admitting-mistakes/.

4. "The First Mover Advantage Isn't Real: Breaking Down Silicon Valley Myths with Adam Grant and Reid Hoffman," Next Big Idea Club, https://nextbigideaclub.com/magazine/conversation-creativity-in-the-age-of-disruption-a-conversation-with-adam-grant-and-reid-hoffman/20491/.

5. Connie Loizos, "Wharton Professor Adam Grant on Creativity and the First Mover Myth," TechCrunch, February 2, 2016, https://techcrunch.com/2016/02/02/wharton-professor-adam-grant-on-creativity-and-the-first-mover-myth/.

6. "The First Mover Advantage Isn't Real."

7. Mark Sullivan, "How Did Samsung Botch the Galaxy Note 7 Crisis? It's a Failure of Leadership," *Fast Company*, October 12, 2016, https://www.fastcompany.com/3064569/how-did-samsung-botch-the-galaxy-note-7-crisis-its-a-failure-of-leadership.

8. Hayley Tsukayama, "How Samsung Moved beyond Its Exploding Phones," *Washington Post*, February 23, 2018, https://www.washingtonpost.com/business/how-samsung-moved-beyond-its-exploding-phones/2018/02/23/5675632c-182f-11e8-b681-2d4d462a1921_story.html.

9. Tsukayama, "How Samsung Moved beyond Its Exploding Phones."

10. Abigail Gentrup, "Fitness Giant Xponential Might Go Public," *Front Office Sports*, April 20, 2021, https://frontofficesports.com/fitness-giant-xponential -might-go-public/.

11. Andy Stenzler, in discussion with authors.

PRINCIPLE #4

1. Sebastian Brandt, *The Ship of Fools, Volume 1*, trans. Alexander Barclay (William Paterson, 1874; Project Gutenberg, December 23, 2006), https://www .gutenberg.org/files/20179/20179-h/20179-h.htm.

2. Konstantinos Pelechrinis and Wayne Winston, "The Hot Hand in the Wild," *PLoS One* 17, no. 1 (January 25, 2022), https://doi.org/10.1371/journal .pone.0261890.

3. Thomas Gilovich, Robert Vallone, and Amos Tversky, "The Hot Hand in Basketball: On the Misperception of Random Sequences," *Cognitive Psychology* 17, no. 3 (1985): 295–314, https://doi.org/10.1016/0010-0285(85)90010-6.

4. Daniel Kahneman, *Thinking, Fast and Slow* (New York: Farrar, Straus and Giroux, 2013).

5. Patrick D. Larkey, Richard A. Smith, and Joseph B. Kadane, "It's Okay to Believe in the 'Hot Hand,'" *Chance* 2, no. 4 (1989): 22–30, https://doi.org/10.108 0/09332480.1989.10554950; Joshua B. Miller and Adam Sanjurjo, "Surprised by the Gambler's and Hot Hand Fallacies? A Truth in the Law of Small Numbers," *Econometrica* 86, no. 6 (2018): 2019–2047, http://dx.doi.org/10.2139/ssrn .2627354.

6. David Remnick, "Bob Dylan and the 'Hot Hand,'" *New Yorker*, November 9, 2015, https://www.newyorker.com/culture/cultural-comment/bob -dylan-and-the-hot-hand.

7. Curtis Stone, in discussion with authors.

8. Karen Gilchrist, "How a 32-Year-Old Turned a High School Yearbook Idea into a $3.2 Billion Business," *CNBC Make It*, January 9, 2020, https://www .cnbc.com/2020/01/09/canva-how-melanie-perkins-built-a-3point2-billion-dollar -design-start-up.html.

9. "From Idea to Billion-Dollar Company: The Melanie Perkins Story as Canva CEO," Kitrum, April 25, 2023, https://kitrum.com/blog/melanie-perkins- story-as-canva-ceo/.

PRINCIPLE #5

1. "Why Does an Empty Vessel Produce More Sound Than a Filled One?," Study.com, https://homework.study.com/explanation/why-does-an-empty-vessel -produce-more-sound-than-a-filled-one.html.

2. Les Fabian Brathwaite, "RuPaul Is Everything: The Rise & Reign of America's First Drag Superstar," *Out*, August 30, 2017, https://www.out.com/out -exclusives/2017/8/30/rupaul-everything-rise-reign-americas-first-drag-superstar.

3. Fenton Bailey, in discussion with authors.

4. Scott Barry Kaufman, "Daydreaming and Mental Contrasting for Goal-Fulfillment with Gabriele Oettingen," *Scientific American*, November 26, 2014, https://www.scientificamerican.com/blog/beautiful-minds/daydreaming-and-mental-contrasting-for-goal-fulfillment-with-gabriele-oettingen/; Gabriele Oettingen and Peter M. Gollwitzer, "Making Goal Pursuit Effective: Expectancy-Dependent Goal Setting and Planned Goal Striving," in *Psychology of Self-Regulation: Cognitive, Affective and Motivational Processes*, ed. Joseph P. Forgas, Roy F. Baumeister, and Dianne M. Tice (London: Psychology Press, 2009), 127–146.

5. Ainslea Cross and David Sheffield, "Mental Contrasting as a Behaviour Change Technique: A Systematic Review Protocol Paper of Effects, Mediators and Moderators on Health," *Systematic Reviews* 5, no. 1 (November 25, 2016): 201, https://doi.org/10.1186/s13643-016-0382-6.

6. Nicole Celestine, "What Is Mental Contrasting and How Can We Benefit From It?," PositivePsychology.com, January 1, 2020, https://positivepsychology.com/mental-contrasting/.

7. David Venable, in discussion with authors.

8. Ryan Serhant, in discussion with authors.

9. Robert J. Shiller, "Three Questions: Prof. Robert Shiller on Bitcoin," *Yale Insights*, October 19, 2017, https://insights.som.yale.edu/insights/three-questions-prof-robert-shiller-on-bitcoin.

10. "Elizabeth Holmes," *Forbes*, https://www.forbes.com/profile/elizabeth-holmes/?sh=6f293c6247a7.

PRINCIPLE #6

1. Ranjay Gulati, *Deep Purpose: The Heart and Soul of High-Performance Companies* (New York: Harper Business, 2022).

2. "Clorox to Acquire Burt's Bees; Expands into Fast-Growing Natural Personal Care," The Clorox Company, October 31, 2007, http://investors.theclorox company.com/releasedetail.cfm?ReleaseID=272197; "Putting Her Money Where Maine's Woods Are," *New York Times*, August 6, 2001, https://www.nytimes.com/2001/08/06/us/putting-her-money-where-maine-s-woods-are.html.

3. Jennifer Wang, "Burt's Bees Cofounder on Why She Gave Away 87,000 Acres in Maine," *Forbes*, October 24, 2017, https://www.forbes.com/sites/jenniferwang/2017/10/24/burts-bees-cofounder-on-why-she-gave-away-87000-acres-in-maine/.

4. Craig Koch, in discussion with authors.

5. Niraj Chokshi and Sydney Ember, "4 Takeaways about Boeing's Quality Problems," *New York Times*, March 28, 2024, https://www.nytimes.com/2024/03/28/business/boeing-quality-takeaways.html.

6. Mark Walker, "F.A.A. Audit of Boeing's 737 Max Production Found Dozens of Issues," *New York Times*, March 11, 2024, https://www.nytimes.com/2024/03/11/us/politics/faa-audit-boeing-737-max.html; "F.A.A. Audit Finds Quality-Control Lapses at Boeing and Spirit AeroSystems," *New York Times*,

March 4, 2024, https://www.nytimes.com/2024/03/04/us/politics/faa-boeing-737
-max-audit.html.

7. Patrick Smith and Rob Wile, "Boeing CEO, Other Executives Stepping
Down amid Safety Crisis," *AOL.com*, March 25, 2024, https://www.aol.com
/news/boeing-ceo-dave-calhoun-slew-121024056.html.

8. Malique Morris, "Can Allbirds Survive Its Own Turnaround Plan?,"
Business of Fashion, March 20, 2024, https://www.businessoffashion.com
/articles/direct-to-consumer/explaining-allbirds-turnaround-progress/.

9. Bethany Biron and Jennifer Ortakales Dawkins, "The Rise and Fall of the
Gap," *Business Insider*, July 26, 2023, https://www.businessinsider.com/gap
-company-history-rise-and-fall-pictures-2019-11; Bethany Biron, "We Went to
a Gap Store and Saw Why Its Sales Have Been Struggling," *Business Insider*,
June 1, 2019, https://www.businessinsider.com/gap-sales-struggling-store-visit
-photos-2019-6.

10. Nathaniel Meyersohn, "What the Heck Happened to the Gap?," *CNN
Business*, July 13, 2022, https://www.cnn.com/2022/07/13/business/gap-history
-old-navy-retail/index.html.

11. WebMD Editorial Contributor, "Goat Milk: Are There Health Benefits?,"
WebMD, September 13, 2022, https://www.webmd.com/diet/goat-milk-are-there
-health-benefits.

12. "Millennials and Gen Z Want to Support Purpose Driven Companies Act-
ing Sustainably," SmartHead, February 26, 2021, https://www.besmarthead.com
/en/blog/post/purpose-driven-brands-younger-customers-look-for.

13. "From Me to We: The Rise of the Purpose-Led Brand," Accenture, December 5, 2018, https://www.accenture.com/us-en/insights/strategy/brand-purpose.

14. "2024 Global Human Capital Trends," Deloitte Insights, https://www2
.deloitte.com/us/en/insights/focus/human-capital-trends.html.

15. "The Purpose Premium: Why a Purpose-Driven Strategy Is Good for
Business," Monitor Deloitte, 2021, https://www2.deloitte.com/content/dam
/Deloitte/us/Documents/process-and-operations/purpose-premium-pov.pdf.

PRINCIPLE #7

1. Emma Baldwin, "You Can Lead a Horse to Water but You Can't Make It
Drink," Poem Analysis, June 11, 2021, https://poemanalysis.com/proverb/you-can
-lead-a-horse-to-water/.

2. Emma Baldwin, "A Dialogue," Poem Analysis, July 9, 2023,
https://poemanalysis.com/literary-device/dialogue/.

3. Ryan Pendell, "Customer Brand Preference and Decisions: Gallup's 70/30
Principle," Gallup Workplace, September 30, 2022, https://www.gallup.com
/workplace/398954/customer-brand-preference-decisions-gallup-principle.aspx.

4. Manda Mahoney, "The Subconscious Mind of the Consumer (and How
to Reach It)," Harvard Business School Working Knowledge, January 13, 2003,
https://hbswk.hbs.edu/item/the-subconscious-mind-of-the-consumer-and-how
-to-reach-it.

5. Abby Ellin, "When WeightWatchers Ended In-Person Meetings, They Held Their Own," *New York Times*, February 2, 2024, https://www.nytimes.com /2024/02/02/nyregion/brooklyn-weightwatchers-meetings.html.

6. Scott Magids, Alan Zorfas, and Daniel Leemon, "The New Science of Customer Emotions," *Harvard Business Review*, November 2015, https://hbr.org /2015/11/the-new-science-of-customer-emotions.

7. H. O. Maycotte, "Customer Lifetime Value—The Only Metric That Matters," *Forbes*, August 25, 2015, https://www.forbes.com/sites/homaycotte/2015 /08/25/customer-lifetime-value-the-only-metric-that-matters/.

8. Jennifer Dublino, "Returning Customers Spend 67 Percent More Than New Customers—Keep Your Customers Coming Back with a Recurring Revenue Sales Model," *Business.com*, January 3, 2024, https://www.business.com/articles /returning-customers-spend-67-more-than-new-customers-keep-your-customers -coming-back-with-a-recurring-revenue-sales-model/.

9. Fred Reichheld, "Prescription for Cutting Costs," Bain & Company, https://media.bain.com/Images/BB_Prescription_cutting_costs.pdf.

10. Conor Begley, in discussion with authors.

11. Stephen Brown, in discussion with authors.

PRINCIPLE #8

1. Yuliya Chernova, "Glossier to Furlough Most of Its Retail Employees," *Wall Street Journal*, May 27, 2020, https://www.wsj.com/articles/glossier-to-furlough-most-of-its-retail-employees-11590617232; Jacqueline Kilikita, "What Went Wrong at Glossier?," *Refinery29*, February 1, 2022, https://www.refinery29 .com/en-us/2022/02/10854189/what-happened-to-glossier; Adrian Horton, "The Complicated Rise and Fall of Glossier: 'There Were Missteps and There Were Successes,'" *Guardian*, September 19, 2023, https://www.theguardian.com /books/2023/sep/19/glossier-beauty-brand-book-emily-weiss.

2. Mary Giuliani, in discussion with authors.

3. Ovid, *Ars Amatoria, or The Art of Love*, trans. Henry T. Riley (1885; Project Gutenberg, December 16, 2024), https://www.gutenberg.org/files/47677 /47677-h/47677-h.htm.

4. "The Ten Commandments," The Church of Jesus Christ of Latter-Day Saints, https://www.churchofjesuschrist.org/comeuntochrist/uk/beliefs/holy-bible /the-ten-commandments.

5. Daniel Kahneman et al., "Would You Be Happier If You Were Richer? A Focusing Illusion," *Science* 312, no. 5782 (2006): 1908–1910, https://doi. org/10.1126 /science.1129688.

6. "Focusing Illusions," *FS*, https://fs.blog/focusing-illusions/ (our italics).

7. David A. Schkade and Daniel Kahneman, "Does Living in California Make People Happy? A Focusing Illusion in Judgments of Life Satisfaction," *Psychological Science* 9, no. 5 (September 1998): 340–346, http://www.jstor.org /stable/40063318?origin=JSTOR-pdf.

8. David Stark, in discussion with authors.

9. Teddi Nicolaus, "Practicing Kindness Is Good for Your Health," *Nation's Health* 53, no. 9 (December 2023): 24, https://www.thenationshealth.org /content/53/9/24.

10. Stephen Brown, in discussion with authors.

PRINCIPLE #9

1. Sally Hogshead, in discussion with authors.

2. Dacher Keltner and Kira M. Newman, "How We Misunderstand Anxiety and Miss Out on Its Benefits," University of California, September 8, 2022, https://www.universityofcalifornia.edu/news/how-we-misunderstand-anxiety -and-miss-out-its-benefits.

3. Tracy Dennis-Tiwary, *Future Tense: Why Anxiety Is Good for You (Even Though It Feels Bad)* (London: Piatkus, 2022); Dacher Keltner, host, *The Science of Happiness*, episode 122, "Riding the Waves of Anxiety," *Greater Good Magazine*, August 18, 2022, 21 min., 40 sec., https://greatergood.berkeley.edu /podcasts/item/anxiety_aparna_nancheria.

4. Keltner and Newman, "How We Misunderstand Anxiety."

5. Adrianne Shapira, in discussion with authors.

6. Jonathan Anderson, "Dan Levy and Jonathan Anderson on Balancing Creativity and Commerce | BoF VOICES 2023," YouTube video, January 12, 2024, https://www.youtube.com/watch?v=HvT42qLovD4.

7. Kathleen Elkins, "Why Mavs Owner Mark Cuban Spent 30 Minutes Signing Autographs for Boston Fans," *CNBC Make It*, December 11, 2017, https:// www.cnbc.com/2017/12/11/why-mavs-owner-mark-cuban-spent-30-minutes -signing-autographs-for-fans.html.

8. Robert Herjavec, "Small Businesses Are the Backbone of Our Economy," Facebook, October 21, 2024, https://www.facebook.com/story.php?story_fbid=10 91022869049562&id=100044255775105&_rdr#.

9. Barbara Corcoran, "The Joy Is in the Getting There!," LinkedIn, November 10, 2022, https://www.linkedin.com/posts/barbaracorcoran_the-joy-is-in-the -getting-there-the-beginning-activity-6996491675283931136-9TSZ.

10. Carol Tice, "Investor Lori Greiner on Her Swim in the 'Shark Tank,'" *NBC News*, March 18, 2012, https://www.nbcnews.com/id/wbna46777153.

11. Kevin O'Leary (@kevinolearytv), "I'd rather invest in an entrepreneur who has failed before than one who assumes success from day one," X, May 20, 2023, https://x.com/kevinolearytv/status/1660046493108039681.

12. Kevin Harrington, *Act Now!: How I Turn Ideas into Million-Dollar Products* (Deerfield Beach, FL: HCI, 2009).

13. Brian Patrick Eha, "Daymond John of 'Shark Tank' on the No. 1 Thing Entrepreneurs Need," *NBC News*, August 31, 2013, https://www.nbcnews.com /id/wbna52892536.

14. Caroline Kelly, "Virginia Governor Apologizes for 'Racist and Offensive' Costume in Photo Showing People in Blackface and KKK Garb," CNN, February 7, 2019, https://www.cnn.com/2019/02/01/politics/northam -blackface-photo/index.html#.

15. Anna Purna Kambhapaty, Madeleine Carlisle, and Melissa Chan, "Justin Trudeau Wore Brownface at 2001 'Arabian Nights' Party While He Taught at a Private School," *Time*, September 19, 2019, https://time.com/5680759/justin-trudeau-brownface-photo/; Kerry Flynn, "Bon Appétit Editor-in-Chief Adam Rapoport Resigns after Brown Face Photo Sparks Anger," CNN, June 9, 2020, https://www .cnn.com/2020/06/08/media/bon-appetit-adam-rapoport-resigns/index.html.

PRINCIPLE #10

1. "Happy Workers Are 13% More Productive," University of Oxford, October 24, 2019, https://www.ox.ac.uk/news/2019-10-24-happy-workers-are -13-more-productive.

2. Nathan P. Podsakoff et al., "Individual- and Organizational-Level Consequences of Organizational Citizenship Behaviors: A Meta-analysis," *Journal of Applied Psychology* 94, no. 1 (January 2009): 122–141, https://doi.org/10.1037 /a0013079.

3. Michelangelo Vianello, Elisa Maria Galliani, and Jonathan Haidt, "Elevation at Work: The Effects of Leaders' Moral Excellence," *Journal of Positive Psychology* 5, no. 5 (2010): 390–411, http://dx.doi.org/10.1080/17439760.2010.516 764; Anna Nyberg, "The Impact of Managerial Leadership on Stress and Health among Employees" (Karolinska Institutet Dissertations & Theses, 2009), ProQuest (28426751), https://www.proquest.com/openview/81ba4c4c58db3f86609d 191d900b2634/1?pq-origsite=gscholar&cbl=2026366&diss=y.

4. "Addressing Employee Burnout: Are You Solving the Right Problem?," McKinsey Health Institute, May 27, 2022, https://www.mckinsey.com/mhi/our -insights/addressing-employee-burnout-are-you-solving-the-right-problem.

5. Brie Weiler Reynolds, "FlexJobs, Mental Health America Survey: Mental Health in the Workplace," FlexJobs, https://www.flexjobs.com/blog/post /flexjobs-mha-mental-health-workplace-pandemic/.

6. Denise Albieri Jodas Salvagioni et al., "Physical, Psychological and Occupational Consequences of Job Burnout: A Systematic Review of Prospective Studies," *PLoS One* 12, no. 10 (October 2017), https://doi.org/10.1371/journal .pone.0185781.

7. James Timpson, "Here's How Trust & Kindness Make a Business Successful | James Timpson | TEDxManchester," YouTube video, April 3, 2024, https://www.youtube.com/watch?v=ioZqYLqfziU.

8. Timpson, "Here's How Trust & Kindness Make a Business Successful."

9. Timpson, "Here's How Trust & Kindness Make a Business Successful."

10. "Many Hands Make Light Work," Dictionary.com, https://www .dictionary.com/browse/many-hands-make-light-work.

11. Christian Stadler et al., "Open Up Your Strategy," *MIT Sloan Management Review*, December 20, 2021, https://sloanreview.mit.edu/article/open-up -your-strategy/.

12. Andrew Hill, "Release Strategy from the Grip of a Corporate Priesthood," *Financial Times*, October 10, 2021, https://www.ft.com/content/ac562c20-5c8c -4fc4-8854-58414f2fc75b.

13. Sydney Finkelstein, "Don't Bother Hiring the 'Perfect' Candidate," BBC, February 23, 2016, https://www.bbc.com/worklife/article/20160223-dont -bother-hiring-the-perfect-candidate.

14. Adam Grant (@AdamMGrant), "Narcissistic leaders are threatened by talent. They want to be the smartest person in the room," X, April 1, 2024, https://x.com/AdamMGrant/status/1774836192220942668.

15. Ben Wigert, Jim Harter, and Sangeeta Agrawal, "The Future of the Office Has Arrived: It's Hybrid," Gallup Workplace, October 9, 2023, https://www .gallup.com/workplace/511994/future-office-arrived-hybrid.aspx.

16. Nancy Baym, Jonathan Larson, and Ronnie Martin, "What a Year of WFH Has Done to Our Relationships at Work," *Harvard Business Review*, March 22, 2021, https://hbr.org/2021/03/what-a-year-of-wfh-has-done-to -our-relationships-at-work; Claire Cain Miller, "Do Chance Meetings at the Office Boost Innovation? There's No Evidence of It," *New York Times*, July 1, 2021, https://www.nytimes.com/2021/06/23/upshot/remote-work-innovation-office .html.

17. Deepak Chopra, in discussion with authors.

18. Ziad Ahmed, in discussion with authors.

PRINCIPLE #11

1. "Ecclesiastes 4:9–12," oremus Bible Browser, https://bible.oremus.org /?ql=163619871.

2. Luke Ferris, "Simon Sinek: Who's the Man behind the Personal Brand?," Foundr, March 29, 2024, https://foundr.com/articles/leadership/personal-growth /simon-sinek.

3. "Shark Tank US | Social Media Star Pitches Influencers in the Wild—the Game," YouTube video, May 6, 2024, https://www.youtube.com/watch?v =5iNapbBqgeg.

4. Tank Sinatra, in discussion with authors.

5. "About Us," The Kimberly Wahlberg Company, https://www.kimberly wahlberg.com/about-us/.

6. Kim Wahlberg, in discussion with authors.

7. Tomei Thomas, in discussion with authors.

8. Kyle Benson, "The Magic Relationship Ratio, According to Science," The Gottman Institute, October 4, 2017, https://www.gottman.com/blog/the-magic -relationship-ratio-according-science/.

9. Alix Strauss, "Their Relationship Morphed from Dislike to Inseparable," *New York Times*, September 27, 2018, https://www.nytimes.com/2018/09/27 /fashion/weddings/their-relationship-morphed-from-dislike-to-inseparable.html.

10. Rachel Feinblatt, "Palm Beach Resident and Founder of NEST Fragrances Laura Slatkin Talks Scents," *Modern Luxury Palm Beach*, April 9, 2023, https://mlpalmbeach.com/laura-slatkin-nest-fragrances.

11. Glossy Team, "NEST Fragrances' Laura Slatkin: 'The Consumer Really Wants a Brand That's Important,'" *Glossy*, January 17, 2019, https://www .glossy.co/beauty/nest-fragrances-laura-slatkin-the-consumer-really-wants-a -brand-thats-important/; Aubree Mercure, "NEST Fragrances Celebrates 10 Years," Cosmetic Executive Women, August 13, 2018, https://cew.org/beauty _news/nest-fragrances-celebrates-10-years/.

12. Strauss, "Their Relationship Morphed."

13. "Interview Nikhil and Alejandro Co-Founders: Back to the Roots," Billion Success Media, https://billionsuccess.com/back-to-the-roots/.

14. "Our Story," Back to the Roots, https://backtotheroots.com/pages/our -story.

15. Mair Allen, "Back to the Roots: From Office Space Mushrooms to a Gardening Revolution," Foundr, January 28, 2023, https://foundr.com/articles /building-a-business/back-to-the-roots.

16. Ferris, "Simon Sinek."

17. Allen, "Back to the Roots."

18. Allen, "Back to the Roots."

19. Anthony D. Smith, "Splitting: It's Not Just for Borderline Personality," *Psychology Today*, December 26, 2021, https://www.psychologytoday.com/us /blog/and-running/202112/splitting-it-s-not-just-borderline-personality.

PRINCIPLE #12

1. Jaclyn Lindsey, in discussion with authors.

2. Seth Borenstein, "Not So Random Acts: Science Finds That Being Kind Pays Off," Medical Xpress, July 2, 2020, https://medicalxpress.com/news/2020-07 -random-science-kind.html.

3. James H. Fowler and Nicholas A. Christakis, "Cooperative Behavior Cascades in Human Social Networks," *Proceedings of the National Academy of Sciences*, 107, no. 12 (March 2010): 5334–5338; https://www.pnas.org/doi/ full/10.1073 /pnas.0913149107.

4. David R. Cregg and Jennifer S. Cheavens, "Healing through Helping: An Experimental Investigation of Kindness, Social Activities, and Reappraisal as Well-Being Interventions," *Journal of Positive Psychology* 18, no. 6 (2023): 924–941, https://doi.org/10.1080/17439760.2022.2154695.

5. Renée Onque, "I've Studied Positive Psychology for 10 Years: This Is the Secret to Happiness—and You Can Start Today," CNBC Make It, May 16, 2024, https://www.cnbc.com/2024/05/16/this-is-the-secret-to-happiness-from-a -happiness-researcher.html.

6. "Pareto Principle (80/20 Rule) & Pareto Analysis Guide," Juran, March 12, 2019, https://www.juran.com/blog/a-guide-to-the-pareto-principle-80-20-rule -pareto-analysis/.

Epilogue

1. Te-Ping Chen, "America's New Millionaire Class: Plumbers and HVAC Entrepreneurs," *Wall Street Journal*, October 12, 2024.

INDEX

ACKNOWLEDGMENTS

We would like to acknowledge:

- Anyone and everyone at every job we ever had
- All of our family members
- Every teacher and librarian from kindergarten through grad school
- Anyone who ever purchased or used a Beekman 1802 product
- Every Team Beekman member that ever passed through our doors
- For this book specifically:
    - Our agent, Tom Miller, who, when we said Harvard Business Review Press was our top choice to partner with on this book, made it happen.
    - Our editor, Kevin Evers, who could envision a different type of business book for the different business times in which we are living, and the entire team at Harvard Business Review Press who got this book into your hands.
    - Abby Ellin, who took our two voices and made them blend into one.
    - Seth Schulman, who helped us go from point A to point B.
- Every reader, dreamer, worker who reads this book and makes it to this page (write your name here:). We see you. Welcome to the Neighborhood.

ABOUT THE AUTHORS

JOSH KILMER-PURCELL and **DR. BRENT RIDGE** are the co-founders of Beekman 1802.

Ridge began his career as a physician at Mount Sinai in New York City and later launched the health and wellness division of Martha Stewart Living Omnimedia. Kilmer-Purcell was previously an award-winning advertising executive and *New York Times* bestselling author of three books.

The pair founded Beekman 1802 in 2008 after purchasing the historic Beekman farm in Sharon Springs, New York, where they started researching the nutrients in goat milk and began making goat milk soaps and gourmet cheeses. Today the company has over a hundred employees and is recognized as one of the most successful lifestyle brands in America by Nasdaq, *Inc.* magazine, and the *Wall Street Journal*.

In 2019, they set the record for the largest beauty brand launch in the combined thirty-seven-year history of both HSN and QVC.

Thousands of people visit their flagship store and enjoy tours each year in rural Sharon Springs.

Ridge and Kilmer-Purcell have been featured in countless media and business outlets.

As the stars of *The Fabulous Beekman Boys*, they were the first gay couple to have their own television series on a national network. They also competed on and won *The Amazing Race* on CBS. They've published four bestselling cookbooks and a home decor book, and they have produced an award-winning quarterly magazine, *The Beekman 1802 Almanac*.

Out Magazine has included them on its Top 100 Influential LGBT List, and they received Farmer of the Year recognition from the US secretary of agriculture.

They sit on the board of the Farmers' Museum in Otsego, New York, and were awarded honorary doctorates by the State University of New York for their contributions to both agriculture and business.

Kilmer-Purcell and Ridge continue to reside on their farm in Sharon Springs and in Orlando, Florida.

To continue the journey of *G.O.A.T. Wisdom* and discover the Bar Soap that started it all visit us at Beekman1802.com